BATTLING DARK FORCES

A Guide To Psychic Self-Defense

TORKOM SARAYDARIAN

BATTLING DARK FORCES:
A Guide to Psychic Self-Defense

Cover Design:	Geralyn Cronin
Printed by:	Gilliland Printing
Published by:	New Vision Publishing
	252 Roadrunner Drive, Suite 5
	Sedona, AZ 86336 U.S.A.

Publisher's Cataloguing-in-Publication

Saraydarian, Torkom
    Battling dark forces : a guide to psychic self-defense / Torkom Saraydarian
        p. cm.
    Includes bibliographic references and index.
    Library of Congress Cataloguing Number: 96-72177
    ISBN 0-9656203-2-8

    1. Good and evil.   2. Occultism--Miscellanea.   3. Self-defense -- Miscellanea.   4. Spiritual life.   I. Title.

BJ1401.S37 1997   111'.84
                                        QBI96-40895

Printed in the United States of America

Table Of Contents

PART 1

THE BATTLEGROUND

PART 2

THE BATTLE

PART 2 (cont.)

PART 3

LIBERATION

ABOUT THE AUTHOR
(1917-1997)

Torkom Saraydarian was a prolific author and tireless teacher. In his lifetime he published sixty books, gave thousands of lectures, and traveled the world presenting the practical application of the Ageless Wisdom. Since boyhood he learned firsthand from Teachers about the everlasting value of principles such as Beauty, Goodness, Righteousness, Joy, Freedom, striving toward perfection, and sacrificial service and selflessly presented this vision to the world.

The author's books are used all over the world as sources of guidance and spiritual inspiration. Many of his books have been translated into other languages including Armenian, German, Dutch, Danish, Portuguese, Spanish, Italian, Greek, Yugoslavian, and Swedish.

In addition to being a prolific writer, he was a composer and an accomplished musician having published numerous recordings as well as a magnificent CD called, "A Touch of Heart." He plays all the instrumentals for his pieces including piano, violin, guitar, and cello, just to name a few of the instruments he mastered.

In addition, Torkom Saraydarian was the founder of the Aquarian Educational Group, established in 1961, which was renamed the Saraydarian Institute in honor of his unending service. Centers are located in Agoura, California and Sedona, Arizona.

Although this book was published posthumously, his vision will live for many, many years through the lives he touched.

. . .Learn the methods of the enemies.

— *Heart*, para. 111

PREFACE

To write about enemies and dark forces as we approach the 21st Century seems absurd. Where are the dark forces? We cannot see them. We cannot register them in our electronic machines. This is what average man and scientists think. But the dark forces are here, around us, in us, and in man's events.

You can see them in operation in obsession and possession, if you examine deeply. If you dig the well of greed, jealousy, hatred, and fear, you can see them.

If you examine destructive events, hunger, and homelessness, you can see the tools of dark forces. If you enter into the secret records of education and government, you see their shadows and their fingerprints. If you examine your life, you can see how unconsciously you are a victim or an agent for them.

A long time passes before you are able to see that your personality is often unconsciously serving evil or encouraging evil through the subconscious mind and mechanical reactions. To eliminate evil in the world means to overcome your personality and enter into the Transpersonal Self. In that consciousness you will be able to see good and evil.

Some people say that God created evil. But God did not create the atomic bomb and all radioactive wastes, pesticides, and other poisons that are here eating our life!

Evil is in front of our noses — exploitation, manipulation, crime, drugs, alcohol, tobacco, and various lawless actions which devastate our world. Our families are in danger of disintegration. Our society is full of conflict and self-interest. All these are the evils we are facing today. Someone must warn about these plagues. A nation's advancement runs parallel to the victory it gains over evil, over dark forces, over obsession and possession.

Many professionals are facing cases of obsession and possession, and they do not understand what is going on. There are many cases of multiple personalities with difficult complications; the present medical profession considers them to be physical or psychological problems. The medical profession does not believe that evil entities exist and that they can possess people. Many people at the time of Jesus believed so. Jesus confronted them and, in many cases, cleaned people from these malignant entities.

This book is an exposé on evil. As much as possible, it is for your guidance.

Torkom Saraydarian
1997

PART 1

THE BATTLEGROUND

1 A Teacher's Tale

Once my Teacher told me that all that exists in the world, in society, in our mind, and in politics is there for a reason, and that life cannot proceed without things existing that we both hate and love. This was a very shocking statement for me, and it stayed in one of the corners of my mind until I slowly digested it. It took me years to control my criticism, pride, superiority, and superficiality and to understand the roles of all that exists in the Divine Plan.

"Teacher," I said one day, *"what about all those activities which are against virtues, spiritual principles, health, and happiness?"*

He answered, "Don't you see that it is because of these things that we develop virtues, spiritual principles, health, and happiness and make breakthroughs from plane to plane? That is how merit is created."

"Are such destructive activities going to be with us forever?"

"Yes," he said, "but in other forms, until one day they

will become conscious promoters of your progress and the conflict will create breakthroughs and actions toward the highest.

"Let me make this clear for you. There are many forces and conditions in the world which seem to act against our progress. We have so-called involutionary forces which run toward materialization, fragmentation, separatism, disintegration, and so on. These forces are not dark forces or evil. They act under the Laws of Nature. Actually, they are in all forms on all planes.

"If our consciousness chooses to follow them, we create friction between the evolutionary forces and the involutionary forces in us, in society, and in Nature. We bring pain and suffering to ourselves because our inner essence now is evolutionary and it tries to make all our physical, etheric, astral, and mental atoms be in line with evolutionary forces.

"Then we have dark forces, so-called, or the evil lodge. Then we have karma. All these are different factors.

"Dark forces or evil can use the involutionary forces to fulfill their plans, but they are not involutionary forces in reality."

"Is there any difference between dark forces and evil forces?"

"Dark forces are those who work for evil purposes behind the veil, subjectively and in secret. Evil forces are those who work generally in the open, in all fields of human endeavor. They work often through mediums, hypnotists, channels, crime, violence, murder, exploitation, hatred, wars, and so on. But generally people do not see the difference between them. The evil forces take their inspiration and energy from the dark forces.

"Dark forces have very ancient origins and they have centers established in etheric, physical, astral, even in the Cosmic Astral Plane. Evil forces have their agents, ancient or contemporary. Most of the evil forces are generated from our humanity in this Round.[1]

"An evil agent has the possibility to work in the dark lodge as he goes step by step onto the evil path."

"Do you mean that dark forces try to slow or prevent evolutionary progress?"

"There are dark forces and evil forces that exist side by side."

"What about all the damage that they do to people?"

"They damage and destroy only the damageable, destructible part of a person or a nation but cannot touch the indestructible part of a person or a nation."

"Don't people fall victim to these dark forces?"

"Only those who were already victims of their inertia. The dark forces may eventually quicken their light."

"Are the dark forces conscious about what they do?"

"It does not matter for us. They may be conscious or unconscious, but our duty is to keep going into light, learning how to overcome them."

"If we overcome them, don't we prevent them from doing what they are doing?"

"Yes, on one level. On the next level they will meet us in another form."

"Do you mean that we must not fight against corruption, hatred, separatism, totalitarianism, drugs, prostitution, and black arts?"

"They are there to make us fight with them, to develop more potentials within us. But they will be there for a long time to keep us going toward the highest."

"You mean that it will be a long time before we will be released from them?"

"There will be times that we will be above their traps, but they will follow us until we unite with the One Self.

---

1. For more information on rounds, globes, and moon chains, see *Hierarchy and the Plan*, p. 15.

The higher we go, the better they may serve us."

"Can we save them too?"

"Yes, we can, if we follow the evolutionary path."

"Can we justify those who are in evil, destructive, harmful activities?"

"Not at all. We neither justify nor condemn them but analyze them to see why they are, how they are, what they are, then to see how we can advance and progress in order to overcome the harm they do and to help them to be of assistance on a higher level. Our intention will be to lead them into the evolutionary path.

"The evil ones are the agents of dark forces and they act under their command. But they can change their position to this or that side. Remember that the dark lodge thinks the White Lodge is its enemy, but the White Lodge is not an enemy to any side. They see what the evil lodge is and what their role is, and accordingly they take their attitude toward them."

"Does this mean that the evil lodge has less intelligence than the White Lodge?"

"I can say that both have intelligence, but the evil lodge uses its intelligence in self-interest. The White Lodge uses its intelligence in the interest of all. But the White Lodge has the advantage over them as the White Lodge has more love and more conscious contact with the Purpose of God than the black lodge."

"Does the White Lodge affect them?"

"Yes, it does, without using their ways and means or methods."

"Why does the White Lodge want to influence them?"

"They want to influence them to increase their sensitivity to the Will of God and make them consciously change their ways."

"Can you clarify the difference between involutionary process, forces of destruction, dark forces, and the

evil lodge?"

"The involutionary process is continuously going on when spirit is proceeding toward materialization, objectification, toward form. This is a natural process. It is a natural process that matter is proceeding toward spirit, through the process of spiritualization. There is nothing evil or good in it. Force is produced when spirit becomes matter, and energy is produced when matter becomes spirit. Actually, these two processes work together under the Universal Plan to create living forms.

"Forces of destruction originate from a very high source. Sometimes this source is called Shiva, Father, Destroyer. It has many agents in all planes. Its duty is to destroy a form when its cycle is over. That form can be a man, a tree, a bird, a group, a nation, an ideology, and so on. The destructive force cooperates with the creative force and both act under a Higher Purpose.

"Dark forces are different from forces of involution and forces of destruction, but they use these forces to act against the Will of the Creator, against the Purpose, and against the Plan. They have their own purpose to stop evolution and to disintegrate forms and unifications. Thus, many forms that are destroyed and put into disintegration are not caused by the forces of destruction but by the dark forces using destructive methods or using forces of destruction on their own behalf. The origin of dark forces can be traced to the moon chain and to the fourth globe of our chain.

"The evil lodge is formed by dark forces and those humans who for ages followed the dark forces and eventually lost their Solar Angel or sold their soul to the dark lodge.

"They use the involutionary forces and forces of destruction, and obey the will of dark forces in order to create all those thoughts, emotions, and activities which hinder the progress of humanity to prevent the unfoldment of divine potentials in man and which lead them to pain and suffering, increasing their vices, hatred, and so on. "The evil lodge is anchored on the earth, is organized better than any other organization, and keeps the world boiling in hatred, revenge, materialism, separatism, totalitarianism, ugliness, greed, and destruction. But this does not mean that they are the victors. The White Lodge is slow in organizing its ranks, but time is with them, and eventually the dark forces and evil will see the uselessness of all their efforts."

"Does the White Lodge, or those who are on the arc of evolution, use the dark lodge or evil lodge?"

"Yes, they may use them against the very army of the dark or evil forces or to reveal to humanity the real face of the evil. Also, the White Lodge learns their tactics and uses them to awaken them from their illusions."

"Do you think that the intention of the evolutionary and involutionary forces is to annihilate each other?"

"They represent matter and spirit and they cannot exist without each other as long as there is *manvantara*, manifestation, creation. They work in the *manvantara* upon the principle of duality. Of course duality will one day cease to be. But the important function in the existence of evil forces is that they come to existence by the misthinking and misaction of those self-interested people who, age after age, built a group of their own to manipulate mankind to create friction. The karma of such people will be awful, as it will lead to the annihilation of their individuality.

"Let me tell you that the White Lodge is the flowering result of the activities of evolutionary forces. They are the flowers and fruits of the Tree of Evolution. Also, the dark forces and evil germinate and come into being through the forces of involution, when human beings changed their course from involution to evolution."

"Can you give me an example of how dark forces differ from the evil lodge?"

"The evil lodge is composed of those who are sensitive to the dark forces for their own transient interest. For example, dark forces intend to capture a city, but evil forces join them to slaughter the people in the city. Evil forces in some way make dark forces succeed in doing their job. Evil forces are the product of karma. They may eventually pay their karma and, with strenuous effort, side themselves with the White Forces. Evil forces sometimes see that their efforts are defeating their own success."

"Is there any philosophical way to explain the involutionary forces?"

"As I said, they use the involutionary fires and matter. They go toward substance. They become vehicles. We each have involutionary forces in us. As long as we are confined in a vehicle, no matter how high-level it is, they are involutionary workers. They are in the process of materialization and fragmentation or separation.

"Dark forces destroy, limit, and try to prevent you from radiating and becoming one. Evil forces create pain, suffering, and destruction when it is not in the Plan. There is conscious destruction and there is deliberate destruction, which is not controlled by the Will of the Logos, Planetary, Solar, or Cosmic. Both dark forces and White Forces try to gain evil forces and make them work for their behalf.

"To make it more clear for you, there is a difference between darkness and dark forces. Dark forces, in reality, are forces that fight against evolution. Darkness is a state of existence that is not revealed yet. It is the matter side of creation. Light and darkness in essence are the same, but in human terms people think darkness is evil, which it is not. But dark forces are evil. The dark lodge is evil."

"What does 'evil' really mean?"

"Evil is those activities, beings, or directions that go against the Cosmic Purpose and Plan and destroy the Will of the Central Command of creative or destructive actions. For example, if you are building a house and some thieves are stealing materials and destroying what you built for their separative, selfish interest, they are assumed to be evil. Thus, evil is that which creates disharmony, destroys cooperation, and lacks the sense of responsibility, cooperation with the Command, responsibility to actualize that Command.

"Evil relates to all those actions which work against freedom, joy, health, sanity, prosperity, progress, transformation, transfiguration, cooperation, harmony, synthesis, and unity. In general, evil works for self-interest at the expense of the interests of others."

"Is there any Teaching that God created dark forces and evil?"

"In reality, there is not. In ancient Teachings light and darkness were assumed to be opposites, and generations of ignorant people took light as being good and darkness as being evil. They thought that spirit was good, matter was evil. Such a mistranslation made people believe that involution and matter are evil, and evolution and spirit are good, whereas matter cannot exist without spirit, and spirit cannot exist without matter.

"Involution cannot exist without evolution, and evolution cannot exist without involution. Even we can dare to say that *light does not exist without darkness, and darkness does not exist without light.* Actually, in some advanced Teachings, the source of manifestation is called the concealed Mystery of Mysteries, the Darkness."

"What is darkness?"

"Darkness has various meanings. For example, it means impenetrable, unrealized, absolute, an existence that does not exist for our senses and consciousness. It also refers to the substantiation of light, when the spirit proceeds toward the involutionary arc to become matter. Darkness is not evil in a philosophical sense. It is the beginning of spirit. Darkness turns into dark forces under evil influences. Evil works against the spirit because spirit reveals it, but evil uses the matter or the involutionary process to hinder its God-destined task."

"Are we supposed to fight against evil?"

"Yes, if we know for sure that it is evil. We must try not to follow evil or not be trapped by it. Any fight against evil creates new evil if we use its methods."

"Does this mean that we let the evil increase?"

"No, instead of direct confrontation with evil, using the same weapons it uses, we must try to expose its ways and means and let people realize and not become trapped in them."

"Do the dark forces have close connections with evil?"

"Of course. The dark forces give every opportunity to evil to work against human evolution, against human development, because what evil forces want is to perpetuate the slavery of people on the involutionary arc. They are associates in this labor."

"Is Cosmic chaos related to dark forces and evil?"

"Cosmic chaos is when the evolutionary forces and involutionary forces are mixing together like hot and cold water in a waterfall, or when the evolutionary forces are in process of construction, as for example in the formation of a galaxy. The involutionary forces present the chaotic side of it until the White Forces gain the battle and the first shape of the galaxy comes into being. But even in this process, evil can interfere and delay the Galactic (or any) Construction, causing unnoticed difficulties."

"Do the evil and dark forces have a center from which they are controlled?"

"Yes. We are told that evil is concentrated in the Cosmic Astral Plane and their victims are everywhere in this world, in all prominent places, even under the disguise of White Forces."

"Would it be possible one day to get rid of them?"

"We are told that Great Forces in Shamballa are fighting against them. As far as dark forces are concerned, their power will decrease round after round and chain after chain, when the evolutionary forces will increase in their progress. Eventually, the involutionary forces will turn into conscious coworkers with the evolutionary forces."

"In the past I thought that there was no difference between dark forces and evil."

"Yes, there are many factors and elements not yet explored and clarified due to the stage of human evolution. Darkness was taken as synonymous to evil. Darkness is a state in which our intellect is not yet able to penetrate. Darkness and light are the two faces of the same reality."

"Is there any connection between karma and evil forces?"

"People think that every time pain and suffering and problems arise in their life they are attacked by evil, but this is not so. Most of our difficulties, pain, and suffering are the result of our thinking, emotions, and actions. If we break the Laws of Love, Light, and Beauty, we suffer in order to see the cause of it. Evil has nothing to do with karma. But every suffering, pain, or problem is not necessarily the consequence of karmic debts. They could also be the result of evil attacks. When evil ones see that a new warrior is on the way to bring Light, Love, and Beauty, they attack him to prevent him from advancing into high positions, positions in which he can be effective. The one way that a person can escape many such attacks is to remain pure, loyal to the laws of his country, and keep his imagination, thinking, and feeling in the light, charged with love and beauty.

"Evil forces even attack a person through his past mistakes, mistakes that he did in past lives, just to create delay or frustration in his life. But on the other hand, when evil attacks an innocent one, the Hierarchy and his Solar Angel protect him as far as is possible. Usually, those who are under such attacks overcome the attackers, and they proceed on the way to victory and light with greater speed and triumph. Often they benefit from the attacks of evil and pass to higher positions and power."

"This is much clearer in my mind because in the past I was confused between dark forces, evil, matter, spirit, attacks, and so on."

"That is true for most of us, but do not forget that, due to the level of development of people, the Teaching is given very slowly until people are able to see things clearly. First there are fairy tales, then stories, then science. Until people show the maturity in understanding deeper issues, there will always be confusion in using words and expressions. For example, in the past the etheric body and the astral body were used synonymously."

"How does evil come into being?"

"Evil is the result of various factors: human ignorance, disobedience to natural causes, self-interest, hatred, anger, and fear, especially fear, jealousy, and separatism. The list is long. Evil starts like a small snowball. As it rolls, it becomes bigger and bigger. People carry their evil into the Subtle World and come back with similar tendencies, until eventually they join the evil army in the Cosmic Physical and Cosmic Astral Planes.

"Of course, some of the evil doers are saved before they fall into the pit. A few continue, encouraged by evil forces and their smart agents. As an army has its gradations, so too has the army of evil. Each soldier follows strict disciplines."

"Can such an army continue to exist forever?"

"Not at all. They try to persist as long as they can, but eventually there are two choices. The first choice is to join the evolutionary forces. The second choice is to enter into the process of annihilation in which they lose their individuality and disintegrate into the forces of chaos. But the most important step to take is to see if we are unconsciously serving evil or becoming its agent. A person must try to increase his harmlessness in all his mental, emotional, and physical activities and words and to purify his mind to be able to see the faintest traces of evil in himself. If we conquer evil within us, we conquer evil in the world."

2 Karma vs. Dark Forces

People think that a person cannot come under the attack of the dark forces if his karma is clean. This seems very logical, but since karma is personal, national, and global, one is always under attack as he is a part of his own national and global karma. However, if a person's karma did not contribute to national or global karma and he was attacked innocently, his rewards will be great in the Subtle Worlds and in coming incarnations.

There are two kinds of attacks. The first kind of attack comes from people in the world who have dedicated their lives to evil. If these people are not directly connected to or serving in the army of dark forces, they cannot attack you if your karma is clean. They can only damage you when you invite them to you by your own weakness and bad karma.

The second kind of attack comes from agents of Cosmic evil. You must be a very influential person to attract such an attack. They attack only if you do not have protection of Christ or the Hierarchy. Such a protection makes your aura invincible. To have such a protection you must advance in your spiritual life and selfless service.

There are also attacks which are accidental. An accident may occur when you are crossing certain currents and wandering unknowingly in forbidden territories.

How can we discriminate between the payment of a karmic debt and an attack? The answer is that karmic payment makes you feel joyful, released, and free. It makes you renew your spiritual striving, become more dedicated and clean from your former vices. On the other hand, a dark attack creates fear and slavery in you. It excites your vices and leads you to confusion, anger, and hatred. It urges you to take actions against freedom, unity, and cooperation. It gives you depression and leads you either to apathy or to the service of the forces of evil.

Karmic suffering transforms your life and clears your eyes to see your spiritual goal. Dark attacks pollute your body, feelings, and thinking. They make you lose your destination and resign from your spiritual striving. But if you are a warrior equipped with spiritual powers, every time an attack comes you turn into a better warrior and learn better the tactics and goals of the dark forces. A warrior clearly recognizes an attack because it is always accompanied with malice, slander, treason, and crime, and it is usually covered with flattery or bribery. It is possible that the attacks of astral evil may incapacitate a person who has no protection for a while, but in the meantime he learns a very precious lesson which he can use in future battles.

It is necessary for disciples of the Forces of Light to belong to groups dedicated to the service of humanity. The group aura, protection, and understanding are precious assets in times of attack. It is also necessary to have a Teacher experienced in battle who can understand your situation and come to your assistance.

Past enemies meet us again in almost every life, and in every life a chance is given to us to change them into friends. This is why when you meet an enemy, remember that you met him because it is an opportunity to change rather than to continue the animosity.

In our life we must try to increase friendship because it is through friendship that we can save money, time, energy, and matter and reach our destination sooner. Friends are like walls of protection; they are sources of experience and wisdom. Friends are those who help you to be healthy, happy, prosperous, and more enlightened.

How do you feel if you are under the influence of the dark forces?

First of all, you feel as if someone else is operating your "car" and running your life. You notice that your mind is being operated by some mysterious force outside yourself. This force thinks for you; it leads your mind toward certain directions. You feel that these are not your thoughts and not your directions. You feel as if your emotions are becoming automatic. You lose control of them and notice that certain emotions control you and your life.

You notice that you sometimes talk without wanting to talk, or keep silent when you intended to say something. You notice at other times how you said certain things which you would never have normally said. You see yourself making certain unconscious body movements and gestures which you did not intend to make. You even notice that your hands and feet are under the control of a mysterious force.

Other signs are that you do, see, or think in contradictory ways, and you sometimes change your position from one camp to another. This eventually leads to insanity, a state in which you lose your bearings and your identity. You lose control over your urges, drives, glamors, illusions, and vanity and turn into a broken branch in the rapids of the river of life. You fall into depression or rise to the summits of hilarity. You become pessimistic, suicidal, and hopeless or engage yourself in crime.

All of these are signs that dark forces are possessing or obsessing you. Dark forces also have more modern ways to enslave humanity. Some of them are

- directed evil thoughts

- radio death-waves

- projected hot and cold waves

- the distribution of radioactive materials and wastes

- the creation of disturbances in certain areas around the electromagnetic sphere of the earth

If people go unprotected, these new methods will result in

- the death of certain people who are dedicated to human welfare

- insanity on a mass scale, which will lead to increasing crime and bloodshed

- economic collapse all over the world due to the destruction of our food sources

If the leaders of humanity stand alert and take countermeasures against such evil attacks, humanity can overcome the adversary and make a new breakthrough toward the future. The countermeasures to be taken are not only scientific but also moral and spiritual.

In eastern philosophy we read about the three *gunas*, which are called rhythm (*sattva*), motion (*rajas*), and inertia (*tamas*). We are told that evil stays away from those who bear the characteristics of rhythm, radioactivity, and liveliness.

Motion has three directions: up, down, and around. Those who move toward higher dimensions of consciousness or toward spiritual virtues repel evil. But those who move in a circle around the axis of their ego are eventually obsessed and possessed by evil. Those who move downward are already the coworkers of evil because they go toward matter, hatred, and separatism.

Evil uses inertia to bring down those who are engaged in hard labor to raise their consciousness, purify their nature, and walk a path of beauty. The method of inertia that the dark forces use is to inspire people to become involved in extensive pleasures, alcohol, drugs, and sex. They inspire people to take it easy and become lazy, careless, or sluggish. Eventually they lead such people into inertia and apathy. Once a person is caught in the network of apathy, he becomes useless.

Evil ones know that when a person believes he is useless he becomes a very dangerous person to the community. Uselessness is a state of consciousness in which evil breeds. This is why the ancients tried to teach their students to be fiery and charged with the divine fire of enthusiasm. Where there is enthusiasm, or the fire of the Gods, no evil dwells because enthusiasm carries with it rhythm, radioactivity, cooperation, unity, and an intense aspiration for perfection. Sometimes dark forces or their agents approach you for your talents and offer money to help you. Often the agent pretends not to care for back payments and continuously loans to you, until you realize that you are so much in debt and without enough income that you work day and night to make the payments. He makes you his slave, and you work with all your employees for him.

This is a very dangerous trap in which individuals, groups, and nations fall into while thinking that everything is well, but the enemy is watching you and waiting for the right time to take everything back that you have and leave you desolate.

To avoid such dark attacks is not easy because they approach you at your weakest moment, or in the moment that you have an enflamed vanity and ego which can be used by your attackers.

Nations become slaves to banks who offer money, and politically-oriented banks make you their slaves. They intend to control you, your group, your nation. Keep away from those who want to enslave you and suck the fruits of your labor and morale. You can take a loan, but pay it back as soon as you can.

Even some dark agents help you build yourself on one side, but on the other side they fabricate court cases against you to take control of you as soon as possible.

This tactic does not give real joy and spiritual satisfaction to the attackers. They only increase their karma, and karma destroys them at the right time.

3 The Nature of Evil

Those who have not experienced evil in their life are lucky people. Evil is an organized army which is interested in material value, making man and woman the slaves of material values. Their intention is to stop the evolutionary process and turn it into involution. Of course, this will create opposition from those who are on the evolutionary arc. Their efforts will be wiped out and all action taken for involution. Here is where the conflict lies.

We say that evil was created when the spirit began to materialize. This spirit descended to lower materialization and became matter. Here is the origin of *evil*. Evil is not matter but the urge to keep matter from turning to spirit.

Thus, materialization of spirit created *limitation*. Limitation is evil because you are not one with all creation, and you think that limitation is you. You are, as a person, limited physically, emotionally, mentally, and these limitations do not allow you to see the actions of law in everything, everywhere. You take all events as separate, and you do not deal with them as a whole. This creates short-seeing, me and you, us and others, and the conflict goes on between these two sides, producing all glamors, illusions, maya, war, blood, suffering, pain, and death.

Thus we have two kinds of people: those who are open to spirit and those who are shut off from the spirit, whose actions cause opposition in those who are open.

We have materialization, limitation, conflict.

Evolutionary people press forward to reach spiritual heights consciously and with the treasures of their experience. Involutionary people try to stop evolution and remain in matter, in material values, and use all their intellect to perpetuate a material life.

Material form by nature does not last long. It cracks, disintegrates, causing pain and suffering. The life leaves the form when it disintegrates, and the spirit builds another form to continue its pursuit on the line of matter. It repeats this maybe a thousand times, continuing to suffer under limitation and matter. Sometimes man awakens. Sometimes he does not. So his suffering continues, also causing suffering to all those who are associated with him and to those who are on the evolutionary path.

The evolutionary process is to create those forms which fit in the perfect rhythm of spirit and to allow the potentials of spirit to manifest through form. This is a continual process. The spirit tries to eliminate limitation on all levels, causing matter to adjust itself to the finer radiation of spirit. Matter for a while rejects such a pressure and continues to remain in the same form.

Spirit gains experience that it is not the material form, that it can survive forms. For man to leave form and assume a better form does not mean suffering but joy.

Evolution emphasizes evil. As one evolves he sees greater limitations in life, greater ignorance, and greater fear of one's own actions and the actions of an involutionary man.

We are told that our Solar Logos in previous cycles and *mahamanvantaras* developed Cosmic Mind. That is in His treasury. And in seven or ten schemes in His solar system He eventually defeated all limitations until He achieved control in the Universal Mind.

At the present, in seven chains in all solar systems, He is developing the love-wisdom aspect. You can see that all limitations are related to love-wisdom, for example in our globe, in the fourth chain, in the fourth globe. Lack of love, lack of wisdom is the source of all trouble in our globe. Wisdom is accumulation of all experiences in the past. Love is utilization of wisdom for all.

The evil in this solar system is hidden in those activities which oppose love-wisdom. Evil ones use their mind, pretending love and wisdom but acting against them.

In the first solar system and in the second solar system those who embodied matter, ignorance, fear, and limitation graduated into the ranks of evil and joined those who are on the line of evil, this time working against love, unity, synthesis, harmony, cooperation.

At this time there is an organized evil on our planet, supported by ancient evil. They have their hierarchy, their commanders, soldiers, and followers. They have their purpose, their plan, and multidimensional methods to penetrate every layer of society.

Those who love humanity must be prepared to fight eternally against this force. Every initiate, every disciple under the Hierarchy of Light, is a warrior. That is why the Great Sage calls all His followers "warriors." All spiritual disciples have the aim to prepare warriors.

Through his experiment, an individualized spirit eventually reaches the level where he is initiated into the deeper mysteries of life by those who are far advanced on the path of evolution, and he learns the secret of how to control matter for the purpose of the spirit and to manifest "beauty" through matter.

A time comes that matter becomes the perfect servant of the spirit, and the spirit can manifest its resources through forms.

Who are all these monsters of evil existing in the history and traditions of the world? They are those people who were trapped for a long time in matter and material values to such a degree that they were blinded to any other values. They turned into a tumor in life and exercised their separative willpower over others.

The evil people in our life are not alone; they are the servants of a huge army and receive energy and power from that army. Essentially, they are spirit but blinded by matter and material values such as

- more land

- more power over others

- more money

- more possessions

- more luxury

- more dominance to force their separative will

- more deception to avoid light, reality

- more pretense to hide themselves

- more crimes to avoid opposition

- more sensuality to be insensitive to reason and logic

Evil walks through all these tunnels and lives in the darkness of its ignorance. Ignorance is the inability to see progress, to be part of the spiritualization process. In fact, ignorance hates so violently any kind of spiritual phenomena because it hurts its ignorance. The Great Sage calls such people who follow the path of evil "ignoramuses" who, wrapped in matter, ignore the fiery values of the spirit.

Ignorance is not a lack of certain knowledge or information. Ignorance is the inability to see the reality of evolution, the reality of a breakthrough into light.

When ignorance continues for many incarnations, there comes another evil that is insensitive, indifferent to any spiritual values, virtues, or aspirations. The spirit is buried deep in matter, and man is approaching the moment when he will lose his soul and turn into matter.

The man, or other disintegrating body, promotes evil. It stimulates material tendencies, separatism, self-interest, vices, and manifold low desires. Every disintegrating form has a similar effect in its environment.

Not only the man, but there are huge constellations in space in the process of decay. Their bodies have a malefic influence upon global and systemic bodies — man included. We are told that the process of their disintegration causes healthy bodies to suffer. Suffering puts a limit on them and forces them to attach to the form side of life.

Evil in its many forms must be recognized as a hindrance on the path of human evolution.

The success and survival of a person depend upon three things:

1. recognition of the enemy
2. learning the ways of the enemy, how he works
3. frustrating the efforts of the enemy

We must try to expose the enemy so that we really understand what he is. We expose the nature of the enemy through Beauty, Goodness, Righteousness, Joy, and Freedom. The enemy can never be exposed except through these five means. If you want to bring out his ugliness, you must really manifest beauty. This is a greater way to fight against enemies than to fight with ugliness. If you fight with ugliness, you increase the ugliness in the world and harbor the enemy within your own system, on all levels.

How are you going to fight using the means of Beauty, Goodness, Righteousness, Joy, and Freedom? For example, the enemy is totally afraid of freedom because freedom means destruction to him. Joy also means his destruction. He always tries to limit you and to bring you grief, sorrow, and pain. He teaches you unrighteousness. He brings evil intentions, evil will, and ugliness. If you can expose him through the five means, not only do you destroy him but also without directly attacking him you reveal his nature to everybody so that everybody else recognizes him. In building Beauty, Goodness, Righteousness, Joy, and Freedom, the enemy will be exposed naturally.

This technique of fighting is Hierarchical. The Hierarchy fights; members of the Hierarchy are called Warriors. They fight not with the techniques used by the enemy, but with the five techniques of Beauty, Goodness, Righteousness, Joy, and Freedom. Of course you will say, "If the enemy is using bombs, I must use bombs." This is logic, but it is a logic totally different from Hierarchical logic.

We are at a certain point in a cycle for this planet and for humanity in which we will make it if we reach certain heights of consciousness by the year 2000. If we do not meet this deadline, we will miss the opportunity for another two thousand five hundred years. Because of this crucial time, you can see increasing activity from both sides. Now you can see that the Forces of Light, the forces of Beauty, Goodness, Righteousness, Joy, and Freedom are increasing in the world. The opposite side is also increasing. This indicates that instinctively, intuitively, the masses know that the time is short.

Whatever is happening in the world is a reflection of that which is happening within our individual psychology. If you want to know what is happening within you, listen to the news. The news is a very good reflector which reveals what is happening within humanity and within individual beings. If we understand what is happening outside, we can understand what is happening inside. We are going to catch the enemy within us. If every individual, group, and nation caught the enemy within itself, then the outer enemy would not have any field in which to operate because its field of operation is the human nature.

Forces of Light and forces of darkness are related to one another, like flame and smoke. They are in every nation, in every race, in every group, in every human being. When we talk about enemies and dark forces, we are not referring to any particular nation, race, or group. It is just like a flame and smoke mixed together. It is everywhere; it is international. It is also in our nature. If we really start observing ourselves, we will see how "mixed" we are. Sometimes we have an idea that we are angels. If this is the case, we should prepare ourselves for a great disappointment. One must really see the other side of himself by asking, "What is the other side of myself that I am not seeing?"

Hiding is one of the greatest techniques of the enemy. It hides behind your emotions, behind your pleasures, behind your goodwill, behind your good intentions — even behind your love. But if you expose it, you will be terrified to see what opportunities you have given the enemy to function within you and how it works in such a way that you did not even let yourself know about its existence. This is what exposure is.

Your greatest success as a human being is to expose the enemy within you. Ask yourself, "What is in me that is creating so many things that are not good and prosurvival?" Your greatest opportunity is to face yourself. In some traditions it is said that man is both darkness and light. This is why we have been given the prayer, "Lead us, O Lord, from darkness to light," from the nature within us that is darkness to the nature that is light within us.

What are those things that prevent us from seeing the enemy? The darkness within a person has a magnificent technique of hiding itself. Darkness projects itself outside onto others so that the person always looks for it within another human being instead of looking for it within himself. Knowing this, we can expose the enemy.

Dark forces have worked very intelligently in the past two hundred centuries. Very slowly, a philosophy has surfaced which says, "There are no dark forces; there is no evil. God has created everything; therefore, everything is good." This philosophy is a fabrication of the dark forces so that they can hide under another blanket. But if you remove the blanket, you will see the enemy beneath it.

There are dark forces. There is a Satan, as some churches emphasize. In all religions and traditions dark forces are mentioned. For example, when I went to Africa I was present at a healing ceremony. The sick man was lying there, when five or six medicine men started dancing around him with swords and arrows to drive the devil out of the man. They wanted to scare the devil away. I asked, "How old is this tradition?" "From the beginning of the earth," was the answer. One medicine man said, "I can see whenever a person is sick. There are entities around him that want to conquer him because he is capable of being their enemy."

This African tradition is very old. Similar traditions are found in the *Bible*, in the Zoroastrian religion, Muslim religion, and Hindu religion. It is a universal tradition. For two hundred centuries, the enemies of humanity have created and emphasized a misleading philosophy to hide themselves. It is now being taught in many churches and groups that there is no evil. When Alice Bailey first published the Great Invocation and people read, "And may it seal the door where evil dwells," they wrote hundreds of letters in protest. I have received many letters saying, "If Alice Bailey was an esotericist, she would know that there is no evil." Some groups have gone so far as to change that phrase to read that evil does not exist. This is why I wrote about evil and its origin in *The Science of Meditation*.[1]

Dark forces are not limited to any particular branch of human endeavor. They are everywhere and in everything. They are found in politics and in education. For example, various schools have been closed in recent years because of pornography and different sexual abuses. What is this? It is more than evil. We can see how evil is operating in education and in communication. It is even in the arts and sciences. For example, there are many dangerous chemicals in your food and cosmetics which cause permanent, lasting damage. In various religious groups evil is deeply rooted. The religions that are supposed to stand for light, love, and goodness have too much evil. I am not saying that religion is evil, but that there is much evil in religion. There are religious wars being fought throughout the world — in India, in the Middle East, in Ireland, to name a few — where people are murdered every day in the name of religion.

What Is Evil?

Evil, first of all, is built by our own evil thoughts. Any time you think evil, bad, critical thoughts about somebody or something, you build a thoughtform which carries a very negative charge. That form is a black entity, a decomposing form. That thoughtform travels faster than light. It can circle the earth three times before you can

---

1. See Ch. 28, pp. 265-278.

blink your eye once, scattering pollution all over the world. Sometimes when you are sitting quietly or engaged in any activity, an evil thought suddenly comes to your mind. That thought is the result of those "thought satellites" which circle the planet and broadcast evil thoughts. Those thoughtforms stick to people when people have similar attractions within themselves. Some people become like snowballs. As they roll, they gather more snow and become increasingly bigger.

This science has not been given to humanity at this point because the enemy tries to prohibit and forbid its release saying, for example, "Evil is superstition or prejudice. It doesn't really exist." But if you ask, "Then why is evil happening on this planet?" they will answer that it is because of the economy or any other number of reasons. Why, for example, was crime only five percent ten years ago, and it is now two hundred and seventy-five percent? It is an expanding snowball, rolling faster and faster.

You attract evil thoughtforms if your aura contains associated thoughts. Similar thoughts are magnetically attracted to each other. They come to your aura, contaminate it, and eventually a part of your aura is decayed.

Our aura is a light-sensitive body. It becomes sick; it decays and becomes polluted. Parts of the aura can collapse. Parts become like a vacuum, while other parts can become occupied by entities. This is why the Great Sage says, "We are living in danger; we are always in danger." The initial action originates within you. If you create an attraction within your aura toward evil thoughts, you will attract them. They are never attracted to a person who does not have associative thoughts within himself.

An evil thought does not land for a while until it pollutes the layers of the atmosphere. Thus, it prevents higher inspirations and impressions from reaching us. This planet has layers upon layers of evil thoughts surrounding it. In a particular layer there may be lots of light and divine impressions. Hierarchical suggestions are accumulated there. The evil thoughtform pollutes that layer and obscures it, preventing the beauty and light from reaching earth. Then it lands. But where does it land? It lands on a special "runway" that has been prepared for it — a personal, group, or national aura. It lands in those nations, groups, families, and individuals which provide a "terminal."

The moment one thinks an evil thought, evil increases in him. This is a very psychological, scientific observation. Why should thinking an evil thought increase evil within a person? Thinking evil thoughts increases evil because the person then creates a magnetic attraction to other evil thoughts. Sometimes apparently innocent people whose minds are not pure become carriers of evil without knowing it.

There are also evil intentions. Intentions are totally different from thoughts. An evil intention is like an arrow. An evil thought is just a form, while an evil intention is a very strong, negative, electrical energy. Every time you have an evil intention, you provide a horse for an evil entity.

Most of the entities in the space around us do not have any particular direction. They want something to play with, just as monkeys do. Give a monkey anything, and he will try and play with it. An evil intention gives direction to evil forces and anchors evil thoughts toward the person to which that thought is directed. If I have a bad intention toward Mr. X, I direct evil thoughts through my intention toward him, thus providing a form, a body that an evil entity can occupy and manipulate.

Negative emotions are the third category of evil. Evil thoughts sometimes live three thousand years. Evil intentions live maybe four thousand years. Eventually, they reach the borders of the Fiery World where they burn and fall as ashes upon humanity. Negative emotions may live anywhere from one day to two thousand years. It depends upon how much energy you put into that negative emotion.

These three evils — evil thoughts, evil intentions, and negative emotions — sap your most precious energy, which we call life energy. I am not referring to prana. It is really your life. Every time you have evil intentions or emotions, or think evil thoughts, you give some of your life to make these entities exist and live. They are like our children. Our real children, however, can survive by themselves once they are grown, while these evil entities cannot. Children can support and nourish their own life after they are grown, but these evil entities continue to survive only by constantly sapping our energies. Our life energy provides fuel for them to act and survive. As an individual, a family, a race, a nation, as a whole planet, we are giving life to these entities.

The fourth type of evil that is prevalent on this planet is called hypnotic or subliminal suggestions which are carried out in self-interest. Any hypnotic suggestion that is used for self-interest is an entity that will always fight against your own free will. Its objective is to prevent you from having an independent will. Anything that prevents your freedom, whether occasionally, periodically, or forever, is your enemy. Hypnotic suggestions keep a person continually occupied in that black spot in his mind. Subliminal suggestion is another very subtle trick to impose things upon one's mind that he would not consciously accept. So you have in your consciousness a conflicting field without being informed of it. This condition reflects in your health, in your points-of-view, in your logic and reasoning without you really knowing what is happening. Some people suddenly feel exhausted; a posthypnotic suggestion is probably in action. Or let us say that you received a subliminal suggestion. It creates conflict within your consciousness about which you are unaware and wastes your energy.

Dark forces and enemies always work in darkness. They work within the unconscious. They work in ways so that you are not aware because once you are aware, you can conquer them. The greatest technique of the enemy is to hide so that you are not conscious of it. For example, how many times have you heard yourself say, "I don't know why I did that" or "I wish I hadn't said that?" Why did you do it or say it then? Who made you do it? What is operating through you that is making you unconscious of your actions, words, and thoughts?

The fifth category contains very evil entities. How did these evil entities come into being in space? Some people living on this planet are criminals; they stay drunk on alcohol or use drugs day and night. They steal, they kill, they are traitors. They are enemies of human freedom. They are strongly pornographic. When these people die, they are exactly the same as when they were in the human body. It is not the human body that gives them their negative qualities but their emotional and mental bodies that urge them to act this way. Just because the physical body is left behind, does not mean that these people turn into angels. They have the same urges, drives, and appetites as before. But because they no longer have a physical body, they no longer have the vehicle through which they can come and do the same things they were doing before. The only method by which they can fulfill their urges and drives is to possess and obsess people. In this way they use the bodies of other people as the vehicles for their own sensations and pleasures.

This kind of evil is very strong and creates a tremendous amount of pollution. Once such an entity sticks to your aura, it enters like a drill and makes room for itself. The quality and condition of your aura determines where it will locate itself. For example, if the entity is sexually abusive, it will come and enter into your sexual aura, your sacral center, and activate it to such a degree that it becomes impossible for you to control your sex drive. Or, if its intention is to break up your marriage and establish disunity, it will make you impotent or totally reject sex. Both of these extremes are created by the same kind of entity. The dark ones are against normality. If they take your normality away from you, they succeed in their endeavor because abnormality is against your own progress.

If your heart is acting evilly, it is possible that an evil entity has blocked the heart petals so that divine grace, beauty, and compassion cannot manifest. You become possessive, aggressive, and destructive. You bring destruction around yourself. Now the enemy can do whatever it likes. For example, if the dark forces want war, they enter your brain and make you a war monger. You begin thinking, "We want war! We want to destroy them!" But if you tell the enemy or its agents, "Come, we will take you to the front lines," they will escape because such entities do not want the ones they possess to die, so that darkness can continue to spread its pollution. It is very tricky. If we could write a book about all the ways and means that the dark forces operate, it would be like an encyclopedia of sicknesses.

The sixth kind of evil, or enemy, is a very dark force. Dark forces are not human beings. They are referred to in the Bible as "Satan and his armies."

At some very ancient date in the history of our planet, a great angel rebelled against the Divine Plan. This occurred on the Cosmic Physical Plane on this planet. Other angels joined him and said, "We don't want to work under the Plan," so they began to oppose the Plan. They were not humans from our planet.

Throughout the history of humanity, the dark forces have been seen by many people. They look like skeletons with very red eyes; sometimes they have horns and tails.

This is not superstition; there are such kinds of beings. In the *New Testament* we are told that Saint Peter said, "Your enemy, like a lion, waits upon your path to devour you." In another place He says, "Our fight is not against human beings, but against dark forces." Whatever humanity does that is evil is mostly inspired by the dark forces.

The seventh type of dark force and enemy are those who are possessed and obsessed by the dark forces. These people are dark forces. If a man becomes a clear channel for a dark force, he is part of their army. We read in *Faust*, for example, of a ceremony in which a man signs a document with his blood, selling his soul to Satan. In medieval history, there are thousands of similar stories in which people have sold their souls to evil. For example, an evil one would say, "You want a pretty girl? Then sign your soul over to us, and we will bring the most beautiful girl to you." People in these stories also sign away their souls for wealth, power, or to destroy a nation. The dark forces say, "We will do it for you, but you must give us your soul."

These examples refer to the renouncement of your Solar Angel. Once you renounce your Solar Angel, you join the dark army. Your Solar Angel then leaves you because you "sold It" to the dark forces. The Solar Angel does not belong to the dark forces, but your agreement with Satan makes your Solar Angel leave you. Once your Angel is gone, you are at the mercy of the dark forces.

Question: *If a person renounces his Solar Angel, is he doing this in ignorance?*

Answer: Not necessarily. This contract with the dark forces is agreed to knowingly; you are signing it. You say, "I renounce my Solar Angel." You are aware of what you are doing. You may be possessed or obsessed when you do it, but this does not matter. You signed the contract.

Question: *I have a question about the horns and tail. What are they? What caused them?*

Answer: These serve as antennas, as their communication system. We think that horns and tails are something that God made as a joke to animals. But they have a purpose. If research is undertaken and people analyze what horns are, we will discover that they are electromagnetic instruments which give direction and convey feelings to the animals. The horns may appear to be made of very coarse substance, but in reality there is no coarse substance in the world — there is only substance. Substance may look coarse, but it is as sensitive as the finest ether, because everything is built from the finest. It can be condensed but not coarse. The tail has different uses.

We have not researched these ideas yet because we are too busy building atomic bombs and wasting time in fruitless activities, in stockpiling munitions upon munitions.

Question: *If someone criticizes a person without the intention of hypnotizing him, can it still be a posthypnotic suggestion if the person is in a psychologically receptive state, for instance, if they are depressed and you criticize them?*

Answer: It can be. For example, if I say, "You are stupid," I have projected an image upon you, and if you are sensitive at that moment, you assume that you are stupid. From that date on you act really stupidly, even though I only said you were stupid.

This is why if we can expose these things within ourselves and in our community, we will have a better chance to survive. However, we are brainwashed and bombarded with hypnotic suggestions every minute from our society. It is very difficult to rid ourselves of these things unless we really want to do it.

Question: *Doesn't a negative thought go out and then return to the sender?*

Answer: Yes, it comes back, but it pollutes other places as well. Most of our thoughts multiply every minute, like ten thousand little germs. This is what pollution is. If you speak one lie, the lie itself does more damage than is apparent. Many people, without knowing it, are harmed by the lie. For instance, you say to someone, "The train is not coming today." The word spreads that the train is not coming. Suppose a man planned to travel on that train because he was sick and needed an operation to save his life. But he did not go to the station because he heard that the train was not coming. The man dies leaving orphaned children, and so on. All of this happened because you spoke only one lie. The dark forces can use that lie to create lots of different "children," so to speak.

Question: *If a person's aura is really strong, is he protected?*

Answer: What does "strong" mean in this instance? There is no aura that is strong unless it is totally charged with the five factors of Beauty, Goodness, Righteousness, Joy, and Freedom.

Question: *Does an aura charged with these five factors repel negative thoughts?*

Answer: It repels them, of course. The negative thought comes and goes away. It may even be destroyed.

Question: *If at death the dark forces have somewhat penetrated into you, is this registered in your permanent atom so that when you return you are already in their clutches?*

Answer: The permanent atom is not activated, but the dark force is in your aura. For example, if you are on the astral plane, you are still possessed. If you are mentally possessed on the physical plane, you will be mentally possessed on the mental plane. You will do exactly the same things on that plane that the possessor wants you to do. And, when you incarnate again it will incarnate with you.

Question: *Is there some kind of psychiatric rehabilitation center on the astral plane?*

Answer: On the physical plane you are not aware of the entities in your aura. On the astral plane, after your physical death, you can see them in your aura so you look for help. There are many so-called clinics on the astral plane. Great disciples and Masters occasionally visit the astral plane. The Great Sage says, "In the astral plane, people know about Us." They know that members of the Hierarchy exist because they can see Them. The Great Sage is a great physician. When He visits the astral plane, maybe once every ten years, people see Him. In the meantime, disciples and nurses work there day and night to clean up the mess. Sometimes before a baby is born, he is cleaned of possession and obsession. But sometimes babies are born with two or three different "faces." I observed one young child who acted like a monkey. He did not know what he was doing. He was divided between several different influences every hour.

Question: *Do Satan and his armies have a particular place of origin or a plane upon which they dwell? Is it beyond our solar system?*

Answer: The dark forces have their headquarters in the lowest plane of the Cosmic Astral Plane which is beyond our Divine Plane. They are very "heavy."

Question: *Do they manifest on the physical level?*

Answer: They sometimes take incarnation. There are examples of this. A man was once knocked down and his soul left. A dark entity immediately entered and occupied that man. He was Hitler. Nero is another example of this kind of criminal.

It is very sad that China destroyed Tibet, but actually, Tibet had become a land of black magicians. When these magicians grew old they used to pull out the soul of a child, leave their old body, and enter the body of the child in order to continue living on the physical plane for another sixty to eighty years, repeating their evil game.

Question: *Is jealousy inspired by the dark forces?*

Answer: I would say that in the beginning human jealousy invites the dark forces, which eventually take possession of the person and leads him into various crimes. Some people think that jealousy is a sign that a person has a sense of value and wants to protect the object of value or that he has a deep love for the object of his jealousy.

But jealousy, in its real sense, is proof that the person is incapable of having a real sense of value because he is destructive toward the value itself.

4 Enemies of Light

We sometimes think that the enemies of light, the dark forces, and evil are so powerful that they are running the whole show. When this impression is given, it creates inertia, disappointment, and hopelessness in us. Actually, the contrary is true. It is Divine consciousness, Cosmic consciousness which has ultimate power over everything. There is a great angelic organization which fights against the dark forces. This organization consists of millions and millions of beings, both on earth and in the heavens. Specifically for our planet, it is very significant that the army of the Forces of Light are under the command of Christ.

In 1941 the war was at a very critical, dark state. We did not know whether Germany, Japan, and Italy were going to conquer the earth or if the allied nations were going to conquer the enemy. Then, at the June Full Moon in 1942, the Great Teacher sent a letter saying, "Today, Christ took into His hands the command of the angelic forces and the war will soon come to an end." Shortly thereafter, the allied forces began landing in Europe and the enemy was defeated. So we see that the upper hand is with the Forces of Light, the Commander of whom is Christ.

As the dark forces try to attack a person, a family, or a nation, angelic forces are ever-ready to give help. They come to your assistance once you shift yourself toward their direction and create some kind of contact with the Forces of Light. Knowing about this creates a kind of balance in our consciousness.

The enemies of Light are against seven principles: Beauty, Goodness, Righteousness, Joy, Freedom, enlightenment, and expansion of consciousness.

1. *Enemies of Light hate beauty.* Wherever there is ugliness, there is also the presence of dark or Satanic forces. It does not matter if that ugliness is your body, your emotions, your thoughts, your plans, or activities; whether it is found in the movies, on television, in announcements, dramas, or history. Wherever there is ugliness, you must feel that it is a fight against beauty. Beauty is the presence of God. Beauty is the path through which man is going to reach perfection. Beauty itself is the symbol, the image of our future perfection, inspiring us to go toward the Source.

If, for example, there is a family where the husband and wife act through ugly thoughts, words, and behaviors, we can conclude that dark forces are operating there. If you commit an act of ugliness, stop it immediately and shift it toward beauty. When you catch yourself in a moment of ugliness, immediately stop because you are opening a path for evil to possess you. You are weakening your own defenses and the evil ones rejoice at this opportunity. They will go to their chief and say, "See how I was able to make this husband and wife fight against each other? Now they are fighting, now they are separating, now they are divorcing, now they are enemies." They will get a nice medal because they created ugliness and disunity within that family.

We must remain alert and awake. Most science fiction and adventure films we see today are psychologically prepared to destroy beauty and express ugliness in the minds of people. Every time you see ugliness represented as being beautiful, be aware that dark forces are within it. There is ugliness in drugs, in alcohol, and in crime. Dark forces fight to increase ugliness because when ugliness is increased, it instantly retards the possibility of your development and unfoldment.

One day a man and his seven-year-old son came to my office. The man said, "This boy wants to kill, to destroy cats and dogs, and he beats other children. Why is he doing this?" I talked with the boy for a while. He seemed very intelligent and healthy otherwise. Then I noticed a certain thoughtform in his mind. I arranged to visit his home, and as I entered the boy's room I saw a large picture hanging on the wall of a tiger devouring a lamb. All the bones and blood were falling to the earth. The tiger had a happy expression, while the lamb looked very pitiful. The image of that picture had penetrated into the mind of the boy. He was playing the role of the tiger, always wanting to create sheep to eat. You cannot be a tiger unless you have prey. The sheep, in the boy's consciousness, symbolized anything that was weak. Because he had this ugly image in his mind day and night, I advised his father to remove the picture and replace it with a beautiful image. In two months the boy had calmed down.

The human psychological mechanism is so sensitive and complex. What was the evil in this case? A dark force noticed the situation and inspired the father to hang that picture in the child's room. It then used the opportunity to inspire crime in the boy. We must remain alert and careful about what we put in our homes and what we see in the movies.

Many women come to me for counseling regarding their marriages. When I asked one woman her reasons for getting a divorce, she said, "Everybody is doing it. Just the other day I saw a movie that exactly expressed my desire for divorce." She did not realize how much the film was influencing her. She was destroying her family because she could not feel joy unless she did exactly what was impressed in her mind. Impressions sometimes work like a tumor or like pus in your mind. Until that pus comes out, you cannot relax. These negative images come out through your behavior.

2. Dark forces fight against goodness. They never want anyone to be good. How do they prevent goodness? They petrify your heart petals. Suddenly you become cold, atrophied, resistant, and rejecting. You become cold to beautiful things, to your duties and responsibilities in such a way that you never think, act, or speak about what is good.

Goodness is something you give to others to increase their joy, their freedom, their beauty, their health and well-being, and so on. Dark forces try to prevent you from doing good not only locally but also in national and international fields. In spite of the tremendous efforts of the dark forces, there is still a lot of good produced from the activities of those who are in the Army of Light. In an individual, or in national and international fields, darkness is fighting against Light, like a flame that is surrounded with smoke — flame and smoke together. You can see it in every field of human endeavor.

3. Dark forces fight against righteousness. For example, they want to put people in positions of high leadership who work for special interest groups, for particular personalities, and for racial interests. Righteousness does not belong to a separate or specific individual, group, race, or nation. Righteousness belongs to everybody and is for everybody.

How do dark forces work against righteousness? First they enter into your brain and affect your judgment. You start thinking unrighteously about people. Consider the following examples:

- Someone tells you a piece of information and you exaggerate it and become unrighteous in your thinking, feelings, and actions.

- A person passes by and does not say goodby to you, so you go into your office and write him a nasty letter. He did not say goodby because he was preoccupied and did not see you, but you write that letter because unrighteousness works within you.

- Your wife is one minute late, so you think she is with another man. You are unrighteous. Wait a little.

- Let us say you have an obligation to someone, and you consider not fulfilling your obligation for various rationalizations. Such reasons are very "sugary" to deceive you. In this way, you are unrighteous with so-called sugary reasons. But the sugar turns out to be poison because it leads you to act unrighteously.

4. *Dark forces fight against joy.* They hate joy, but they inspire hilarity in people. Hilarity is senseless and purposeless happiness. They hate joy because joy is Divine essence. Joy is from God. When Christ says, "I give My joy to you," He is sharing His Divine blessings. Satan hates this. He wants people to be sick, depressed, beaten, angry, hateful, jealous, revengeful. He wants people to criticize each other, to separate from each other, to always sit on the fence, so to speak. This is what Satan wants. So whenever you see that you are taking joy from a person, you are under the influence of the dark forces.

Joy is not happiness. Joy is Divine satisfaction; it is beauty. For example, I was listening to two men talking at the dinner table. The older man, who was eighty, was telling the younger man, "You know the God you believe in does not exist. There is no God. There is matter; there is pain and suffering; there is death. That is all there is." The young man looked at him and said, "Do you really think so?" "Yes, my son," he said, "this is life. Believe what I am telling you." The older man took away the joy, the subtle joy of the young man's awareness that God exists. Do not take the joy of others and destroy them.

Another example is when a young girl says, "I want to be really pure when I marry," and a so-called friend says, "You are stupid. I was fourteen when I had sex with many boys and became pregnant. It is so delightful." The girl replies, "No, I don't want to do that." See how the friend is taking the joy of purity from the young girl?

In still another illustration, a young man in the army says, "I don't want to kill people," but his commander says, "You must kill. Here is the science of killing." Eventually the soldier becomes a professional criminal, even though originally he did not want to kill.

Do not take joy from people if they have joy. On the contrary, increase the real joy in others, not their superficial or cosmetic joy. Taking the joy of people is like extinguishing a fire by pouring water on it. Increase the joy of other people. When you take the joy of others, your joy will be taken from you and dark forces will replace it with their gloom.

5. *Dark forces are totally against freedom.* In the name of freedom, dark forces fight to destroy freedom in a way that you do not feel it. They propagandize for freedom, but they totally work against it. For example, they say that you are a free person, but that you cannot do certain activities in many areas of your daily life. Now where is your freedom? In what ways are you free? You can do whatever the dark forces tell you to do — that is your freedom. You can see how your freedom and the freedom of the world are slowly evaporating because of dark attacks. Are they going to be successful? They are not! There is a great secret which the evil ones are not aware of. This secret is that evil will eventually destroy itself. This has happened repeatedly throughout history, and it will happen again. Somewhere, somehow, their faces, their activities will be exposed, and light will once again be triumphant.

6. *Dark forces are against enlightenment.* They do not want you to be enlightened. What is enlightenment? The first step of enlightenment is to see your responsibilities and duties. If you do not have a sense of responsibility and duty, you are not enlightened. Whatever your position is — husband, wife, laborer, office worker, or whatever — if you do not have a sense of responsibility toward your tasks, toward human and planetary survival, toward the unity of mankind, then you are acting under the influence of the dark forces.

7. *Dark forces do not want your consciousness to expand.* How do they accomplish this? They cram so much knowledge in your mind that you do not have time to digest and use it. While in Europe I gave a lecture attended by many scientists, doctors, and other professionals. They were asking questions at a child's level even though I spoke to them at their level of understanding. Finally I said to them that they may be very advanced in their education, in their diplomas, degrees, and positions, but that they lacked understanding; their consciousness was not liberated.

Wrong knowledge is poisonous, but poison also

exists in right knowledge. For example, someone asks you for directions to a certain place, but the directions that you give are so complicated that he loses his way. These are the tricks of the dark forces. That is why Christ warns us to be careful of hypocrites. Hypocrites are those who give you something for reasons other than what they say. In other words, the bread they give you contains poison instead of nourishment and energy.

Once while lecturing at a university, I noticed something very interesting about the students. They were acting like automatons. They had so much knowledge that they could not stand apart from it and be themselves. One can know so many things that he loses the power to effectively use the information he has. Congestion of the mind is very harmful; simplicity is much better. Simplicity, clarity, directness, straightforwardness, and cleanliness are ideal.

I attended a seminar at the same university given by three instructors. The first session was very good. The second lecturer presented one hundred exercises, which confused the audience. During the final session a lady said to me, "I am totally confused. I don't know what to do." I told her, "It was the teacher's intention to confuse you so that you would never do the exercises again." One exercise would have been enough.

Another example of confusion would be if you gave someone five tickets to five different movie theaters, each featuring a wonderful movie, all for the seven o'clock show on the same evening. He will not know which one to attend. He will probably not attend any of them. I was once given three tickets for three different football games, all for the same day, at the same time. By the time I decided which one I wanted to attend, the doors were closed.

When you think about the psychological basis of confusion, it is interesting to observe how this "game" is played in the stock market and in politics. When you become aware of what is taking place in relatively small situations, then what is occurring in the larger picture becomes more evident. "As above, so below." It is an analogy, nothing else. If you know human psychology, then you will better understand the "game" we call politics.

Dark forces are totally against anyone making contact with the Inner Guide, the Inner Self. They make every kind of fabrication — psychological, scientific, historical — to prove to people that the Self does not exist.

A scientist once tried to convince me that the human body was nothing more than an accumulation of twenty-one elements, which, he said, were only worth a total of one dollar and ten cents. Unfortunately, once this kind of teaching is spread in our schools and universities, evil will be able to possess us from every side so that we become its servants and act against Beauty, Goodness, Righteousness, Joy, Freedom, and enlightenment. Under these conditions we are less able to establish contact with our inner conscience, the Solar Angel. When a person severs his relationship with his Solar Angel, he cuts his communication with his conscience. If you sell your conscience, you cannot operate as a soul anymore. You become a machine in the hands of the dark forces.

The conscience is the presence of the Solar Angel within you. The dark forces make great efforts to impress your mind not to pay attention to your heart, to your feelings, or to your conscience. They say, "Just do it. Why should it bother you? It is only ten cents that you stole. It is not a big deal. You made that girl pregnant and then you deserted her. What's wrong with that? Everyone does it. You became angry with your wife and said terrible things to her. These things happen every day. You gossiped? Well, why are you bothered about that? Everybody gossips." These are subtle examples of how they operate. Through such methods, the dark forces begin destroying your conscience so that you no longer have any contact with it. They attempt to close off your conscience so that you do not feel bad about having negative thoughts, feelings, speech, and motives. They say, "Don't feel bad about your actions. You did it, and now it's finished." They may even lead you to a psychologist or psychiatrist who eventually takes your conscience away from you, someone who will say, "You did it; it is finished and gone. Why worry or feel guilty?" You eventually become a zombie who thinks all of his sins have no impact or that they have been forgiven. Or a person goes to a priest and asks that his sins be forgiven, and the priest gives him absolution by saying, "All the sins on earth and in heaven are now forgiven you." Why not tell the person, "You did wrong; don't do it again. I am glad that you are worrying and in a panic about it." This is the action of light. The other that hides and covers your conscience is the action of darkness.

One must really suffer with his conscience without exaggerating the situation. Through exaggeration, the dark forces totally destroy your conscience by making it overly sensitive. For instance, you think that with every little mistake you make you are going to end up in hell. This can lead to insanity because you are in a panic and think that you are condemned to hell from then on. I visited a mental hospital and talked with two Christian girls who had been committed. One of them said, "I am going to burn in hell because I kissed a boy. My priest told me I was going to hell." The other girl kept repeating, "I have lost my soul; I have lost my soul." "Where did you lose it?" I said to her. "You are here, talking with me. You are the soul, understand?" Evil forces can magnify your mistakes and sins in a way that you lose your mind.

Another very subtle technique or device of darkness is to exaggerate your virtues in such a way that they eventually become vices. For example, fanaticism is an exaggeration of something you love. Because you love it the evil ones make you fanatical so that, eventually, you lose your common sense and become a ridiculous person.

Question: *What do the dark forces gain by doing such things?*

Answer: When they take from others they increase in wealth, just like human beings. If you take a portion of someone's territory, so to speak, you become richer; your side increases while his side decreases. Dark forces prevent the Divine Plan from manifesting. They prevent enlightenment, beauty, and goodness. When they prevent these things in you, you become their slave. For example, they begin by creating two slaves. These two slaves can multiply into thousands of slaves until eventually the dark forces possess the earth. By this criteria, the earth becomes a possession of Satan's instead of God's.

Question: *Doesn't Satan know about the eventual degeneration of the dark forces?*

Answer: According to my information, a portion of the evil forces are beginning to see it now. One of my Teachers told me that certain groups of evil ones now have an opportunity to turn to light. For example, if you can change the minds of alcoholics, drug users, sex abusers, criminals, traitors, and so on, it is possible for them to become responsible human beings. It is even possible to talk with them at certain levels and say, "Your way is wrong." However, they are so scientific and intellectually sophisticated that you have a very difficult time talking to them. For instance, if you ask a military commander why he destroys a city, he will tell you it is because the enemy lives there.

Question: *What benefit can the dark forces possibly gain if the earth becomes an asteroid, or if the whole solar system is destroyed?*

Answer: It would be the greatest victory for the dark forces. They are quartered in the astral plane. Their greatest victory would be to frustrate the evolution of this planet and disturb the Plan of God. In this way they would be able to prove that they could successfully work against God's Will. If we lose the opportunity to fulfill the Divine Plan, it will be another two hundred and fifty thousand years before the Zodiac comes into a cycle again in which humanity would have another chance.

Question: *To carry this question to a logical conclusion, if they keep frustrating the Divine Plan and win, will all the galaxies crumble and everything end up in total chaos?*

Answer: No, not to the extent that you think. Dark forces are influential only in those areas where they have stations with which they can tune in. Because of our globe's racial condition and tendencies and its particular stage of evolution, it is vulnerable at this time to the efforts of the dark forces. But on other globes in this solar system or in other solar systems in the galaxy they do not have too much of a chance to be influential.

There are many people on our planet who have tendencies toward crime and evil. I have had the experience of counseling people who would not change their minds to be healthy. For example, I observed a man on television the other day who had been convicted of abusing over fifty young children. The commentator asked him, "What do you plan to do after you are released from prison?" "The same thing," he answered. All his psychiatrists, psychologists, and medical doctors could not convince him to change his mind. There is some devil sitting in him.

Question: *Is there any technique that can be used to help such people and those who are attached to the dark forces?*

Answer: Early education and a noble environment will help. Pain and suffering also can change the orientation of people who cannot be helped otherwise.

We are also told that a ray, similar to a laser beam, will be found that will penetrate into the etheric centers and burn any tumors or cancers forming there. This instrument will also be able to penetrate into these areas and burn away hatred. Hatred is a sickness just as real as any physical illness, but it exists in the subtle planes. When you have conflicting urges, drives, and emotions, you dump loads of poison into your aura even though you are not aware of it. One day that poison must be destroyed scientifically.

The Masters can destroy this poison by using Their eyes to project a specific ray that burns the seeds of sickness, if a person's karma allows it. But sometimes even the Masters are not able to clear away the poison. For example, before the betrayal of Christ, Judas was agonizing with himself because the time had come for him to go to the high priests and betray his Lord. Judas was in pain. Christ turned to him and said, "Go do what you want." Judas ran to the priests and said, "Give me thirty pieces of silver. This is where the Lord is. Go and catch Him now." Even Christ was not able to change the mind of that man because the time of change had not yet come. If you are involved in one line of allegiance for many ages, it cements in your psychology.

There is an example of a man and his wife who are greedy materialists. At the mention of a single penny they tremble. Their two-year-old child is already developing the same characteristics. Greed is a cancer eating all of them. How is it possible to destroy their greed?

The Great Sage was once asked how to develop compassion. He smiled and replied, "Compassion is a labor of ages of incarnations." One must work for ages to have compassion. It is not acquired through reading books. You cannot simply read about compassion and become compassionate. You must develop it, like a career. For instance, you decide to become a psychiatrist, a scientist, or a judge. After you graduate from school you think you know everything, but you do not. You need until the end of your life to learn the profession that you have chosen.

Consider nationalism. Let us say that a young man is a citizen of a particular country. If he is put in the same grinder for five hundred years he will say, "This is my nation" when he emerges. You can say to him, "You are now an esoteric student; now you are a disciple, an initiate. Think in terms of one humanity. Forget about your race and your nation. Be part of one humanity." But at the end, when he is dying, he will say, "Bury me in my national cemetery." You could not make him universal; you could not give him Cosmic consciousness. You could not destroy the tumor that tradition, religion, or nationalism instilled like a capsule in his mind. This is the way that evil forces perpetuate separatism, war, revenge, and destruction.

Question: *Do you think that we must not have close feelings about our nation and country?*

Answer: It is natural to love your country, your nation, and be faithful to the interests of your country — but not at the expense of other nations and their rights. Our racial or national feelings must expand to involve all races and nations. This will give us everlasting joy.

I used to be very nationalistic and racist. I would speak to hundreds of people, shaking them with words like, "Our nation, our race, our blood." It was not until 1963 that for the first time I felt like a human being and nothing else. I worked very hard to accomplish this. Most people die with tumors of nationalism. What is your nation or your race in terms of the Infinite? You are a beam of Light from the Divine Sun, nothing else. Do not label yourself as this or that. Because of these labels we are ready to annihilate all life on this planet. We need to think in terms of oneness, and that oneness must not be artificial.

For example, people talk about how they are one body, one spirit. But, if they are asked to make a financial contribution to support their claims of unity, they separate themselves from unity with others and disappear. This idea of separatism is illustrated in the following story:

A group of mice were looking for a way to protect themselves from a cat. They decided that one of them would have to put a bell around the cat's neck so that when he was close by they could hear the bell and run for shelter. But the mice could not agree on who would be the one to bell the cat. While they were busy arguing, the cat sneaked up on them and ate them all.

In the future, humanity must not be based on separatism. Of course, we must be noble, faithful, and obedient to the nation in which we live; we must not fall into spying or treason. We must be faithful and watchful citizens because our karma has placed us there.

5 Methods of Attack

Dark forces use numerous methods to attack the Forces of Light. The following are just some of them:

1. Dark forces charge objects and places with their negative energy, such as a statue, a picture, eating utensils, plates, cups, and so on. Once they charge an object or a place with their energy, you feel repulsed by that object or place. The dark forces demagnetize or magnetize places and objects with their pollution. For example, if ten people who carry the intentions of evil or darkness attend a church, that church will eventually fall apart because the dark forces emit magnetism or substances that are destructive to unity.

This is why some houses must be thoroughly cleaned before you move into them. A house where a murder has been committed or where there has been divorce or meetings held with criminal intent is polluted. If you buy that house, before you move in you need to clean it because the evil thoughtforms and patterns of thinking are still there. These patterns, if left behind, eventually penetrate into your bones unless you are extremely strong and pure.

If you buy used clothing of any kind, it is important to know from whom they came. Clothing carries the aura of its wearer. The total charge of the aura, whether good or bad, is contained in the clothing. If an advanced man gives you his shirt, that is good. If a criminal gives you his shirt, do not bother to wear it because eventually his criminal thoughts will penetrate into your aura.

Question: *What if you are pure and you give your old clothing to a goodwill organization and someone very negative buys your clothes?*

Answer: It will help the negative person a little bit, but it may overstimulate him and drive him crazy, make him a fanatic, or make him lose control of himself. Overloading certain people with gold will create the same damage as if you had overloaded them with trash.

Question: *Does it reflect back upon you?*

Answer: Not necessarily. If you are strong enough, it will not affect you. But if you are not strong, it will create a relation between you and the negative person. When the evil influence of the person increases and surpasses the power of your goodness, his negativity will come to you through the clothing you gave him. A communication line is built between the two of you.

Question: *Then should we not give our clothes away?*

Answer: Some Hierarchical sources advise us to burn our old clothing or give it away to spiritual people.

Question: *How do you clean a house that has negative thoughtforms in it?*

Answer: Spray it with eucalyptus oil on the first day.

Spray it with peppermint oil on the second day. Then for one month burn sandalwood incense in all the rooms. This method cleans away many problems. The greatest cleaning agent is prayer. If you read prayers aloud, such as the Great Invocation, the Lord's Prayer, certain verses from the *Psalms* or mantrams from the *Vedas* for a few days, for a week or a month, you will observe how the atmosphere in your home changes. Family relationships will improve. You can feel the way it changes you.

The blessing contained at the end of *Spring of Prosperity*[1] cleans negative thoughtforms. It is a very strong mantram. Any time you withdraw money from the bank or receive money from other sources, repeating this mantram will clean the money and totally change it. As it is now, money passes through millions of different hands and carries with it a lot of trash.

Question: *You said that negative thoughts travel around the world. Do positive thoughts do this as well?*

Answer: Yes. Positive thoughts travel faster than negative ones, but negative energies have more receiving and broadcasting stations than the positive ones at this time. Remember that both energies are fighting in man, in nations, in the solar system and Universe. We must be agents of light or generators to increase light, Divine potential, and Divine energy. Each of us is a generator. You must take in a little light, and then increase it by a factor of ten. You must also increase love. You must take beauty and then create more beauty. For example, if we listen to a beautiful lecture, we must take that information and teach it to other people so that light is increased everywhere.

Every object that you use must be blessed before you use it. You can use a blessing which magnetizes or

---

1. Written by the author.

demagnetizes the object, just by looking at it. You can energize an object in the same way. Eyes have the power to do good or bad. There is such a thing as a "good eye." There is also what people traditionally refer to as an "evil eye." A person with evil will says, "What beautiful clothes you have." Two days later you tear your clothing. Or they might say, "What a beautiful vase," and it cracks the next day. Powerful evil is within such a person.

Dark forces can harm your health. My mother used to take the flat base of a bunch of garlic, dry it, and put it in our pockets so that evil would not affect us.

There was a very evil woman who lived in our area. I did not believe how evil she was until I saw her do something. We had a very special jar for cooling water. This woman paid us a visit one day and said, "What a lovely jar that is!" It cracked immediately.

If you carry a copy of the *New Testament* in your pocket, or a cross or holy object, it gives you conviction, strength, and faith that nothing will happen to you. It is this kind of faith that repels evil.

Blue stones are also used against the evil eye. In Asia, for example, many girls place a blue stone upon their forehead so that the evil eye does not make them sick.

Question: *What kind of blue stone?*

Answer: Any simple blue stone, not a precious gem.

Question: *In* Altai Himalaya, *Nicholas Roerich talks about the evil eye. He says that people can look you in the eye and make you sick. How does this process work?*

Answer: A negative force enters and destroys your aura. When you look at another person, you pour something out through your sight. This substance touches people. It is not just a reflection; something is actually poured out.

I read a book which described certain people's psychic abilities. It gave one example of a man who could look at a road and crack it. Another man looked at a woman and raised her three feet off the ground. Both men did this through their eyes. It is energy. This occurs throughout the world and has been witnessed under strictly controlled scientific research. Qualified Americans visited these areas to test the scientific validity of the experiments and wrote a book on their findings.

2. Dark forces build thoughtforms and send them out. They can send you thoughts about your health, your success and prosperity. If they do not want you to be successful, healthy, or prosperous, they will build and send an opposing thoughtform to you.

Once on a visit to Mexico City, I met a person who invited me to attend a special meeting. The meeting was attended by some powerful men and women who intended to kill a few select people. They began the meeting by distributing a victim's photograph to each person present. Then they imagined that the person had a heart attack and was taken to the hospital where he died. They then imagined his funeral and so on. After building these thoughtforms for twenty-five days, the victim would eventually become ill with the symptoms and die. Undercover agents in many countries work in similar ways to harm national leaders or influential citizens, using negative thoughtforms to control them.

War will someday be fought on the mental plane. If you can fight mentally, then you are going to fight. It is very close to this situation now. We are either going to fail mentally or conquer mentally. This is why you must never think evil of anybody. Thoughts such as "I wish that person would fall down and die" or "I wish that you would lose everything you have. I hate you. I don't want to love you" must never be thought or verbalized. Any expression of this kind builds a thoughtform which goes to the person and hits him. The damage that you send the person is recorded in your "account," and you will pay for it at the time of judgment. If you committed two tons of damage, you will have to pay for it with interest. There is also a system of taxation in spiritual realms, so be clever and intelligent and do not think negatively about others.

Gossip is the result of wrong thinking. Slander is even worse. Malice is very bad, and treason is the very worst. Do not occupy your mind with these things. You will pay for it severely. That is why Christ said, "Bless those who curse you and slander you." By thinking this way you do not become involved in karmic debts. Just say, "God bless you," then remove yourself from the situation. If you curse, you react in the same manner as those who curse you. You both will be debtful.

Current political practices throughout the world are based on retribution and revenge. "You killed our people, so we will kill yours!" This policy see-saws continually. A time must come when humanity ceases from doing these things. In the *Bible* it is written, "Revenge is Mine, sayeth the Lord." No person must take revenge upon another. Revenge must only be taken by God, meaning that karma will take care of it.

Question: *Is there any way in which a leader can protect himself against destructive thoughtforms?*

Answer: Of course. In the *New Testament*, one of the apostles said, "Pray for our leaders." For example, if one million people pray for the president, he will be a better leader than if everyone hates him. Leaders must be protected by our prayers. When you hear that a leader is doing something wrong, do not be full of malice, hatred, and revenge against him. Instead, pray for him. Take the leader in the light and ask for the blessing of a Great One so that the person is in light and not in darkness. In very critical times your light will help; the leader can suddenly make the right decisions.

If you fabricate things about your enemies, you make the situation worse. For example, if you make a comment about your enemy, saying, "He is an animal; he cannot understand. He is really dark, a criminal, a traitor," all of these thoughtforms will go to him and nourish his mind, unless he is equipped with goodwill or a radiant aura.

We think that our enemies are always evil. Often our enemies are better people than we are. When people oppose or restrict our forceful demands and exploitation, we consider them our enemies, while in reality we are worse than they. When a person's mind is nourished with negative thoughtforms, he will be an even more negative man. That is how we make our enemies worse than they were. We are the ones who are doing it!

Politicians do not know about these matters because they have been brainwashed by the old technique of "an eye for an eye." This approach has never worked effectively. That is why Christ said, "Love even your enemies." This is the way to establish peace and unity. But where is peace? The law of "an eye for an eye" was given in the right way. Karma works in the same way, but it has been distorted and used in the wrong way to the point where it has become a superficial law. Be very careful and work with divine principles such as Beauty, Goodness, Righteousness, Joy, Freedom, and so on. In doing this, you will be healthier, more successful, and your enemy will be less dangerous than if you think of him as being evil.

To illustrate this method of the dark forces further, let us assume that you continually tell your son that he is a bad boy. By saying, "You bad boy! Why did you do that? You bad boy! Why didn't you eat? You bad boy! Why don't you smile?" you turn him into a criminal. He will be a very bad boy to justify the thoughtforms he received from you.

3. *The dark forces work through the controversial issue of abortion.* Abortion is the result of the activities of the dark forces. Abortion must never be performed unless the mother's life is in danger. Dark forces are especially against those souls who are spiritually advanced. Evil forces work to prevent advanced people from taking incarnation. They want to send an advanced soul to the Subtle World so that there are fewer soldiers of Light to fight against them on the physical plane of the planet. In the future we must not even think about abortion, but find solutions to avoid it.

Question: *What about China's current efforts to limit its population problems with abortion? What about birth control in general?*

Answer: Birth control is all right, but the best method is discipline and natural methods. Even so, you are still trying to limit the number of people being born on the planet, which includes advanced people as well as premature incarnations. This planet could hold another two hundred billion people, if we lived correctly. But because we do not live correctly, there is not adequate space or food for them. If we lived according to the doctrines of Christ, Buddha, and Krishna, we would have plenty of life's necessities. Actually, humanity is currently wasting ninety percent of its natural resources. If we look at the situation scientifically, we waste for the most part; we are involved in greed, competition, jealousy, and the "mine-yours" psychology for the most part. Animals know their sexual purpose more than we do. We are perverted and brainwashed. We look upon sex as a daily necessity, like eating. Once our glamors and illusions are gone, sex will be regulated so that it will be used only in need. We will eventually come to realize that sex is necessary only to bring in a child. How can we reach this awareness if our mechanisms are distorted and disturbed? We must accommodate and compensate until we reach the ideal. Sex, as we think of it now, is only a glamor, an urge. We do not need it, but we crave it because our movies, newspapers, parents, loneliness, and propaganda urge us toward excessive sexual activity. If we attain a natural, clean consciousness, however, we need much less sex than our current habits. It is a waste. The fluids involved in sex are Cosmic substances which are given to humanity to connect the Intuitional Plane to the human being. When this substance, this precious energy, is wasted, it cannot do the work for which it is intended. The best policy is to use common sense and be as clean and pure as possible.

When I first came to the United States I was surprised to find that twelve and thirteen-year-olds were having sex. A person should not have sex before age eighteen, and then it must be in a marriage.

There is some tolerance that we can allow to a certain degree, but not too much. We not only tolerate following our own sexual urges and drives, but also we encourage others to do so. Eventually, however, a time comes when we see how we misuse ourselves and others. This is the moment that we crush our sexual glamor and stand in light. Of course we regret what we did in the past, but we think about the future and plan our life to handle our energies more creatively.

In Atlantean times, syphilis, gonorrhea, and AIDS were so widespread that they destroyed that civilization. The safest route is purity. Have sexual relations only with your husband or wife. Be very careful that you do not indirectly force your marriage partner into unhealthy sexual practices. In everything you do, use your higher concept, your higher intelligence. Using this method you can more easily detect the hands of Satan sitting in your sacral center controlling you.

4. *Evil works with disunity through thoughtforms, emotions, writings, and so on.* Everything that disunites us as families, groups, and nations is from evil, no matter how sugary the form of disunity is presented. Separation stems from evil; unity is from God. In everything there must be unity. Even if you have an argument, the common denominator must be in the best interest of both parties. The common denominator must win, which is for the good of both parties. When you see disunity, especially in groups, families, children, and so on, some dark entity is working there. You must be very cautious to stop it so that you keep the family together. Do not forget that disunity starts with sugar-coated words, intentions, and ideas. As a family member, you might think that you have the right to do whatever you want. This is self-deception. Your good intentions and good thoughts were sugar-coated instruments from the dark forces. Your only right is to maintain the integrity of the family, nothing else; otherwise you become a victim of the dark forces.

In groups one must be very careful not to express criticism and various acts of treason behind the back of the leader, the teacher, the group itself, or behind the interest of the whole. This is a sure sign that some evil has penetrated into those traitors.

Traitors often carry on their destructive work in the name of justice, but all their intentions are to gain superiority over their victims and satisfy their revenge, hatred, and hurt feelings. Most traitors cover their past ugliness and corruption with a blanket of purity and holiness, under which they attack others in order to serve the dark forces. In attacking others for their personal ends they delay their evolution for many lifetimes and perpetuate their suffering.

Possessed ones try by every means to justify their actions, slandering somebody else and declaring that their actions were taken because of the weaknesses or supposed failures of others, to protect their "holiness" and "immaculateness." Such people usually ignore the "long tail" of their failures and misdeeds that hangs from their own back.

Regarding such an example, one Teacher wrote, "The difference between me and you is that in spite of all my weaknesses and faults, I am guarding a palace of highly beneficial ideas, visions, and the Teaching, and with all my humility and dedication I am serving those who need my help. But you, knowing of the palace and its treasures, escaped because you could not use the palace and its treasures any longer for the gain of your own selfish interests, and you could not stand the pressures placed upon the palace by its enemies. The ugliest thing was that instead of seeing your shortcomings, failures, and stupidities, you hid yourself behind an alibi that the guard of the palace was imperfect and that his imperfection hurt you. What a pitiful excuse this is to hide your utmost ugliness! I will ever stand guard, even until the last hypocrite leaves the palace to serve his vanity!"

5. *Dark forces create doubt:* doubt about God, immortality, the Teaching, about the concept of group, about Christ, faithfulness of loved ones, or anything precious. Once doubt enters your mind it eats you. Do not establish your reason and logic upon doubt. Be certain that what you are thinking and seeing is scientifically and logically right or wrong. You need to be certain of what you are doing.

One of the most efficient ways of erasing doubt is to be very accurate in all your actions. Are you doing things consciously, or are you an automaton? If you are being pressured into taking certain actions, for example, entering into the swift currents of a river and being involuntarily pushed by this force, you must be very careful because it is a sign that you are not your own master. You are being a slave to some unknown agent who is very careful not to reveal his face. Once you start observing these things, the cause of your behavior becomes clear. You must ask yourself, "Why was I doing this or thinking that?"

Doubt is a very strong force. For instance, I remember a situation in which an organization was going to purchase a forty-acre parcel. The selling price was four-hundred thousand dollars. A man attended the meeting and scattered doubt about the owner, so the organization did not purchase the land. Three years later, that property sold for five and a half million dollars. To undermine a situation all you need to do is spread doubt because, like germs, doubt quickly multiplies. One little doubt is enough. That is why the Great Sage calls doubt "the coffin of the soul."

6. Dark forces use confusion. Dark forces work through confusion. For instance, I told a group of teenagers that marijuana was no good and not to smoke it. Five of them immediately said, "We have medical evidence which proves that it is not harmful." Others said, "Some sources say it is very harmful." At this point there was confusion in the group.

When a person is confused he continues doing whatever it was he was doing originally, and that is exactly what the dark forces want. This is referred to as being "lukewarm." It creates a very bad condition in your consciousness.

At present, dark forces do not attack the Teaching; instead, they confuse the Teaching. For example, they say, "Karma is good," so that people think they believe in karma. Then they subtly add a few definitions that change the quality of karma, and people swallow it because they did not speak against it. They distort and confuse the issues with the purpose of confusing and manipulating you. This technique is used in politics, psychology, economics, communication — everywhere.

For example, let us say that Italy is a strong ally of this country, so for ten years we talk about Italy as a nation which is friendly to our interests. Those who wish to confuse us show up and say that Italy is secretly preparing to attack us. Once this information is expressed we start mobilizing, whether we like it or not. Then Italy becomes aware of our mobilization and makes counterpreparations. Once this psychology is employed, we are involved in an arms race, and a dark devil will be very happy about this situation. He will receive a medallion because he was able to create so much doubt and confusion.

In *The Republic*, Plato speaks about future government, saying, "Future leaders of humanity must be philosophers." He means that our leaders must know exactly what their duties are and must know about the secret layers of human psychology.

How can a man rule a nation righteously, or be a good congressman or senator, if he does not know these things? In the future, people will elect philosophers into public office, people who know the secrets of life. These philosophers will know how a devil can attack them. All leaders must learn the science of the dark forces or their leadership will not be righteous. How can a captain direct his ship in the ocean if he is not aware of the dangers inherent in every wave, wind, tornado, or earthquake? He must know about the dangers he might face in order to be a good captain. Likewise, the leaders of humanity must know about the tricks of the dark forces so that the ship can be guided in the right way. Our present leaders know nothing about the dark forces.

In still another example of disunity and confusion, a treaty is signed but at a later date that treaty is ignored, even though it was a good treaty. The dark forces are always in favor of confusion and against unity.

7. *Dark forces mix fact with fiction.* This is such a subtle procedure. For example, I saw a movie in which an actor was masquerading the words of Christ. People in the audience knew he was talking about Christ, but in a way, the actor was speaking totally against Christ. This is a technique in which the dark forces are really proficient. First they present the facts, then the falsehood. They gain you with the facts, and then defeat you through the falsehoods.

This method is also used in our everyday relationships. For example, a man says to you, "Didn't I tell you that five years ago your husband went with another woman and then shortly after that with another woman?" "Yes." "Well, now he is with a third one." This time he is lying, but you believe him because he was correct the first two times. He seems reliable to you, so you do not see the poison in the capsule. That one little capsule is enough to create trouble between you and your husband. This is how the Satanic army operates.

8. *Dark ones degenerate the images of Great Ones.* For example, I once attended a play about Goethe, where Goethe was presented in such a ridiculous and dirty way that no one in the audience would want to read what he wrote. A recent movie about Mozart depicts him as a disfigured, ridiculous, and dirty man, who just happened to write beautiful music. The dark ones used Mozart's great music as a trap to impress in you an ugly image of his personality. You will never again have the same image of that artist because of the way they destroyed his image. In another film, the Virgin Mary is depicted as an ugly prostitute. It was terrifying to see this sacred symbol of purity so horribly defiled. Another film depicts a saint engaged in homosexual activities. That saint has been worshipped for hundreds of years, and now they are presenting him as a homosexual. Anyone who hates homosexuals will now hate that saint. And the evil one responsible will say, "I did it! I created disrespect for a worshipped image." As if asleep, people pay millions to view these dramas and films which encourage them to create more and more damage to the human race.

This is a technique that the evil ones use. Who are they? Not a particular nation or tradition is responsible, but people found in all nations and all traditions.

Try being a teacher and you will see how very difficult it is in this day and age to deal with children. It is a very difficult duty. You must be a psychologist to do it. There are lots of disturbances in the psyches of children because of the movies and television shows they watch. Television and films are wonderful instruments for education, however, if they are used properly.

9. *Dark forces are very much interested in the period of adolescence* because it is in this period when physical, emotional, and mental changes occur and when sexual temptations and crises are revealed all around the person.

Adolescence is a period in which you either build your future or destroy it, or create hindrances that will meet you in the future in front of each step you take.

10. *Sexual perversions and unnatural sexual acts are very damaging to human beings.* These practices are forbidden in all religious literature.

11. *Dark forces work through alcohol and drugs.* Alcoholism is totally under the control of the dark forces. In bars and nightclubs where alcohol is consumed you can find millions of dark forces and entities. Drugs are another extremely harmful agent.

12. *Greed is another effective instrument of the dark forces.* Dark forces stimulate greed in you. Whenever you see yourself becoming greedy for anything, be careful. You are coming under their control.

13. *Dark forces work through hatred.* Hatred is a device in their hands to destroy nations, countries, everything.

14. *Revenge is an everlasting calamity for humanity.* Revenge must not be allowed in our personal lives, in groups, or in national and international fields. Revenge has far-reaching and destructive effects.

15. *The dark forces create the instrument of "earth-boundness."* People are stuck to earth, to their property, as if it is their only hope in life. Actually, it is the least hope, the weakest hope. Still, people continue to buy and buy, have and have, which makes their mind and whole psychology earthbound. They say, for example, "That river is ours. This lake and this mountain are mine. This acreage is also mine." This continues until they eventually become earth, nothing else.

16. *Materialism is a tool in the devil's hand.* Materialism means that you give matter the highest value in the world. You believe in nothing else. In doing this, you put your focus in the wrong place.

17. *Another instrument of the dark forces is the operation and maintenance of so-called pleasure establishments.* For example, there are clubs which feature nude male and female performers. This brings not only a lot of money to the proprietors but also destroys many families. For instance, a man sees pretty, naked girls and then goes home to his wife and says, "I don't like you anymore," but he does not really know why. Then he starts looking for a woman who is more like the naked model in the nightclub.

This is what the dark forces are doing, and we are paying for it. These pleasure palaces with their liquor, drugs, lust, hatred, and crime are destroying our children and our family structures.

18. *The dark forces use many other activities which occupy or waste our time.* For example, watching television for several hours a day is a common practice. If those hours were accumulated you would have had enough time to study to become a doctor or a teacher. But the dark forces do not want you to do anything worthwhile. They want you to waste your time and energy. It does not take much effort on their part to do this because suddenly you realize that you are fifty years old and have no time to study to become something better. It is finished because they kept you occupied.

19. *Dark forces impress your mind with the superiority of luxury or laziness.* Once they create a craving within you for luxury, inertia, or laziness, they have achieved a great goal. Forces of Light want you to be active, diligent, and working every minute, using your time to do something very beautiful. Against this, the dark forces use fabrications, such as, "Buy luxuries. Push buttons will do all the work for you."

Take, for example, microwave ovens. They cook in just seconds or minutes. This gives you another ninety minutes to chase pleasure. You have more time to waste on unimportant things, not more time to do better things. Actually, it will be seen in ten years how microwave ovens have created another ten million cases of heart disease. Food prepared by microwave is trash. This is a perversion of science.

20. *Dark forces create irritation.* They annoy your friends, your marriage partner, and associates to irritate you. In this way you also become a source of irritation to others. Irritation creates a contagious poison. When you receive a dose of irritation, you share it. Then many become poisoned. The dark forces like this. They say, "We played a nice game with them."

21. *Dark forces work by passing private and secret information to others.* This is an effective way to create cleavages. For example, someone obtains secrets of the

United States and sells them to another nation. Someone else takes secrets from Russia and sells them to another nation. The secrets of private citizens are obtained and sold. In this way the dark forces can create bad relationships between people. This is their goal.

When bad relationships are created you no longer have right human relations. This is what the dark forces want. They are against unity and understanding because in unity and understanding they cannot live. They cannot set up business in unity and understanding.

22. Dark forces work for the prevention of future vision. Most dark forces try to prevent your eyes from looking to the future. Dark forces work in the present. For example, they say, "Just enjoy it now. This is life. Enjoy, eat, have, do. There is nothing else." If you talk about the future they ridicule you and create confusion in your mind so that you no longer think about the future.

Once you stop thinking about the future you become an earthbound criminal. Observe your friends. Those who are preventing the future are not really your friends; they are not really working for your own good. Someone might say, "Forget the future. We are here now. Let's enjoy it." Such a person is working for the past, and the past means evil. The past belongs to evil; the future belongs to Light. Observe whether a person is working for the past or for the future.

When you read magazines, books, or newspapers, observe if the author is bringing your attention to the future or to your past failures. If he focuses on your past failures, he is a servant of darkness. Dark forces never focus on the beauty of the future. They have no future. Darkness dwells only in the past.

Question: *What about people who study archaeology or history?*

Answer: To study archaeology or history does not mean to live in the past, just as to study the phenomenon of cancer does not mean to have cancer.

History is either unbiased or it is changed by nations or historians for many reasons. In archaeology we see the path of life; we see causes of our failures and successes and the results of our education and creativity.

The present recorded history of humanity is a history of the crimes we committed. Read it and you will see that it is mostly crime. From the viewpoint of the future, many of our national heroes would be considered criminals because their heroism was achieved by killing others to make their nations greater. In future judgments people will ask, "Why did you do that? Your right hand was killing your left hand, and you were enjoying it." When a person has the consciousness of the whole he will say, "That was stupid. I was cutting my right hand with my left hand."

In a true historical account, we would see the psychology of leaders and people and learn precious lessons that could be used in the future. But unfortunately, most often the history of an event is not written by someone who is able to see things as they really were, and the author is often commissioned by those who have personal gain and interest tied into presenting history in a specific way.

Archaeological treasures do not belong to the past but to the ever-existing present. We are advised in esoteric literature not to look back at the past and not to be attached to the past, but people do not usually understand this advice. It means simply that one must not be trapped in his past failures, successes, limitations, wealth, or with his painful relationships with certain people. Instead, one must press forward with a spirit of adventure and striving and, with full spirit and mind, forge ahead toward greater success and achievement.

Comment: *One of the great early American historians wrote history showing how God's Plan was being worked out through the American nation. Current historians say to ignore him, that he was wrong, superstitious, and not on the right track.*

Answer: According to your own interests you approve or disapprove of things, which does not mean that you are right or wrong. You must have principles. Measure what you write and speak according to those principles. If you do not have any principles, you will be just like a pendulum, swinging from side to side. We know that one of evil's techniques is to destroy the principles within you.

What is a principle? Let us take one very clear principle — unity of the family — as an example. Nothing must interfere with family unity. If you do not have this principle in your essence, which the church brings through its prayers and blessings at the time of marriage or which the judge impresses upon you at that time, then you lack this principle. You act every which way according to various stimuli, urges, and drives. You must first have a principle upon which to base your judgment. A principle is always prosurvival, individually or in a group.

Principles stand behind the law because the law is a translation of those principles. This is what laws are. If the law says not to drive over fifty-five miles per hour and you speed, you are doing wrong. If there is no law, then you are doing neither wrong nor right. You can go one hundred miles per hour or one mile per hour if there is no law.

Why are laws established? Let us make a general statement and say that laws exist to give everyone a chance to be happy and protected. This is the principle. What is the law? All the regulations and rules that we make to provide for and protect our principles are the laws. That is why we say that every human being must have principles, and those principles must be based in spiritual realms, like those principles found in great religions, great traditions, or in great scientific discoveries.

Question: *Sometimes dark forces can get into a nation and pass laws which contradict principles. What about this?*

Answer: Exactly. For instance, a special interest group can infiltrate into a legislative committee and create certain laws favoring its own future advancement and destruction of group members which the committee represents. This happens in every nation and in many organizations. This is especially noticeable before revolutions. Evil ones create the kinds of laws in which their crimes cannot be caught. But generally speaking, the law must be obeyed because ninety percent of the law is good for humanity. In the *Bible* it says, "Follow the laws of the nation. Do not break the laws of the nation." In some way, national laws are under the guidance of Divine Will. Where are the defects coming from? They come when we misuse and misapply the law. Mistranslation of the law or misusing it through various means of power creates suffering. A judge once told me that fifty judges will meet sometimes for as long as five hundred days to define one word. That word is law now, but before it was defined it could have been misinterpreted.

The origin of law is based on benefiting every human being. Sometimes, however, people distort this original purpose. Fanatics and special interest groups can create laws biased in their favor, as mentioned earlier. For example, the laws of a little country in the Middle East were changed in such a way that the king suddenly realized that all the laws were against him. To counter this, the king changed all the laws to support his wishes. This is another extreme.

SNEAKY METHODS OF ATTACK

Dark forces often use a very sneaky method in order to follow their victims. When their agent, for some personal reason, cuts his relation with someone to whom he was carrying destructive venom, the dark forces can be hindered by such aloofness. What they do to again establish a connection and have a way to pour the poison into their victim is to make their agent try to contact the victim with cards, letters, or telephone and establish a new relationship with the former victim or with his closest friends. Once the relationship is established, the agent traps his victim, slowly pours heavier poison into him, and damages the victim to such a degree that the plan of the dark forces reaches its destination.

Extreme caution is needed not to restart communication with the agents of evil. Their intention is not to cure, to heal, to uplift, to harmonize but to have a chance to release more poison.

Of course it is possible that the agent of dark forces can change, realize his mistake, and feel sorry about his past destructive labor, but one must have proof that such a transformation or change occurred in the heart of the agent of dark forces. The change can be witnessed if

- the agent regrets the past and realizes the extent of the damage he did

- he asks forgiveness without justifying his past action

- he never mentions the cause of his slander and treason and sincerely asks to be forgiven

Even if such an event happens, the victim must be very slow in accepting his contact and must give a few years' time to see if the agent is again in his sad business or not.

Of course one must always be forgiving, but forgiveness must not be used by the agent as a new opportunity to poison the victim or a new chance to sow a few seeds of new evil.

The wisest technique in relation to those people who acted as the agents of dark forces — demonstrating ingratitude, slander, treason, hate, malice, jealousy — is to completely isolate them. Cut all communication with them, keeping a very sensitive eye on all their activities. Wakefulness is extremely important because an agent of evil can appear in a thousand forms and can act in a thousand ways to keep himself always covered. Naïve and stupid people, with all their good intentions, can play with such rattlesnakes and get beaten, destroy themselves, their loved ones, and their future plans for the Forces of Light.

An adversary is charged with hatred and separatism, and his intention is to hurt, to destroy, and to take revenge. Giving an opportunity for an adversary to contaminate groups is just like opening a box of germs which may contaminate weak minds.

If anyone has a problem with anyone in the group and is really seeking constructive actions and settlement, his duty is to see the concerned person and try to reconcile with him or see the leader for constructive direction. If his intention is group welfare, he must act in a way that he does not create disturbances in group unity. But if his intention is to punish, to devote to his ego and vanity, he must be guarded.

If an adversary is filled with love and goodwill, he cannot remain as an adversary but turns into a wise counselor and friend and helps those who made him "an adversary."

Encouraging adversaries is an action to open the door to dark forces.

It is true that lots of mistakes are made in various groups, by various members and leaders. But those who were hurt need not turn into adversaries but into men or women of loving understanding. They can make their points heard but without destructive intention. When adversaries, who are charged with jealousy, revenge, and criticism, gain ground, no good comes into being but bitterness and an increase of adversaries instead.

The defeat of an adversary is an action which makes him more explosive in the future.

With group problems the best way is to approach the problems with the light of higher principles such as

- forgiveness
- mutual respect
- sincere communication
- absence of jealousy and revenge
- the Common Good
- humility
- loving understanding
- cooperation in progressive improvement

If an adversary is attacking from the outside and trying to penetrate the group through his slanderous talk or planting mistrust within certain members, he must be immediately cast out.

It is possible that leaders and members may err, but in order to correct a situation one does not become an adversary. On the contrary, one can deal with the people involved as a friend and with loving understanding try to correct the situation.

Many adversaries are adversaries because

- they feel they are superior
- they have hatred or anger
- they are jealous
- they are hurt
- they crave recognition
- they crave position

If people give a chance to such persons, listen to them and honor them, but know that they encourage them in their destructive activities and thus delay their evolution for ages.

Dark forces easily possess people who, through malice, slander, and treason, try to serve their self-interest at the expense of the destruction of others.

Once a victim is possessed by dark forces, he will suffer and be haunted, life after life, through his malice, slander, and treason.

EVIL INTENTIONS

In this century, the dark lodge uses a new technique to combat higher ideas, principles, and standards.

In the past the dark lodge fought higher ideas, principles, and standards face to face. Now it uses the technique of distortion. For example, the dark lodge fights against freedom by teaching about freedom, using the principle of freedom in such a way that people are trapped in the prison of freedom, and freedom is used to prevent freedom.

They made the planetary life a big concentration camp, singing for freedom, politically, economically, and financially. Take the idea of art and beauty, and see how art and beauty are prostituted in modern films and plays, how beauty is used to advertise sex and crime. Take love, and see how love is distorted and turned into sexual license. Take health, and see how much the idea is exploited both in orthodox medicine and so-called new age medicine.

The dark lodge also learned patience. If it cannot win a war, it can win ten years later by steady pursuit and by preparing for its victory. The dark lodge currently does not hate any good action but cooperates with it to inspire vanity, ego, jealousy, self-interest. Soon good action turns into corruption.

My Father told me that there was a saint whom an evil one visited every day in the form of a friend. The evil one spoke to him about the beauty of forms, such as

- flowers

- trees

- architecture

- furniture

- arts

- the human body

- a woman's body

Then at the end he brought with him a beautiful girl. The saint was intoxicated to see the beauty of the girl. That moment the evil one departed leaving the girl with him. Ten days later the saint was no longer a saint.

In another story my Father told how greed was introduced to a saint under the idea of building a temple for the congregation.

Only a few people smell the intention of evil ones because now they pack their gifts with luxurious papers and flowers.

The new era disciple must cultivate himself to see the essence through the forms and the methods the evil ones use to deceive their enemies.

6 The Ways of Evil

There is no end to the ways evil is promoted on the planet. We are seeing the disastrous results of many of them.

1. *Dark forces work for pollution* — pollution of the body, emotions, mind, water, air, and earth. Only through pollution can they prevent the development and health of our bodies, our brain, and our nervous system. This sets us back on the path of evolution. Every human being who works against pollution works under the Forces of Light.

I was in Switzerland when a man came to me and said, "Can you talk with me? I feel something very bad in my conscience. I am an agent who sells five thousand tons of poison every year to certain factories. I know what these poisons do to human beings."

"Be very careful for your karma," I advised him. "If I were you, I would discontinue doing that."

Later, when I was giving a lecture in Zurich, he attended. Afterward he told me, "I quit selling the poisons. It is going to cost me half a million dollars a year. Is this better than selling poison?" "Good man!" I told him.

Whoever is selling poison, producing poison, polluting the planet, polluting the human mind, the human emotions and heart is working either directly or indirectly for the dark forces. We all want to drink good water, but there is little good water to be found anymore. This means that life is going to be shorter and shorter and increasingly painful. Because of this, our evolution is not progressing. We are destroying our health. A person can fight against the destruction of his body and evolve, but it is extremely difficult to do. He needs Divine Power to do it.

2. Dark forces build destructive thoughtforms. What is an evil thoughtform? If you think in evil, destructive, and harmful ways, your thoughts take the same shape as the objects about which you are thinking and the manner in which you are thinking. Take the example of a man who thinks that California is going to sink into the ocean and that ten million people are going to die. He writes a book, which thousands of people read. Because of what they read, they imagine exactly what he wrote. All these people start to be scared, and they panic in their imagination. This man's thoughtform is now growing and growing; the forces of the earth will begin to be controlled by his thoughtform, and an earthquake, even if it is not due, will eventually come.

Dark forces build thoughtforms in the same way. For example, they sit five people together who imagine that Mr. X is getting sick, that he is gradually getting paler and more unhealthy, weaker and weaker. They imagine him dying, then in his coffin at the funeral. This thoughtform is an active electrical form in space. It gains strength from all associated thoughtforms and eventually hits Mr. X, who then has a stroke and dies. Dark forces use such thoughtforms in politics and other fields. At some future time, when atomic bombs and other such weapons can no longer be used, the dark forces will carry on their battle through mental telepathy. Evil thinking and good thinking will clash.

War that is waged through thoughts is more destructive than atomic war. A nation can be annihilated with evil thinking. This is the motivation behind the use of propaganda. Evil propaganda aimed at various people, nations, and races develops thoughtforms against their targets and mobilizes the human mind against them. Eventually, a very dark army will be created to act against the targets of the propaganda.

There is no cure or protection against this except to create the opposite camp and help people think in sanity, in exactitude and clarity — in "as-is-ness." This kind of thinking is very difficult to find now because people's "computers" are so distorted and misprogrammed with polluted thoughts that they cannot even recognize the "taste" of a good thought.

3. *Dark forces use abortion.* Dark forces want people to have abortions, especially if they see that the aura of the future child is beautiful and that he is going to work for the Forces of Light in the future and become a great hero. When they see a child like this, they want to kill him before he can be born and make the mother read and listen to advice that will influence her to abort the baby.

Abortion is a crime against an incarnating soul. This soul will be thrown into the etheric plane, where he will suffer for as long as he was intended to live on the physical plane if he had not been aborted. Often those who commit abortion are acting under the force of possession. It is also observed that the incarnating ego is possessed, and this possession influences the mother to have an abortion so as not to give the incarnating one a chance to free himself from his possessor.

The possessing entity differs according to the level of

the one who intends to reincarnate. Sometimes possession is temporary, and if the mother is pure and strong, she can make the entity escape from her child. This is often accomplished by continuous prayer and meditation.

People who are proabortion are not necessarily evil people, but abortion is an evil act. It is a crime against a soul who wants to incarnate. Dark forces encourage women to have abortions, especially if they know that an advanced soul is coming to earth. Who knows how many geniuses, talents, and leaders have been lost through abortion! Instead of fighting for abortion, men and women must exercise mastery over their sexual urges and find healthy, scientific ways not to become pregnant.

I asked a young girl who was preparing to have her third abortion, "Don't you think you are hurting your own mechanism as well?" She looked at me and said, "It isn't costing me a single penny. I can have another abortion." How can we help such people from continuing to have abortions? When and how will such people learn to use their bodies more purposefully, creating less karma?

Those who are proabortion fail to consider the consequences that will befall them in future lives. It is better to control sex than to register yourself as a future candidate for the forces of darkness. In having an abortion you may seriously damage your physical body, cloud your conscience, and load your mind with various disturbances. You can never strive toward perfection and light if abortion is fun for you. Through disciplining yourself and gaining mastery over your urges and drives, you can achieve greater intellectual and spiritual heights.

Women must be very careful about this issue. Men must not suggest or encourage abortion unless the mother's life is in danger. If you have had an abortion in the past, unconsciously or innocently, then do not repeat this action because you do not want to become an instrument of the dark forces.

If you have had an abortion in the past, do not repeat it. Maybe you were ignorant, or forced by circumstances and other people, but never do it again. Feel proud that you have the honor of being a mother, and you will see what great lessons you will learn in being a mother.

Those who have no qualms about using bombs and violence, about hurting or killing people, or who believe in abortion, cannot stand before Christ and justify themselves. Such violent procedures increase the numbers of those who seek to protect their "freedom" — whatever that "freedom" is.

The solution to the problem is not violence but education. Educate your children about the value of life. Teach them the path of sexual purity, abstinence if necessary, and discipline. Motivate their minds toward forming families. Teach them how precious sex is and how one must use it for higher purposes. If our sons and daughters are properly educated and protected from negative influences, we will not have to worry about them having abortions. They will know what to do with their lives.

The difference between a woman who has an abortion and one who has the baby and raises him in honor is immense. The one who has an abortion will have more blockages and complexes than the one who has the child. The one who has the baby and brings him up in honor will find more joy and happiness. Irresponsible people grow in their irresponsibility. A person who is responsible for his actions will grow in beauty and spiritual achievement.

In the Army of Light, abortion is forbidden and considered a crime. Abortion is the reflection in the physical plane of the actions of the dark lodge in the Cosmic Astral Plane. Just as the dark lodge prohibits and forbids any Spark from proceeding on the evolutionary arc, the mother prevents the soul of the child from coming into incarnation.

Evil has two ways of acting in this respect: it prevents certain Sparks from taking incarnation; it prevents incarnated souls from proceeding on their evolutionary path. This is another form of abortion.

4. *Dark forces create disunity* between friends, wives and husbands, and within churches, groups, nations, and humanity as a whole. Dark forces hate unity because unity is diametrically opposed to their intention — which is to divide. The intention of the Forces of Light is to unite, to bring people together and create such organizations as the United Nations and other united groups, united humanity, and united planetary lives. Dark forces work against such unity.

Any time you catch yourself thinking in terms of cleavage and separatism, stop yourself. When your feelings and your heart are separative, change them. Your intention should be to work to transform those who are evil, to clean and purify them, because they do not know what it is they are doing. Christ said, "Father, forgive them, for they do not know what it is they are doing." Your intention should not be to criticize or use malice or slander against them, but as much as possible to be an example of Beauty, Goodness, Righteousness, Joy, and Freedom. You must try to understand the ways and means of the evil ones and then try to prevent them from affecting your life and the lives of others.

Do not read any book that encourages disunity. You can read books that reveal the techniques of the enemy, but do not read books which encourage their techniques. Try to live for the unity of your family, your nation, and your race. Do not create separatism and cleavages. The world must work toward unity and synthesis. This is the Divine Plan which the dark lodge works against.

There is a hierarchy of darkness, just as there is the Hierarchy of Light. Great Masters are members of the

Hierarchy of Light. The Hierarchy of Light has a Plan, and the evil ones have their plan. It is the plan of the dark forces to destroy humanity by separating, dividing, and then conquering it. The Forces of Light want to unite humanity, to make people happy, healthy, and prosperous so that they can evolve and achieve perfection.

5. *Dark forces flatter you* and make you feel so important that you begin to disregard your elders, your parents, and teachers and develop a rebellious spirit against them. After they detach you from your source of spiritual or moral nourishment, they lead you into gossip, slander, treason, and crime. Sometimes your Soul warns you, but you feel that it is too late to turn back.

The dark forces try to divert you from any person who could possibly help you find the right path in the future. They especially target your spiritual teachers and do not lose any opportunity to turn you off from them by fabricating stories or by pointing out the personality weaknesses in them. They even compare your teachers with World Teachers just to minimize their value in your consciousness. They also use the same kind of technique to attack any book which is a source of inspiration to you.

When successful, they attack your value structures and slowly turn you away from any value which, in the future, would help you free yourself from being a slave to the dark forces.

To protect yourself from such attacks you must not allow your friends or enemies to attack anyone whom you love, trust, or respect. Sometimes dark forces choose your friends for this task, rather than an enemy, so that they trap you through your friends. It is sometimes better to cut off such a conversation before they go on because, no matter how strong you are, they can sow certain seeds which will make it easier for them in the future to regroup and attack again.

Remember that those whom you love, trust, and respect are the energy sources of your life. If you desert them, you will be in the hands of the enemy. Such attacks are carried out by dark forces through gossip, slander, malice, and treason using your friends or close associates. But sometimes these attacks are carried out in the form of impression or even through a direct voice which you hear in your head.

Remember that it is the same enemy using a different approach. Beware of him.

6. *Dark forces spread doubt* — doubt about yourself, about your family members, your Teacher, your government, your nation, and God. They create doubt by distorting facts and presenting you with false concepts about things. If someone creates doubt in you, confront him immediately and try to find the reality, the facts. Whoever creates doubt in you is not your friend.

When I was young my Mother gave me a small edition of the *New Testament* to carry with me in my pocket. She told me to read it whenever I was lonely. Years later, while I was traveling in the Middle East, I met a priest. He saw the *New Testament* in my pocket and said, "I am a priest and I am telling you that everything in that book is trash." I became very depressed when I heard this. That little book was something in which I had placed my hope during many times of darkness; now my hope was destroyed. For three or four months I was depressed. Then one day I closed my eyes and prayed, "God, show me the truth." I opened the *New Testament* and put my finger randomly on the verse which reads, "And when they were crucifying Jesus, He said, 'Father, forgive them, because they know not what they do.' " I said to myself, "This is the kind of man that I am seeking. This is the Greatest One." I regained my faith, and my doubt was dispersed.

Do not let people create doubt in you. Always fight against doubt because doubt is an agent of the dark forces.

7. *Dark forces create confusion.* I once saw a television program where several doctors were having a discussion about the use of marijuana. One of them said, "It is excellent. It is a cure for many things." Another said the exact opposite, "It causes insanity, and there is some proof that it harms unborn children." These confusing and conflicting statements lead people into confused thinking. Then according to their mood and outer pressures, they follow either the positive or the negative statement. If facts are presented in a scientific way after conducting a full investigation, the presentation will not be confusing.

Confusion is a very powerful tool to manipulate people. Confusion is a tool of darkness. Confusion is used extensively in politics, religion, and education. People are tossed from one opinion to another, and eventually they become dizzy and lose all their discrimination. Once a person loses his discrimination, an opportunist can use him any way he wants for his own self-interest.

Schools are supposed to be places where the moral character of the child is built, but dark forces work to plant confusion in the minds of children, presenting them with ideas about drugs and pornography and injecting hatred among ideas of decency and loving kindness. Confusion mixes facts with illusion. Right and wrong are presented in such a way that the child cannot reach a conclusion, so he gives up and follows the path that the majority takes. The greatest weakness of a person is not to have a direction based on Beauty, Goodness, Righteousness, Joy, and Freedom.

You can find confusion in consciously written articles. For example, an article says, "Jesus said many beautiful things. Although I do not believe what He said, it sounds wonderful. Perhaps it is beautiful to believe it, but it is good also not to believe it." Sometimes ideas are very beautiful on the first few pages. Then as the book progresses, there is a paragraph or two that really shocks your mind and confuses you. The dark forces often mix reality with falsehood in such a way that they desensitize the power of your discrimination.

I was reading a story about a man who saved a young girl from drowning. After she was pulled to shore and was trying to express her gratitude to the man who saved her, someone said to her, "Be careful; he saved you only because he was attracted to your sex." The seeds of doubt and confusion were planted in her mind and the flow of her gratitude was blocked. You can find many such instances portrayed in movies and in various writings. Confusion is a mixture of reality and illusion.

8. *Dark forces distort the images of Great Ones whom you worship.* This is carried out either by direct attack or through subtle diplomacy, talking, and writing about the Great Ones in such a way that the public develops rejection toward Them.

Direct attack is more obvious, but when people try to destroy the image of a Great One in subtle ways, dishonoring Him by relating Him to people in ugly roles, then the subliminal message is deeper, more effective, and harder to see. For example, in one movie the Holy Mother is portrayed using cheap and ugly expressions, which cause people to laugh. People laugh at the jokes and comic expressions without seeing the tragedy behind the laughter.

Great images like Krishna, Moses, Jesus, Mohammed, and Buddha are inspiration for millions of people to live a better life. Because the dark ones know this, they want to take such sources of inspiration away from people in order to use people as slaves.

9. *Dark forces give you the impression that you are free, while they actually make you a slave.* For example, they say, "Buy this house. The payment is only two hundred dollars a month." You buy it and find out that you must work fifty years like a slave to pay off the mortgage; all the while you do not own anything but a mortgage. Then you say, "I own a house," but you only own your debt.

Another example of false freedom is when you go to church and the minister tells you, "Kneel down and be saved so that when you die you will go to paradise." Nobody can send you to paradise. You must work hard in order to go there yourself. Only the dark forces give you false hope and false freedom.

Whenever you see someone giving false hope and false freedom, know that he is an agent of the dark forces. Such agents can be found in your family, in your group, religion, or nation. Millions of these agents are scattered everywhere. Whenever you accept false hope and false freedom, you can be controlled by the one who gives it to you. You must be your own boss and lord; no outside power must control you.

10. *Dark forces work very hard to make you fail in your responsibilities and duties* toward your family, teacher, group, or nation. Whenever you fail in your responsibilities and duties, you fall under the influences of the dark forces. Once you start to awaken to this, you will see how your life becomes painful whenever you obey the suggestions of the dark forces and ignore your responsibilities and duties. The moment of failure in responsibilities and duties is the moment that your name is registered in the army of darkness.

When I was nine years old I had a friend, but I did not know that he was a crooked boy. Once we were at the market when he suddenly stole a watch from the merchant and put it in his pocket. "What are you doing?" I asked. "We can sell this and make money," he said. "I don't want to do that," I said. "Well," he said, "if I put it back they will catch me, and it will be worse." We separated from each other because this boy wanted to serve darkness. He ignored his responsibility of being honest and righteous with people.

We have five main responsibilities, which are symbolized by the five-pointed star.

- We have the responsibility to be beautiful.
- We have the responsibility to be good.
- We have the responsibility to be righteous.
- We have the responsibility to be joyful.
- We have the responsibility to be free.

11. *Dark forces lead you into sexual misuse.* The higher mental body is not yet built in most human beings. When sexual energy is economized and sublimated, it provides material to build the higher mental body, as well as the intuitional body, with the related centers and senses. All Great Ones teach the importance of not wasting sexual energy, especially in masturbation. Masturbation is forbidden in Hierarchical levels.

Sexual energy is so precious. Only one drop of it forms a human being. Sexual energy must be sublimated, assimilated, and used for the construction of the higher bodies and the Antahkarana. A person who wastes his sexual energy or masturbates will never achieve continuity of consciousness. Many holy people who were celibate for ten to twenty years started seeing and hearing in higher dimensions because their higher senses started to form.

Oral sex is inspired by dark forces, and it is a very repulsive act. Through oral sex the throat center is distorted. When the throat center is distorted, the intelligent forces of higher centers cannot manifest within you in creative, constructive, and uplifting productivity.

12. *Dark forces create the urge for alcohol.* Alcohol kills your brain centers and makes you do destructive things which prevent the evolution of other people. Alcohol creates a vapor around your aura in which entities from the lower astral plane enjoy living and possessing you. Every alcoholic is very close to possession. Every bottle is a hook of darkness.

Alcohol damages the solar plexus, both in the etheric body and on the fourth mental level where the mental correspondence of the solar plexus exists. This center in the mental plane is used to create causes or those thoughts which will put forces or energies into action.

Alcohol paralyzes such a process. Instead, it opens the path of the possessing entity to use the man to express his destructive intentions.

Alcoholics will come back mentally retarded in their next life. But if they quit drinking and have ten to fifteen years to heal themselves, they may possibly avoid the tragic consequences waiting for them in the next life. If they do not overcome their drinking and die as alcoholics, they will be born without direction, initiative, and striving, and thus will work for others as slaves.

Once a hypnotist told me that he had hypnotized an alcoholic and suggested to him that he could drink but would not become drunk, and it happened. The hypnotist asked me the reason for this. I told him that alcoholics are already obsessed and that the real soul of the human being is not at home. The person is controlled by an entity who uses the person to enjoy liquor but does not become drunk because he has no physical brain. Thus the man, under hypnotic suggestion, drinks but acts normally because he is not there. It is the entity using the personality of the man through his etheric brain, nadis, and nervous system.

Entities know how to bypass certain mechanisms and keep the man looking normal. Depression is the result of an attack on the life thread, but the primary cause of depression is due to the cut on the consciousness thread which entities make. Epilepsy is also the result of such an attack. When the Monad cannot transfer enough energy to the mechanism, the mechanism becomes depleted and falls into inertia or heavy depression.

The quantity of alcohol consumed is not the decisive factor in determining the effect of alcohol. Sometimes one cup of wine will destroy the brain; sometimes a person will have to drink for ten years before he destroys his brain. The damage accumulates and hits the person at a time when it is unexpected.

There are centers which are healthy and those which are already sick or are highly sensitive. Sometimes one cup of alcohol is all that is necessary to ruin a man or draw an evil entity into the person. The best policy is not to use alcohol at all, not even to please other people.

Alcoholic egos attach themselves to those who have the same vice and they often travel with each other, possessing each other alternately.

13. *Dark forces create the urge for tobacco and drugs.* Smoking tobacco or marijuana dulls the pineal gland and the sensitive cells around it which transmit communications from the Solar Angel. It is a very slow process, but eventually the damage reaches large proportions. Chewing tobacco kills the hemoglobin of the blood and opens the person to the invitation of awful devices.

People do not really realize the damage that has been done to our nation through the spread of hallucinogenic drugs. Between 1960 and 1980 close to an entire generation was destroyed. Drugs remain in the brain for years. It sometimes takes as long as twelve years for a person to finally come to his senses after he has used drugs.

The future lives of drug users will be very hor-rible if they do not take drastic actions in this life to rid themselves of drugs and their effects as much as possible.

If you have used drugs in the past and you want to purify your body of them, drink lots of cranberry juice, run two or three miles daily, and sit in hot water up to six hours, with intervals of rest. If you analyze the tub of water afterward, you will find particles of the drugs are floating in it. This treatment becomes even more effective if baking soda and salt are added to the water. If you have used drugs in the past and have been clean for seven or eight years, take a bath once a week in valerian root tea. Add two or three cups of very strong valerian root tea to your hot bath and try and stay in the tub for up to twenty minutes. This is especially helpful for those who have suffered nerve damage because of their past drug use.

14. *Dark forces make you greedy.* Millions of crimes are committed because of greed. The dark forces rejoice in this. Whenever you are greedy, be careful. Your tail is in their hand.

Once I knew a seventy-six year old man with heart trouble. He came to me and said, "The doctors gave me six months to live. What can I do?" "You have lived a full life," I said, "but since you ask I will tell you something. I heard that you are a rich man. You should distribute your money before you die. Give it to worthy charities and other service organizations. Send some needy students to college." "I can't do that," he said. "I must buy some land, and I need all my money. If I buy this land, I will make five million dollars in one month." "You are crazy," I said. "You already have millions of dollars. How many more years are you going to live to use that money?" "You don't understand the value of money," he insisted. "Money is important." "Well," I said, "then God be with you."

One week later he dropped dead of a heart attack while he was out inspecting his properties. All his money went to Uncle Sam.

15. *Dark forces work to make you hate.* They have taught people very well. You hear people using the expression, "I hate" all the time. The dark forces work to make you hate your friends, your nation, other nations, other religions.

Do not hate. Hatred is an indication that you are falling into the network of the dark forces. No matter by what name they encourage you to hate, when you hate you are joining the Satanic army. Try always to love because hatred will never help you proceed on the path of evolution.

16. *Dark forces work to make people take revenge* — religiously, politically, personally, and economically. Do not forget the words of the *Bible* — "Revenge is Mine, sayeth the Lord." Karma will take care of things. Leave revenge to God. You are a traveler on the path of life, and you must be very careful that on this path you are not caught in the net of the dark forces. You are on a battle-field. If you fall in battle, they will win. If you stand on your feet and project Light, Beauty, Goodness, Truth, and Joy, you destroy the dark forces and do a great service for humanity in doing so. Every victory you achieve within yourself is a victory for your nation. A nation is not saved except by individuals. When the individuals of a nation are saved, that nation is saved.

17. *Dark forces make you earthbound.* They try to make you earthbound by attaching you to possessions and material values — lending and borrowing, cars, money, sex, houses, land, investments, insurance — until you are caught. Once you are stuck to material values, higher values will never dawn in you because you are spiritually dead. You can have the best car, lots of houses, and expensive jewelry, but do not be attached to them. Be ready to renounce them at any moment, if necessary.

Identification with your properties is one of the worst forms of being earthbound. Can you be like Leo Tolstoy, who, as a rich nobleman, left all his properties to others and lived the last years of his life in seclusion as a very simple man? We can be wealthy, but everything we have must be used for the perfection of life.

18. *Dark forces make a plan and then get you to help in their plan.* Their plan is related to those issues which are close and dear to your heart. After the plan is set and the issues that are close to your heart are found, they try to deepen the issue in your consciousness and inflame your emotions to such a degree that you are no longer interested in their motives but only in the issue. Here you assist them one hundred percent to achieve their goal.

For example, a man wants to buy a mansion and an airplane for himself and also have some money in the bank. So he tries to sell an idea to the public, such as, "We must stop pollution." Because millions of people hate pollution, they cooperate with his plan. His plan is to raise two hundred million dollars to stop pollution. All those who hate pollution contribute or participate in selling the idea. He asks for twenty-five dollars from each person. Suppose one million people contribute twenty-five dollars each. This will generate an enormous amount of money. Now he demands a salary of one hundred thousand dollars a year. His coworkers will each receive thirty thousand dollars a year. Then there are the expenses. Now he has a team whose success depends upon his success, so they continue to support him. After more money is accumulated, he takes all legal steps to continue his project, printing articles against pollution to keep the money flowing in. Because his income is perpetuated by the existence of pollution, he outwardly fights against it, but in reality he allows pollution to increase. More pollution is poured into the air and water, and he has stronger reasons to collect money to fight against the increasing pollution.

We find a similar situation in our war against drugs. How will the salaries of the thousands who fight against drugs be funded if they are successful in stopping the drug traffic?

This is how Satan organizes many jobs. Engaging

itself in such labors, evil tries to discredit those who might organize such activities in the future with right motives and selfless dedication. One can protect himself from falling into such traps of manipulation by

- knowing exactly who the organizer is

- examining the organizer's life history and past business records

- observing who his coworkers are

- thinking about how to protect the accumulated money from wrong usage

- procuring governmental control of all expenditures of funds

- reporting to the public about the success of the labor put into the project

19. *Dark forces send their agents to join those circles engaged in the true Teaching.* Such agents manifest an intellectual grasp of the Teaching, but they live a ridiculous, insane, and often obnoxious life. They always speak about the Teaching, but they distort it through their behavior and expressions. Thus, through their words, life example, and expressions, they invite hatred of the Teaching and make it an object of ridicule.

You see prostitutes and drug users talking about karma and reincarnation. You see mentally disturbed people writing about the Great Ones and describing their affinity with Them. You see wisdom mixed with curses and malice. You see criminals reading books of higher wisdom. It is through this comedy/tragedy that the most sacred Teaching is rejected by people in general, and the secret agents of the enemies of the true Teaching, hidden in various churches and organizations, find the opportunities to mobilize crowds to attack the Teaching.

It is unfortunate that many churches nourish the enemies of the Teaching in their hearts. Gradually, these enemies of the Teaching take over the church like weeds and mobilize it as an army of hatred. Whenever a church turns into an army of hatred, an army of bigots and fanatics, it becomes the body of Satan. This is why, in the Book of Revelation, the seven churches were seriously warned by the Spirit. The qualities a church must have are love, understanding, nonjudgment, and a life of service in love. When these disappear, Satan enters the church.

7 Techniques of Evil

There are numerous techniques which the dark forces use to control and manipulate humanity. **1. *There is a technique called the use of promises.*** This technique states: give in such a way that taking more later on will not only be possible but also will not meet much resistance. This technique is the use of promises. A promise always gives hope for the future. With a promise, people and governments collect a great amount of money, but then do not keep their promises. On the contrary, they legalize their fraud and punish those who no longer believe in their promises. **2. *Dark forces like to play tricks which pleasantly control you.*** For example, in certain countries they place heavy taxation upon the people. Then before public resistance can mobilize, they remove certain taxes to give people the impression that the government really cares for them. This technique is also seen in our homes where, for example, the husband collects all the money and then offers token gifts to his wife and children, giving them the impression that he cares for them. Certain families obediently follow the boss, in spite of the severe financial limitations he places on his family, year after year.

3. Deception is the royal road for the agents of the dark forces. They deceive you in the news, in business, in their products, and in the objects they sell. Their techniques of advertising have now become a tool which can be used to sell almost anything they want, by taking the legal precaution of warning you not to harm yourself.

People must become alert to the products they buy and the prices they pay. Certain materials are sold cheaply to deceive people, while other objects are sold at a high price to give the impression that they are very valuable. Discrimination and an observant approach are essential in order to use your money wisely and not waste your money on something which is not worth the price.

4. Dark forces give you the wrong idea about freedom. People think that freedom is related to their bodies, activities, expressed emotions, and thoughts. This is a very limited concept. Freedom is related to consciousness. If your consciousness is free, you are free. Con-sciousness is like a concentric circle in space: the greater the space which the circle of consciousness occupies, the more space you encompass and the freer you are.

The space of your consciousness is limited if it is identified with your body, emotions, urges, drives, glamors, illusions, vanity, and ego. It is also hindered by the special illusion that you cannot be free so long as you are stationary. When your consciousness is really free, you do not need to act physically, emotionally, or mentally. You can make things move without moving. You can contact anything you want and enjoy anything you want without possessing it. You do not need to make your body run; you do not need to talk. When you are free, your lower self enters into silence and rest, while your consciousness penetrates into greater and greater areas of space. You are your own consciousness. Wherever your consciousness reaches, you are there. Your consciousness can put into motion things that your physical body and other mechanisms cannot do. You can be in places or spheres where even advanced spacecraft cannot penetrate. This is why many holy ones have retreated to distant mountains and caves, while remaining more active in the life of the planet than any one of us. They can do this because their consciousness is emancipated, and they participate in the causal world to help humanity reach higher perfection.

Freedom is the ability to be conscious and active without the limitations of the body and its various activities. Disciples must continuously strive toward freedom. Often, the more they advance, the less physically active they become. They even slowly retreat to enter greater freedom in their consciousness and assist the labor of humanity in more efficient ways. This is not a form of escape, even though it may seem as such, because most worldly activities hinder their usefulness. Escape is accompanied by indifference, rejection, carelessness, and selfishness.

The withdrawal of a disciple is a sign that he is engaged in a more serious and important labor. Disciples learn to work with the souls of men rather than with their personalities. This gives them more time and a greater opportunity to reach a greater number of people.

One of the secret methods of the dark forces is to slowly take your freedom away from you. Evil does this by spreading false ideas about freedom. For example, it says that you are free to use drugs, so you use drugs and find yourself in jail or you destroy your brain. Evil philosophizes about freedom and then builds prisons and chains to prevent freedom.

Freedom cannot be understood by speaking or writing about it. It can only be understood when one makes another person, group, or nation free. Personal freedom and group freedom can only be achieved by making other people free.

But fear controls man. Because of fear people do not allow others to be free, although they preach about freedom. They think that freedom of others will deprive them of their freedom. When fear controls a person, he must never expect to understand what freedom really is.

You can start to free people when you no longer criticize their religion, their beliefs, or their way of contacting higher values. You can start to let people be free when you do not preach to them that your way is the only way, when you no longer exploit them or use them for your selfish interests. As long as the world turns on the axis of your ego, you are a slave — and a slave is the most dangerous being in the world. If you want to enjoy life and evolve, avoid any effort that creates slavery. Your freedom begins when you free others and yourself from any kind of slavery.

You may ask about the definition of slavery. The best way to define slavery is to examine your own habits, hangups, dogmas, doctrines, fanaticism, and your efforts to impose yourself and your desires and vanities upon others. Another way to understand the definition of slavery is to analyze your fears. This can be a painful process. You can also question your motives and actions. Most of our actions are efforts to build prisons for our conscience, to mask our ego, and to deprive others of their essential freedom.

The definition of slavery cannot be given to you by others. You must find it by observing your thoughts, words, and actions in order to formulate and understand it. Once you understand the meaning of slavery you will understand the meaning of freedom, and you will be able to see the comedy and tragedy that is going on in the name of freedom — which is inspired by evil. Freedom can be achieved by letting others be free. Slavery becomes rooted in your life every time you try to make another person, group, or nation your slave. The companions of freedom are peace and joy. The companions of slavery are pain, suffering, and war. But if a bird is used to being in a cage, you cannot make it free, even if you leave the cage door open.

5. *Dark forces play other tricks.* For example, they find words and expressions which help people find direction, inspiration, and unity and then relate these words to painful, ugly, or criminal events so that people instinctively reject these words and lose the keys to certain doors on the path of their lives. Some of the words they have tried to distort are: discrimination, nobility, virgin, sacred, wise, and so on. If you see how much these words are prostituted in the movies and literature of our day, you will get an idea about the intentions and motives of the dark forces.

The dark forces work through so-called innocent words, such as the word *pity*. One needs to meditate a long time to understand why Satan wants us to pity, but here are a few examples:

A family was driving along a California highway and saw a man trying to hitchhike. The woman said, "Poor man, the sun is so hot. Let's give him a ride." "No," said the husband. "We don't know who he is." "Well," the woman said, "do we have to know him to give him help?" She finally convinced her husband to give the man a ride. Ten minutes later, the stranger put a gun to the husband's head and demanded that he pull off the road into the bushes. He shot all of them and escaped with the car. Only a small boy survived to tell this story.

It was a cold winter day when a stranger came to a home and asked, "for the sake of God," to be allowed to spend a night of shelter with them. They did not have any accommodations, but after hesitating, pity forced them to take the stranger in. The next morning they woke to find the stranger gone along with the jewels and expensive coat of the woman.

A factory foreman saw that one of his worker's behavior was not so good. He called him into his office for a talk. The next few days the worker did very well, except that he stole a few dollars from the cash register. That evening over dinner, the foreman was discussing the situation when one of his daughters mentioned that the worker in question had a son who badly needed money. The foreman went to work the next day and gave his worker some additional money. Several weeks later the foreman arrived at the factory to find that very expensive equipment and many precious things had been stolen. And, of course, the worker had departed, never to be seen again.

A friend of mine, for the sake of pity, married a prostitute. Three years later the prostitute killed him and his child.

Pity is a dangerous feeling which can be used by the dark forces. Pity is not compassion; it is a kind of emotional blindness. Compassion has love but also intuition and intelligence. One can sacrifice, but one must not pity. Sacrifice is conscious, and one needs to prepare himself for sacrifice. A person should not risk his life to save a rabid skunk from a trap; neither should he pay one hundred dollars for a sack of potatoes.

Some governments act with pity and give political asylum to certain people. Then a few years later, they see the headaches they have created in their country. Not only troublemakers but also dangerous spies are welcomed because of pity. Pity must never be a controlling factor in our decisions. The controlling factors should be intuition, experience, and pure logic.

There are other words that Satan puts in people's minds. For example, he says, "Be tolerant, forgiving, and silent" on occasions when tolerance will encourage crime, when forgiveness will inspire exploitation, and when silence will destroy higher principles. *One should know whether words are given to him by Satan or by his own Soul.*

6. Another technique is to assign their agents to enter certain groups and slowly gain higher positions by doing everything possible. After they establish a foothold, they spread certain ideas and goals in the group which have nothing to do with the group's real purpose. These ideas are often sugar-coated and ornamented with flowers. Often these goals even demand "sacrifice and service" to actualize them.

Through words the dark forces excite the group members and slowly create separate sections which follow separate goals. What was once unified ends in fighting and dissolution. In this technique, dark forces use mostly bribery, flattery, malice, and treason to make the group members develop doubt about each other, making room for hatred and repulsion.

Agents of darkness also enter into religious groups "to save their souls." But slowly they trap the leaders or followers of the leader through sex or other temptations. Once their victims go along with them, the agents of darkness expose them and create various damage in the group. Eventually, either the agents take total control of the group into their hands or totally disintegrate the group.

Agents of darkness do not hesitate in exposing their own dark deeds together with the deeds of their victims. It is not easy to discriminate and detect such people when one innocently wants to "save their souls" without feeling that he is becoming a hostage in their hands, going along with them.

For the dark forces any means is justifiable as long as they reach their objectives. Great works of light are delayed for many centuries because leaders were weak enough to fall into temptation. Agents of darkness often expose the failures of others, not because they like to emphasize virtue or because they follow a path of virtue, but because they want to destroy a future warrior who is against the dark forces.

Every time a sincere but immature leader fails, he learns the most dangerous lessons of evil, and in future opportunities he becomes a warrior, an invisible warrior of a true cause. Evil agents may win temporarily, but they lose in the long run.

Evil even uses prostitutes to hit certain targets. There was once a village where the boys were the best athletes and warriors. Another village had the most corrupted youths who could not fight against the first village in sports or in economics. An evil person thought of a way to destroy them, suggesting to the leaders of the corrupt village that they organize some festivities to which they would invite the boys from the good village, as well as certain girls who had incurable sexual diseases. The plan worked, and in ten years the good village buried many of its young men who had fallen victim to the hands of the corrupt village.

Girls who were drug addicts were also used to destroy handsome and promising young men. There were two very handsome brothers who became involved with a dark agent who was so wretched that she destroyed them both with her vices, suicidal tendencies, and criminal plans. Dark forces do not spare their own followers if they think they can achieve their goals by "sacrificing" them.

7. *Another technique the dark forces use is to divert your focus into activities and objects which will consume your time and energy, which otherwise would be used for your unfoldment and spiritual labor.* Generally, they create opportunities which promise you money, position, fame, ego, and vanity, making them so attractive that you find them difficult to resist.

8. *The dark forces have specialized traps to suit specific prey.* Many youngsters lose their path by falling into these specialized traps. Once they are trapped, the dark forces create those conditions which gradually involve them so deeply in the trap that it becomes almost impossible for them to gain their freedom. Examples of such traps are fear, sex, money, and position.

Some agents of darkness sneak in by using the game of sex and love, tying you to them with pregnancy. Or they use bribery and flattery, bringing you gifts and offerings to blind your discrimination. Others present nice lectures and worldly experiences to gain your trust. Still others try to weasel in with pretend idealism and visionary behavior. They are wolves in sheepskins. Others attract you through physical power, the beauty of muscles, or through money. There are also enemies who attack people through more subtle methods, such as making promises or creating a connection with you through court actions or business involvements. You must develop discrimination to conquer all of these.

Even if a person is successful in freeing himself from a trap, the guilt feelings and failure images are impressed upon his consciousness to such a degree that he often becomes a useless corpse for the remainder of his life.

123

Many people realize that they are trapped, but they find it very hard or impossible to release themselves from the trap.

Step by step, mankind followed the path of Satan and misused his power of thinking to please the directions of Satan. This is how pollution and the contamination of Nature came into being on our planet. As man advanced in his thinking, he began to play with elements and created some unnatural combinations that have far-reaching, destructive, and harmful effects on life-forms. These combinations are the result of his impure nature and unclear, confused thinking. Man created poisonous gases, liquor, and drugs, then introduced them into the system of Nature, thus polluting the earth, water, and air.

All chemical elements are created by thought. The Great Chemist knows about all chemical combinations, and He made them in such a way that the progress of life-forms is not hindered but assisted. The order of Nature is the fruit of the all-seeing Thinker.

Scientists feel smart and proud when they discover certain secrets of Nature. To provide or obtain interest for their discoveries, they interfere with the way Nature functions. One of my Teachers used to say that scientists have the biggest noses, like elephants, which they put in many kinds of holes. Some holes provide food or water for them; other holes harbor scorpions and poisonous snakes. Present-day scientists are working in a similar way. They are changing the ways that Nature works — its insects, vegetables, bushes and trees, men and women — introducing artificial ways in them and then calling these ways improvements or outstanding achievements.

Natural ways are tested for billions of years and improved upon cycle after cycle. Nature does not change anything unless that change is considered from the angle of all kingdoms, the planet, solar system, and galaxy, while our poor scientists try to change the ways of Nature after considering only a very few mundane viewpoints.

There was once a great master scientist who built a pump which provided millions of tons of water for a field in the desert. One day a young scientist, who had just recently graduated from the university, visited to observe how the pump was operating. During his observations he saw a loose nut and thought, "Aha! The invention of this so-called masterpiece has a flaw. Let me correct it." And he tightened the nut and proudly went his way. Two weeks later, news arrived to the master scientist that because of a malfunction in the pump, all the fields had dried up. He hurried to make an inspection and found the nut tightened, but he could not figure out why it had happened. Eventually, he heard about the young scientist who had visited and observed the pump and traced him. When he was finally found the young scientist vigorously defended himself, saying that he had tried to improve the pump.

This is what our modern scientists are doing. Instead of learning the ways of Nature, they try to change Nature, protected by their diplomas and certificates. Such actions will be considered criminal in the future generations of scientists who will be surprised why, in the past, ignoramuses played with Nature behind which the Cosmic consciousness operates.

With all that scientists are doing with Nature, there are also those scientists who, inspired by the spirit of Nature, are aware of what their brothers are doing. The hope of the world will come from those scientists who try to restore Nature. They will be great heroes and the foundation of the future. Their work will be very efficient, as they will fight not only against the misuse of science, but also against great monopolies and inventions that support the misuse of science. They will also labor intensely to prove to humanity the dangers that are created by the misapplication of science.

9. *A method used by the servants of darkness can be called "reversing the polarity of the servant of light."* This makes the servant negatively polarized. Dark ones continuously attack the personality weaknesses and failures of the servant of light, exaggerating these weaknesses and failures and blowing them out of proportion to such a degree that the person either identifies with this failure image or strongly resists it by using negative methods against his attackers.

Once the polarity of a servant of light becomes negative, his defeat begins. Fortunately, most experienced warriors know about this technique. They either remain indifferent to the attacks of the dark ones or respond with a positive attitude so that their polarity does not become negative. Dark ones need negative excitement or identification with the failure image to carry out their destructive work.

10. *Dark forces use mediums and channels to communicate with humanity and to create those thoughtforms which can be used as vehicles to spread hatred, separatism, and war.* Dark forces have already placed these representatives in the fields of politics, education, philosophy, art, science, religion, and economics. In all areas, mediums and channels are distributing pseudo-information, disguised with the cosmetics of mental games to appear scientific and realistic. Many mediums at this time are working in scientific fields, pretending to have access to classified or advanced information in order to deceive the public. However, their information and "scientific" data are collected from books more commonly written by scientists who are not up-to-date and who present their books as a message from an unseen ghost.

These communications create alarm in people in such a way that they mobilize their hatreds. Such mediums and channels never propose peaceful, constructive, or creative solutions because they do not want solutions. The hatred and separatism they create will produce a preprogrammed "solution" — more armament and war. Such literature is often published by mediums who work in certain churches or spiritual organizations. They appear to be highly prophetic; they use the *Bible* a lot with their distorted minds and motivations. If you compare these communications as they appear in many fields, you will see how clearly they resemble each other and how much they urge people in the same direction — toward separatism, self-interest, hatred, and war.

At this critical time in humanity, necromancy in its various forms must be stopped. Love-wisdom, clear thinking, and group consciousness must replace it if humanity wants to survive. Humanity is under heavy attack by invading forces from the astral world, via the door of mediums and channels.

11. *Evil works through many ways and in many colors; one of them is prophecy.* Prophets charged with pessimism, personal failure, and self-defeat prophesy about the end of the world and the destruction of culture and civilization. This creates a huge thoughtform toward destruction. If this thoughtform grows out of proportion, it may paralyze all efforts toward peace, harmony, prosperity, and survival. Thus, in translating obsolete prophesies or creating new ones, these so-called new age prophets spread fear and negativity and make people think that there is no hope.

A human being cultivates a garden to enjoy it, and he makes every possible effort to protect it from various dangers. What about the Great Presence Who created this garden? Why not bring His vision and His joy into our hearts and cooperate with Him to create a beautiful world and a humanity striving toward cooperation and harmony? But the servants of evil are against such cooperation. They prophesy destructive conflicts, as if they really knew. Beware of all who cultivate cleavage, despair, and gloom.

12. *Another technique of the dark forces is to mobilize hatred within certain segments of humanity so that they act against those who are enemies of the dark forces.* Let us say that a certain segment of humanity, which we will call Segment A, is devoted to high principles. The dark forces create untrue stories, revealing how certain members of Segment A tortured and killed people in Segment B. These stories contain the philosophies and high principles espoused by Segment A but show sympathy toward Segment B. They even quote from certain books and speeches, just to make others believe that their intentions are the highest and that what they have written is authentic. In this way they mobilize a great deal of hatred toward Segment A, which is the real enemy of the dark forces, and Segment A comes under attack by public opinion or by economic and political means.

13. *People's superstitions, prejudices, and hatreds are a great resource for the dark forces.* Dark forces use this resource however, wherever, and whenever they can. If you meet someone who hates your enemy, you have a greater chance of manipulating him to work with you against your enemy. Unfortunately, world politics is guilty of such an undertaking, being heavily influenced by mediums, channels, automatic writers, and so-called astrologers.

14. *Dark forces teach that wisdom and knowledge must be given to all.* The Forces of Light teach that wisdom and knowledge must be given only to those who are ready. To be ready means to be harmless and that the imparted knowledge and wisdom will not hurt the person's body, heart, or mind. It means that he will understand the imparted knowledge and wisdom and apply them creatively and constructively.

The readiness of people should be tested scientifically, observing their auras, the development of their chakras, and their behavior in relationships. When wisdom and knowledge are given to those who are ready, they are used to assist life in further developing group formations. When wisdom and knowledge are imparted to those who are not ready, they are distorted. Unprepared people hurt themselves and others. They create illusions; they produce ugliness and fabrications; and they force others to delay their evolution.

Readiness is not entirely a mental facility but a combination of three factors: intellect, morality, and physical constitution. One must be ready to understand intellectually. One must be able to see certain implications and the significance of the knowledge and wisdom given to him in a moral sense. Also, his physical, emotional, and mental natures must be pure enough to hold the charge induced by wisdom and knowledge. Wisdom and knowledge are energies. If they are not used properly, they damage people.

It is important to give knowledge and wisdom only to those who are free from self-interest, separatism, glamors, illusions, ego, and vanity because all such impurities will force them to use their knowledge and the accumulated wisdom of the ages for destructive purposes, which will delay the transformation and improvement of others as well as themselves.

Dark forces are very careful not to impart their knowledge to anyone other than those in their army. With every advance a dark brother makes, more knowledge is entrusted to him. But the dark forces try to make students, aspirants, and even certain teachers spread their knowledge and wisdom without discrimination, so that the dark forces increase their own store of information and use it to their own advantage.

This is why the Forces of Light have certain mysteries and secrets which can be given only after certain initiations. This is why Christ advised us not to cast our pearls before swine.

15. *The agents of dark forces try to approach people not only through their vices but also through their virtues.* For example, they use your forgiveness to hurt your labor. They use your love to make you accept an agent of the dark forces. They use your tolerance to talk about their evil intentions. They use your sense of responsibility so that you protect them in time of danger.

This does not mean that people should not develop virtues, but they must be very awake and discriminative to see the motives of people and not be manipulated by their own virtues. Most people are proud of their virtues and expect recognition and flattery because of them. The agents of darkness know this and approach such people through flattery and recognition.

A wise person must develop insight with every kind of virtue that he tries to develop. Insight is the ability to penetrate into the motives of dark agents who want to relate themselves to you for special reasons. Insight is called "the watchdog of virtue."

Our virtues are our treasures. They must be used with wisdom, economy, and to meet a real need. If our treasures are stolen by thieves, they will be resources in their hands. This is why we are told that the greatest virtue of a disciple is his ability not to be deceived by any person or by any force of deception and temptation latent within his subconscious.

Many wealthy people with virtue fall into the traps of the dark forces only because they did not develop insight and an ability not to be deceived.

The moment a person tries to show off his virtues, he opens a gate for the enemies of light. A virtuous person must also feel that the acquisition of virtue is like the acquisition of a precious gem; he must be aware that because of his acquisitions, he is attractive to his adversaries, and be extremely careful to guard his treasure lest it fall into the hands of the enemy.

People sometimes think that teaching about forgiveness, brotherhood, tolerance, and unity brings a rich harvest. But if these virtues or qualities are taught to those who are naïve and without insight and sharp discrimination, they create a hotbed for germs to develop. There are people from all religions, races, and nations who have the same frequency, or cunning nature, and who can use other people's goodness to enter their ranks in order to exploit and manipulate them.

Such people want you to speak intensely about brotherhood so that they can find a chance, with all their separativeness, to be accepted. They want you to speak intensely about tolerance, so that they have a chance, with all their ugliness, to be accepted. They want you to speak about tolerance and make you a tolerant person, so that they find a chance to plant their seeds of greed, fanaticism, and hypocrisy.

When you speak about beauty to people, explain what ugliness is and how to recognize the carriers of ugliness. When you speak about goodness, explain what evil is and how it operates and sneaks in. When you speak about tolerance, explain that tolerance is not blind acceptance of destructive thoughts and conduct of life but an ability to see, to discriminate, and to avoid those who use your tolerance to rape you or exploit you. When you speak about brotherhood, speak also about those who, in the name of brotherhood, gain entry and destroy your home. When you speak about international unity, speak also about those who are eager with their words to be a part of that unity — so that they can destroy it in the future. Many beautiful ideas are used by evil ones for their nourishment and for the destruction of those who want to plant those ideas in the consciousness of humanity.

Evil forces also use associative techniques to degenerate the consciousness of humanity. For example, they create a movie in which a person acts as a hero. This hero saves people's lives, sets an example of righteousness, protects the poor, and demonstrates superhuman qualities, but he smokes, drinks heavily, and lays with various women and prostitutes. Thus, evil ones impress people's consciousness with these vices through creating a hero who is a slave to his vices. This technique works well by impressing in the minds of young people that it is marvelous to be a hero, but one who drinks, dopes himself, and falls into the hands of prostitutes, and with all this he is still able to be superhuman.

When you watch movies and theatrical performances, try to find the technique of association being used and find out which poisons are being sold in sugar-covered pills.

16. *Dark forces try to prevent people from contacting or spreading new ideas which better fit the new conditions of the world than the old ways of thinking.* In the name of religion and tradition, they organize various movements which prevent the spread of new ideas. They even use crime.

The greatest crime to the Forces of Light is the prevention of the spreading of new ideas and the suppression of truth. New ideas eventually find their own ways to succeed, but it often costs the lives of those who promoted them. When a new idea is suppressed and the carriers of that idea are beaten, the world or nation loses; time and energy are wasted until the new idea is accepted. Reactionary forces and deniers of truth cause great damage on the path of progress.

There are new inventions which cannot be put to use because the forces of darkness, working in human form and in all fields of human endeavor, do not want human progress. There are breakthroughs every day in scientific fields which would benefit humanity, but the prison bars are so thick that these inventions cannot reveal themselves and find the fertile soil to flourish, at least for the time being.

17. *Another technique of the dark forces is to have a sublime cause or idea presented by a mentally unstable, obnoxious, or crooked person* so that he creates rejection of the idea in people's minds because of how and by whom the idea is presented. We see this often. Whenever a great idea is presented by a Teacher to humanity, the dark forces immediately mobilize their agents and make the idea look so ridiculous and unwholesome that those who would otherwise be positively influenced by the idea feel a natural rejection, even if afterward they meet the true representatives of the idea. It is important for a higher idea to be presented by a representative equal to the virtue of the idea. The higher the idea is, the nobler its representative must be.

When Teachers began to speak about the reappearance of Christ, we saw the appearance of many "Christs," each proclaiming either that he was the Christ or His representative. They have created such a comedy and tragedy that intelligent people no longer want to hear about the reappearance of Christ. Through all their endeavors, however, the dark forces are doomed to failure. No cloud forever resists the rays of the Sun.

Dark forces want us to be prisoners of the past, of our past achievements, our past religions, sciences, and politics. We cannot surpass such limitations until the prison bars of our crystallized minds are opened. But evil tries to keep us locked up as long as possible.

18. Dark forces have more subtle ways. *At first they help you advance on the path of the Teaching, on the path of your evolution, but then they try to lead you into becoming a "Dweller on the Threshold."* You become a person who prevents other people from proceeding on the Path. Because you already know the Path, you become an able and trained agent to mislead others on the Path. For example, I heard such a man speak who said, "I have studied the *New Testament* and many Eastern scriptures for many years." He then gave quotes and lectured about the philosophy concluding with, "In all of these, I received no assistance. They are all useless dreams." A similar agent once said, "Christ told us to love each other. What He really meant was that we should make free love with each other." After lecturing for a while, he convinced a group to turn off the lights and begin making love to each other. The most dangerous agents of darkness are those who have studied religion, philosophy, and science and who use them for destructive ends. In the Teaching they are referred to as "half-way servitors."[1]

19. *Totalitarianism is one of the most advanced tools of Satan.* Satan knows how to put such tools in the hands of those who supposedly are fighting against totalitarianism. Totalitarianism appears in a family where either the woman or the man tries to be the absolute boss. Totalitarianism appears in churches or groups where the leader wants absolute authority. Totalitarianism appears in beliefs or faiths when a religious person demands that all others follow only his faith. Totalitarianism appears in the media, in secret organizations, in science and medicine, and in organized crime.

Freedom of the people guarantees their unfoldment and progressive achievement. Every totalitarian activity is like a bonfire which dies down only after it has consumed all the fuel. Totalitarianism in political ideologies tries to impose its doctrines and dogmas upon the world. Totalitarianism is found in schools and colleges and in finance and economy. It is found in those governments

---

1. Agni Yoga Society, *Hierarchy*, para. 302.

which impose their will upon people and try to make them cattle, denying them any kind of freedom. Totalitarianism is an effort of Satan to take control over vast masses of people and use them against their own good.

20. Dark forces also encourage the art of distortion, fabrication, and alteration. One of my Teachers wrote a book and later passed away. Some of his followers stole it and changed the words, sentences, and paragraphs completely. When it was finally published, it was a completely false fabrication of his Teaching. The publishers were even praised for their sacrificial work. When I protested the distortions, alterations, and fabrications, they replied with, "The copy you have was not revised by the Teacher. We used the revised copy." The interesting consequence was that they were ultimately unsuccessful in their fabrication because they left many contradictory statements in the book, which eventually led people to doubt the publishers. Twenty years later, the copy I kept was published. After making a comparison, one of my friends said, "This new publication is like a human being; the old one is like a monkey."

Every distortion and fabrication creates dangerous tension in those who are engaged in this labor. Those who follow the truth have a healthier and a more joyful life out of the reach of dark forces.

Dark forces have no principles or laws. Their principles and laws change according to their interest on any plane or level of existence. They do have one goal — to prevent humanity from entering the path of perfection or holiness.

On the other hand, the Forces of Light live and have their existence in principles. *A principle is the manifestation of the direction of the Cosmic Magnet.* When we say that a person has principles and lives by them, we mean that he is sensitive to Cosmic direction and his consciousness is now capable of registering the frequency and direction of the Great Spirit.

Without such a power of registration, people become the slaves of the three worlds. All our vices and failures result from a lack of principle or a lack of contact with the Higher Self, the Spirit within us. Once we have a principle, our mind formulates a way which the principle should manifest and a way its expression must be protected. These formulations are called laws. Those who have principles set standards and formulate laws.

In being subject to principles and laws, man is obliged to observe the laws and even be disciplined by them. Dark forces, however, do not follow laws. They try by all means to create a population that does not believe in principles and does not obey the laws, so that the population will obey the will and interests of the dark forces.

21. *Dark forces use dreams to impress people. They especially use in your dream the etheric or astral replica of a person you love and respect to come and give you certain messages.* Through that image they mislead you and confuse your decisions.

This is carried out mostly by dark entities who live in the astral plane and are trained in imparting certain dreams. Some of these entities entertain you in the lower planes to prevent your ascent into higher planes. Others keep you busy with sexual or criminal events, to occupy your attention or to make you a regular customer of these planes. They also try to introduce you to those who are engaged in dark business because they want to hook you through them.

This is why it is necessary to elevate your soul to higher planes before you sleep. You can read spiritual books, meditate, or use the evening review[2] to raise your consciousness and not be trapped on the lower levels of the astral plane after you fall asleep.

---

2. See Ch. 80, "Evening Review," in *The Psyche and Psychism.*

22. *Another way that agents of darkness work is by making people dependent upon them.* Creating dependency is a very subtle technique of theirs. They like you to depend on them financially, physically, emotionally, and mentally so that they can control your destiny. They intend to create habit and addiction in you. Once you are addicted or have formed a habit, they can easily control your life, your emotions, and your thoughts.

Not only individual agents of dark forces but also corporations and governments work to create dependency in you. A dependent person is a slave. Real democracy is to make people independent and the government the servant of the people, not their boss or dictator.

Certain governments are possessed by evil. They make people less and less independent, sometimes under the illusion of democracy. Great corporations and utility companies, such as the telephone, water, and electrical companies, become totalitarian powers which no one can fight. They can also be used as agents to fight against the independence of people. The urge that mega-corporations have to unite contains a secret motive of exploiting greater areas, rather than serving people and keeping them independent. The more corporations we have, the greater our chance is of being less controlled because they will compete with each other to maintain their existence. If they join together, we lose our chance to remain independent and choose between them.

Dark forces make you dependent upon drugs, cigarettes, alcohol, vitamins, and so on. Once you become dependent upon these items, you become more and more dependent upon them; their power over you grows as you continue to use them.

It is also very interesting to note that the dark forces use religion and so-called spiritual groups to cultivate dependency in people and enslave their souls. Dark forces build such dependency in people that they turn into automatons. People lose their independent thinking, feeling, and acting; they become the tapes of the orders of the dark forces. This is the greatest calamity that can befall a person who starts his spiritual quest in an independent spirit and then eventually turns into an automaton. Certain religious groups inspire the idea that whoever loses his independence advances more on the spiritual path. We must come to the realization that true progress is not achieved through imposition or making the people around us slaves, but by giving them total freedom and an opportunity to educate themselves. The greatest treasure of a person is his independence.

To be an independent person, one must know how to think and how to be free from the control of his urges and drives, his habits and glamors, his ego, vanity, and illusions. Independence leads to conscious harmony. Dependency is not cooperation but imposed slavery. A unification process must not become a totalitarian mechanism.

Dark forces are against democracy and freedom, but they choose to operate under the name of freedom and democracy. *By their fruits you shall know them.* Any imposition in any field of human endeavor is a path leading to slavery.

23. *Dark forces try to penetrate into any community or group, in all fields of human endeavor, directly or indirectly, to make that community or group fail because of accumulating complications, and fall into the hands of the dark forces to be used for separative interests.* For example, their agent may marry someone who has an important position in the community or group, and through that agent, they gain control of the affairs of the community or group. This method is widespread throughout the world. This method is also used in spying and is effective in making a good citizen perform treason against his country. They have even been known to take entire governments and armies into their hands through this method. They try to find people whom they can use as keys to a door. If the person in the position becomes aware that he is being used by his spouse to serve separative or criminal interests, the first thing he must do is not follow the advice given to him by his partner. Then after watching the behavior of his partner, he must ascertain the validity of his suspicions. If they are confirmed, he must take immediate action against the person.

24. Dark forces gain your friendship by protecting you on certain occasions, by giving you asylum, and by standing by you in critical times. But this costs you heavy taxation. Once you are under the protection of evil, you slowly become its servant. Dark forces use various tactics to gain you and eventually make you depend upon them. They will create hatred and anger against you so that you become closer to them and farther away from those who stand for righteousness and justice.

Dark forces also inspire you with certain thoughts that make you feel as if an injustice has been committed against you, and that they are the only protection you can find. This is why the Ageless Wisdom tells you not to justify yourself when you are guilty or to run to the caves of your enemies to hide. It is better to pay for your guilt than to be shielded by the evil ones.

25. The dark forces spread terror about themselves. They try to make it appear is if they are almighty and that they have total control over this planet. We cannot deny that they have power and that they increase in power by making people afraid to stand against them. Thus, they paralyze millions of people, spreading fear in them.

26. Dark forces are against cooperation. Wherever there are sparks of cooperation they try to snuff them out by creating personality tensions or stimulating self-interest. There is a story about this that my Grandmother once told me.

Three dogs were playing together one day when a devil saw how happy and friendly they were toward each other. The devil did not like it, so he decided to create animosity between them. He went to the meat market and bought a big bone which he threw to the dogs. One of the dogs jumped up and began sniffing the bone. The others followed suit. Suddenly, they all began to growl at each other and a fight broke out. They bit each other and fought until each dog was totally exhausted and bleeding.

Grandmother concluded, "Friends, families, groups, communities, and nations become divided when bones are thrown to them. Beware of becoming involved in fights when bones are the issue."

"Bones" are symbols of the objects of self-interest which make cooperation almost impossible until human beings stand above their "dog" instincts. "Bones" can also stand for a position, an object of interest, money, jewelry, flattery, showing off, and so on.

There are people who are very talented and creative, but whose personalities are built in such a way that they cannot cooperate with people. Their personalities prevent them from offering their higher gifts. The dark forces use such cases as opportunities. They try to overstimulate their personality hang-ups to prevent the expression of higher gifts. Some people could do miraculous service to humanity if they could cooperate with certain groups of people. But immediately when the group welcomes them, their glamors, vanities, ego, or various habits begin to create problems and repulsion. Many lives are wasted in this way.

Once there were three highly-educated young men who were engaged in a great service for their nation in the political field. They were planning to bring reform by introducing a certain bill into Congress which was backed with very intelligent arguments and visions. While the work progressed, a very pretty girl appeared and showed attraction to each of them in a way that she gradually created a "she is mine" feeling in each of them. This feeling turned to jealousy, then fighting began. Eventually, the young men parted company in grief and hatred. Their labor was halted, and they began planning how to knock each other down. If they had been more experienced in the ways and tricks of evil, they would have stood above their sexual urges and accepted the girl only as their coworker.

Evil is very cunning and intelligent, but it lacks intuition. Cooperation is a phenomenon of active intuition. Once intuition is active, evil turns into a servant.

The dark forces have other methods of attack. Actually, one of their methods is to change their ways and techniques so that they confuse you and get you. That is why Christ always repeated to His disciples to be extremely watchful and alert.

27. *One of their ways is to create depression in the links or ranks of coworkers who are doing any great labor on behalf of light and beauty.* They arrange a drama in such a way that the coworkers become involved and waste their time and energy. They create tension so that constructive plans and labor are postponed, mistakes are made in discussions, and eventually repulsion is created between the coworkers.

At the same time, those who were once inspired by the coworkers become discouraged. If depression continues or if the effects of depression — self-condemnation and tension — continue, the dark forces begin planting other destructive ideas in the minds of those coworkers who have been weakened because of the disharmony that has set in, in order to try to set them against each other. This is how time, energy, and opportunity are lost.

We can combat such an attack first of all by knowing that dark forces can attack when we are identified with our physical, emotional, and mental desires. Carnal desire is a rope with which they bind us. If we let go of desire, the object of the desire drops and they no longer have a chance to manipulate our feelings and thoughts to create depression.

Coworkers must be very careful that their personal problems do not affect the group work. Sometimes affected members think that the best way not to involve the group is not to talk about their personal problems with other group members. This is good, but the best way to combat the situation is to detach oneself from the object of desire and let it go. If this lesson is not learned, it will repeat itself year after year, again and again, until the subject is able to detach himself from the object of desire and step away from it. The whole problem can be physical, emotional, and mental, and strong will must be exercised to overcome it.

Coworkers can also be affected by various situations of their family members, by their husbands, wives, boyfriends, girlfriends, even with their neighbors, if any attachment or affiliation exists between them. They are also affected by the members of the group to which they belong.

It is impossible not to be a part of some group, party, or family, but coworkers must have the shield of insulation. They must be capable of stepping out of the traps and not become involved and sucked into them. Advanced coworkers handle their problems with others in such a way that they leave their group uninvolved and unaffected by them.

We had a Teacher who was a very joyful and enthusiastic man. I studied with him in a small class for one year. After graduation, I met his son one day in another city. The conversation turned to his father and his family. The son told me that his father went through a great crisis while I was studying with him. In that very year he lost his wife and another son in an accident, his neighbor seized five acres of his land by changing the landmarks, and someone stole his wife's jewelry during the funeral arrangements. The son concluded, "My father is a great man because he knows how to detach himself when he is called for spiritual duties. He can act as if nothing has happened to him."

28. *Another card that the agents of evil play is to wait until doubt forms in your mind toward a principle, friend, or coworker. Then they increase that doubt.* They take actions to increase doubt through the use of various expressions and suggestions. They try to make your doubt so real that you eventually believe that your doubt is based upon total reality. They operate on your doubt, especially if it will create separatism, destruction, and agitation among friends, family members, and coworkers. In increasing your doubt, they create tension, conflict, and irritation and incapacitate you to meet your group responsibilities.

This does not mean that every doubt you have is from evil sources or from your own inner trash can. A doubt can also be a warning to be careful about certain things. In general, such a doubt is directed toward negative things. For example, you doubt that a person will be a good worker because he uses dope or wastes his energies, or you doubt that your own pretension and showing off will work. One must be careful to discriminate between these two kinds of doubt. Usually the agents of darkness know the difference between these two kinds of doubt. If the doubt is not in favor of their plans, they will try to influence you to eliminate that doubt.

29. *One of the techniques of the dark forces is manipulative confession,* which makes people play with the trash of the past and restimulates the trash in others in the name of confession. They make people feel as if they are free from the deeds they committed in the past so that as "free" people they regain the right to be respected. In this way, the dark ones save their "tools" so that they can be used again.

A person who looks behind is a person of the past. Renewed striving must show what he became through all of his past experiences. Washing old clothing does not make them new; the "dirty water" remains in the person's psyche.

Our past experiences can be used as stepping stones. Counsel with your Higher Self or with one who represents your Higher Self, and see how much you have learned from your past experiences. If you spread them to others as sins or weaknesses, you are condemning everyone who is going through similar experiences.

One of the jobs of the dark forces is to spread your trash. When you are tired the dark forces possess you and, in the form of confession, they spread your past failures. Working with trash spreads the trash. Working on higher levels annihilates the trash. Work on higher ideas and the lower trash will be annihilated.

When people do not like you because of your ugly dress, you change it in order to be loved again and to be able to manipulate people again. You change your old clothing by making a confession that you are not the old person but a new one, and you have a new way to deceive people. True confession is not a way to impress people with your ugly past and with future promises, but a way of sharing an example of total humility and long years of striving to prove your change in character.

Once you are possessed by an entity who wants to spread your trash through a form of confession, it makes you turn against whatever you loved in the past and against whatever you worshipped in the past. In this way the dark forces destroy precious images and principles in the minds of others through your hands or example.

Confession must not run on the pathways of self-justification or condemnation of others for your failures. It must not be a comedy to make people laugh at you in order to gain their sympathy so that you can repeat your exploitation. Confession must be used as a technique to meet your True Self. You can confess to rocks, rivers, and trees. Thus, sometimes this saves you embarrassment and saves others by protecting them from contact with your dirty clothing.

The most dangerous and destructive servants of evil are those who eventually hide themselves in religious and spiritual fields. This is why many Teachers of Wisdom taught that religion was no longer a road to God but a road to materialism, self-interest, hatred, exploitation, power, and totalitarianism. Of course, the servants of light are also found in most sanctuaries along side the servants of evil. This will continue until the spirit of Christ smites all servants of evil.

Dark forces are very interested in politics because this is a field which has a decisive effect on the destiny of humanity. Dark agents push their candidate and prepare and present him in such a way that he becomes elected. The candidate of the dark forces uses your love of freedom, prosperity, and health, but once they are in authority, you see the departure of your wealth, freedom, and health.

Never vote for a person who has a record of possession or mediumistic business, who was a drug or alcohol user or seller, who was in the business of prostitution or was a prostitute. Beware of those who were traitors in the past or who were busy slandering people in various ways. Voting for such candidates is an act of participation with the work that the dark forces are going to do through possession or obsession.

If, at any time, you were trapped in the nets of the evil ones, and you consciously hated it and found the ways and means to emancipate yourself, you can be trusted and you will not regret your failure if you now fight with all your might to frustrate the efforts of the dark ones. You must know that any dark agent imitates and pretends that he is transformed as a new person. You will not be one of them because their future will be pain and suffering.

It is very interesting that evil uses a lot of the same methods as the children of light, but it uses those methods for its evil motives. For example, evil always tries to unite, to be a partner, and to be a coworker, not because it wants to help you or have mutual benefit, but because it wants to use you and your facilities, powers, and possessions to make itself grow and eventually take over.

An evil one is not creative. He does not usually create unity or groupings. His method is to infiltrate groups, unions, churches, cooperatives, and organized entities and work his way up until he and his coworkers, like an increasing weed, take over the mechanism of the group, association, or corporation of any kind.

To do this, evil first uses *intelligence*. He gathers as much information as possible about the leaders and their supporters. He systematizes all the information which can be used against the leader and his support staff when the time of attack approaches.

Second, he uses *bribery* and *flattery*, mostly through giving gifts and rendering services "without expectation."

Third, he tries to *gain the confidence* of the leaders and their supporters in order to be able to penetrate into their personal and business secrets and gain authority to run their businesses in case of their absence.

Fourth, he tries to be *seen in the company of leaders* and their supporters in public on as many occasions as possible in order to gain public support and recognition.

All his intentions and plans are to take over a ready-made organization. Thus, an evil one saves time and energy by waiting until a group is formed. He even encourages the formation of groups, knowing that most groups will not be able to resist his techniques and weapons.

When someone 'speaks about unity and cooperation, first of all watch him closely and discover his real motives. An evil one will try to increase his territory and influence and bring in new agents in order to facilitate the process of the takeover. On those occasions when you feel his motives and catch him in his wrongdoing, he may play another game: He will confess, show extreme humility, and pretend that he is very sorry for the "accident," and say that he is now ready to correct himself in whatever ways he can. Then he makes himself subservient. Be cautious and do not act out of pity because he is hiding his venom in order to attack you at the right moment. Observe him in all his actions before you lose your power to stop him.

The agents of darkness show great interest in you when you are in trouble or under attack. They try to help you and make you feel that you were not wrong and that you did not fail in your responsibilities and duties. They shut your eyes toward your weaknesses and make you feel that they are your friends and that you can entrust your secrets to them. Thus, in gaining your confidence, they learn all about your problems and become acquainted with those who are against you. Once they know all about your enemies and their powers, your weaknesses and secrets, they slowly withdraw from you and take the side of your enemies, or remain with you and work on behalf of your enemies.

In order to protect yourself from such a situation, try not to allow such people to come closer to you when you are in trouble, and reject them if they try to justify your errors and actions which break moral or civil laws.

In reality, the dark forces are in the minority compared

to the Forces of Light. They only have power because they always try to hold key positions. Their power is based on the sandy foundation of lies, exploitation, crimes, dishonesty, greed, hatred, and so on, which cannot provide them with a strong foundation for perpetual success. Sooner or later the human mind will develop discrimination and see their faces, no matter what form they take or under what mask they hide.

The Forces of Light are mobilizing their power through goodwill, right human relations, and pure thinking in all departments of human endeavor. Like a shield, the Hierarchy of Light is protecting humanity, letting humanity grow in discrimination, right judgment, and clear thinking. Forced or imposed conditions eventually make the human spirit rebel. Education based on freedom, challenge, and the example of striving creates those conditions in which growth and unfoldment of the human soul become possible.

In spite of the hatred and separatism spread by dark forces, there is at this time a sense of global unity and an organized, worldwide effort for peace, right human relations, and goodwill. In spite of the efforts of darkness to keep the world population in ignorance and slavery, there is clear evidence of increasing knowledge and education and a tremendous effort toward freedom of all kinds.

As we speak of dark forces we must not forget to mention the labor of the Forces of Light, which has inspired us and encouraged us to create splendid cultures and civilizations on earth throughout the ages. The Forces of Light are just as active as they ever were. Their agents are everywhere. They are recognized by their clear thinking, impartiality, serenity, faithfulness, trust, sense of unity and synthesis and, above all, their humility and harmlessness.

30. *Dark forces also use a so-called "positive" technique* which is to make certain people praise those individuals who are in sensitive positions and blow their minds out of proportion to such a degree that they develop incurable vanity. After their vanity is formed, these individuals will reject the discipline of group consciousness and become units which separate, divide, attack, and want to dominate. Such a situation creates unprecedented chaos in a group or organization, feeding the appetite of dark forces.

31. *Another technique that is very prevalent these days is called a "you know, you are" technique.* Dark forces, seeing that in the future you can be a leader of light, slowly inject into your aura the feeling that you do not need to study, learn, search. "You know already; why waste time," as if you had more important things to do! They also suggest that you do not need to work on yourself because "you *are* already. . . ." Years pass and you remain ignorant, and your beingness remains the same. You become an obstacle on your own path and on the path of others.

32. There is another way that dark forces operate. *They lead you into temptation.* They make you associate and relate with people by the body, self-interest, and karma from which you will be trapped. Once you are trapped, they can use and manipulate you against your interests and make you a servant of darkness.

The dark forces have another game. If a person tried to heal someone who was possessed or obsessed, the dark forces try to make the victim hate the healer, counselor, or doctor so that they prevent future help when they re-possess that person.

Once there was a woman who had a nice husband, but she was possessed by an entity craving sex. So she secretly went with many other men using various excuses. Eventually, in desperation, she found a man who could help her come to her senses, and she went back to her husband.

Years passed, and one day a slanderer went to her and slandered her healer. The woman felt full of hatred and the spirit of revenge. She said, "I will fix him." She wrote to him the most nasty and obnoxious letter that one can imagine. The lines of communication were broken between them. Six months later she was repossessed, and she left her husband and went with other men. Someone advised her to see her healer again. "How can I when I wrote such a shameful letter to him?" And no one came to help her. The dark forces were successful in creating a drama. One must always remember not to destroy bridges and always leave a door open for future communication. Such an action can be possible only if one has the spirit of gratitude.

TARGETS OF DARK FORCES

The dark forces have many agents in the movie industry. They know that this industry is a great device to influence masses of people.

In most movies, you are strongly impressed with crime, destruction, murder, extreme violence, beating, and killing. You are impressed in various ways about loose sex. This is the moral side of it. They also make political suggestions, which subtly sink into the bones of the audience.

In many movies you see that even if a person is right in his opinion or judgment and stands against those who violate the rights of people, the police are called upon to solve the problem instead of justice. The police will be victorious in the end, even if justice is buried. Such movies influence you to be extremely careful not to think and act beyond the limits of establishments and interests, even if all your efforts are directed for the good of your nation and humanity. This is a powerful effort by the dark forces to kill every new idea that the youth might have to change things and lead the national or global life toward a happier condition. After watching such movies one thinks, "Why should I attempt something new, if the end is destruction?"

Dark agents even whisper, "We tried through these movies to awaken resistance toward injustice and showed how cruel some authorities can be." Secretly, however, they mean, "Try to oppose authority, but remember all the shooting and killing that will result. That will be your destiny and the destiny of those who follow you."

Dark forces create deep sympathy through these movies toward those heroes who are working for the Common Good. The sympathy of the audience reaches such a degree that they begin to identify with the "good guys," who are eventually killed and mercilessly destroyed. Thus, the audience is psychologically defeated. In no way will any member of the audience try to institute a new change because he is already killed psychologically.

When you watch movies try to observe this point and see how, with all subtleties of techniques, they are created in such a way to defeat in you all that is really human, warning you not to dare, and showing you that in the end your destruction is inevitable.

Another target that the dark forces aim to hit is art objects and books or manuscripts of rare beauty and value. They want to annihilate, if they can, all art objects that inspire humanity to transcend its present level of consciousness. They want to annihilate or hinder the circulation of those books and manuscripts which bring meaning and direction in the life of humanity or that reveal facts which awaken the minds of people and urge them to adopt new attitudes.

Dark forces stand against anything that expands human consciousness and leads people into right action. If they do not succeed in destroying art objects, books, and manuscripts or preventing their circulation, they play another card: They try to disqualify the author or artist and create stories about him which will confuse the minds of those who appreciate the work and make them turn their faces from the objects of value. The ways of the evil ones are many, and they never stop repeating their games until people turn numb toward finer values.

It is known that people full of jealousy, fanaticism, and ignorance search for books that teach how to recognize people who are jealous, fanatical, and ignorant. When they find these books, they publicly criticize them or deny their philosophy, just to hide from the increasing light of public awareness. But now the public is becoming more informed and aware, and it will search specifically for those books which are criticized by fanatics, hypocrites, and jealous people because it knows that the real Teaching exists in those denied and highly criticized books.

It is true that bad books exist which may lead people to moral degeneration and mental confusion. It is not necessary to fight against such books, but rather to build higher characters and noble souls who will not read such books. Once such books are not read, the authors will realize their failure.

Fanatics believe that all they say is the absolute truth. They never feel that they could be wrong. To exercise pressure on people to believe what you believe is an act which stops the progress of others and turns them into machines. The greatest enemy of the Teaching is one who is artificially built-up or forced to believe things for which he is not ready or to accept things under the fear of threats.

One of the targets of the forces of evil is the Teacher, the guru, or leader. Evil hates these concepts and tries by all means to attack them because evil knows that without a Teacher, without a guide, without a leader, one becomes lost in the darkness of the desert and becomes the prey of the wolves of evil.

The path of perfection is a dangerous path. There are physical, emotional, and mental dangers which no one can imagine until he confronts them. Evil forces try to discredit Teachers, guides, and leaders in the minds of neophytes so that they can become the leaders themselves, leading people toward materialism, crime, and horror.

Evil forces also speak against the Transpersonal Self so that you do not stand on your own feet and ask for help from your inner resources. They do not want you to learn how to think. They do not want you to think about lofty subjects, about great heroes and leaders. They want you to be helpless so that you fall into their hands. For this reason, they try to provide you with those conditions which eventually make you helpless and unprotected.

Whenever you feel helpless and unprotected, cry for the Lord and never fall into despair because that is the moment when evil ones come to present their help. Faith and belief can save your life. This is why throughout centuries the servants of darkness tried to destroy your faith and belief. They even entered into the sanctuary to bankrupt your faith and make you a spiritual orphan.

Many beautiful souls fell from grace by obeying these wolves in sheepskins who worked in the sanctuaries. These wolves taught disobedience and made the meaning of obedience so ridiculous. They proved their point with distorted examples, and in doing so won many souls and stopped their progress on the Path of Light.

8 The Battleground

A man or woman is a battleground of forces. You are the field of battle. Your physical body, your emotional body, your mental body, your spiritual realms are all battlefields on which various forces fight to gain victory.

In your physical body, health and disease fight against each other continuously. In your emotional realm, negative and positive emotions are fighting continuously. In your mental nature, good and bad continuously battle. Your inner being is also a field of conflict in that the directions that you have are either right or left; they are constructive or destructive.

Any future progress, any advancement, joy, health, peace, and enlightenment in the future are the result of your decision as to what forces you are going to deal with to fight. Your blood cells fight; your thoughts fight; your decisions and motives fight. Your success and liberation depend upon which side you choose.

If you choose negative emotions, your body, mind, and emotional nature will eventually be destroyed. If you choose positive emotions, your body will be healthier, your emotions more calm, your mind more rational and logical, and your direction correct. You are going to choose on which side to stand. This decision is the main theme of the *Bhagavad Gita*. Arjuna, the human soul, stands between two armies. One army is the forces of darkness, the other is the Forces of Light. If he joins the side of darkness, he will lose forever. If he joins the side of Light, he will conquer darkness. His future depends upon his decision.

Everything that you do, every physical, emotional, and mental condition in which you find yourself is the result of your choice. For example, if your body is not healthy, it is because you chose something in the past or in the present that was harmful to your body. If you are emotionally upset, you have committed an emotional wrong. If you are not mentally bright or enlightened, then you made choices that led you toward darkness. Whatever you sow, you reap; this is the law. If you are unhappy, there is no one to blame but yourself. If you are sick, do not blame anyone but yourself because you made a wrong decision and that is why you are what you are now. You are the plane, the field of conflict. Every minute, you must choose which side you are going to join.

If you choose the wrong side, you will pay for it. You start driving sixty-five miles per hour, then seventy-five, then ninety, one hundred, when you see two red lights in your rear-view mirror. The officer says, "You were enjoying the speed, weren't you?" "Yes, sir." "May I see your license?" "Yes, sir." And you end up paying a ninety-five dollar ticket. You chose the wrong speed. Another example of exceeding the speed limit is when a young woman once came to me and said, "I am reading *Cosmic Fire* and meditating for two hours each day." I told her, "You will get a ticket and have to pay for it because you are exceeding the speed limit of the freeway." You can also violate the law by proceeding too slowly. You must be careful what speed you choose and what freeway you travel.

You are the battleground and all these clashing forces fight within and around you to win you. It is important to learn what or who the enemy is. Maybe you will ask, "What is the real origin of evil, of the enemy?"

The enemy is any person or force which retards your evolution, growth, unfoldment, and beauty. There are five things that we can say about the enemy. First, the enemy or evil is a force which makes you ugly. If any force makes you physically, emotionally, mentally, or spiritually ugly, then it is a dark force. You are yielding yourself and cooperating with it. Second, if any force takes your goodwill from you and replaces it with evil, it is the enemy. Third, if anyone or any impression or suggestion makes you fight against righteousness or forces you to be unrighteous, it is evil. Fourth, if anyone or anything tries to take your joy away from you and load you with grief, fear, or depression, know that it is evil. Lastly, if anyone or anything takes away your rights or freedom and tries to make you a slave or a hostage of his self-interest or beliefs, know that it is evil.

These forces are everywhere. Because they are everywhere, you are used to them and so you can no longer see them. They are even present in your food and water, in your churches, in your sacred literature. They have penetrated into all layers of human experience. If you are smart, you will develop the great sense of discrimination.

When we say "discrimination," people often think that we mean the kind of discrimination which separates blacks from whites, Europeans from Americans. This is wrong usage of the word, which is again the work of evil.

Discrimination means to know exactly which path leads to your destination and which path leads to your destruction. For example, two pills may look very much alike, but one will poison you while the other will heal you. Discrimination means to discover which pill will give you vitality and energy. In Sanskrit, discrimination is called *buddhi*, which means "to have light." *Buddha* means "One Who has Light." If you have light, you know where you are going and where to go. It is important to develop discrimination every minute.

What will discrimination do? Say that I am sitting in bed and watching television while I have some wine. As I drink, I start hallucinating and thinking evil, bad thoughts, then good thoughts, then bad thoughts. Now I am going to discriminate which thought is leading me to darkness, into ugliness, ill will, injustice, slavery, pain, and suffering and which thoughts lead to beauty.

Good forces always have five characteristics which make you beautiful, good, righteous, joyful, and free. If your discrimination is really active, you can see in each word, book, newspaper article, radio program, or lecture which is leading you toward ugliness, slavery, ill will, hatred, and revenge and which is leading toward light. All these forces are fighting for your soul.

There is a Mongolian tradition which says that when a baby is born, God sends two angels. One sits on the child's right shoulder and the other sits on the left; one is light, the other is darkness. These two continuously watch and inspire the person to follow their path; the child is the fulcrum of these two forces.

Sometimes you wonder, "Should I kill that person or save him? Shall I lie or speak the truth? Shall I love or hate? Shall I take revenge or forgive him?" The dark angel says, "Hate him, take revenge, destroy him, rob him, kidnap him, kill him," while the angel of light says, "No, no!

Save him, forgive him, bless him, give to him, uplift him, enlighten him," and you do not know what to do. If you have discrimination, the right-hand angel will be so happy, and eventually it is this angel of light that will take you through initiation after initiation, leading you into greater light. After you pass away, the two angels pull you and push you. Eventually they put you on a balance, a spiritual balance and try to determine your "weight." If you weigh too much, that means you are going to hell with the dark angel. Weight consists of everything that is connecting you to earthly values — your checkbook, money, titles, land, alcohol, drugs, rock 'n' roll, and disco. You are getting heavier and heavier, going down, down. If you are light, it means that you have less matter and more spirit. When you have less matter and more spirit, your soul is elevated like a balloon. When this happens, the angel of light is so happy, while the dark angel is angry. He says, "I couldn't do it. For eighty years I tried to inspire trash in the mind of this person, and I could not win him because he was too smart to be trapped in the traps of the dark forces."

Every time you think, speak, write, or do anything, first check to see whom you are serving. Are you serving materialism, hatred, revenge, separatism, or anger? Or are you serving Light, Love, Beauty, Righteousness, Joy, and Freedom. Which are you serving? Maybe you are blind and are forever serving the armies of darkness and have never realized this. But the moment you find out what you are doing, free yourself because you will be led into greater darkness.

Let us say that you sold your soul to the dark forces. Eventually your physical, emotional, and mental bodies will disintegrate in space, and the soul that you are will eventually evaporate. You will lose your individuality. This is what is meant by "losing the individuality," or the soul. The Universe is very economical; it dissolves and makes fertilizer out of anything that is no longer serving Its purpose. If a leaf can no longer fulfill its purpose, it falls to the ground and becomes fertilizer; it is gone forever as a leaf. You lose your individuality forever and evaporate if you follow the path of darkness.

You may incarnate three, four, five hundred times, as long as there is still a chance. But if your evaporation is at hand, you are finished. There is no incarnation because incarnation is an opportunity to awaken and come to your senses and say, "Let me choose the right path this time." But teachers, ministers, and priests do not discuss these things because their congregations would be afraid.

You think that you have a soul, that you are immortal. But this is a false doctrine, a false religion and philosophy. You build your soul. You are a ray of Divine Light. That Light comes to the mineral kingdom and slowly passes into higher kingdoms, eventually building itself into a soul. Unless you build your immortality, you are not immortal.

You have so many teachers and books that you fall into the wrong lane — the lane of darkness. The dark forces penetrated into the Teaching and are telling you things that do not exist.

Dark forces are scientifically trained professionals. They have great certificates and diplomas. They are very smart. Unless a person is very smart, he cannot be a part of the dark forces. When the human soul does not develop to a certain stage of trial and error and is stuck in the traps of the dark forces, the human soul gradually disintegrates. The human soul is nothing else but a focus of energy which is developing consciousness and mind. When this is not accomplished, it disintegrates and once again becomes part of the chaotic forces of Nature.

How Evil Comes Into Being

First of all, does evil really exist? Evil, in essence, does not exist. In most cases, it is a man-made creation; we create it. For example, you desire alcohol or drugs, and eventually this desire becomes a glamor in you, an urge, a drive within you, a madness in you, and it starts to control you. This is an evil that you have created. Another example is when you do not like someone, and that dislike slowly turns into hatred which becomes deeper and deeper. It might even become a crime, a strong crime, a dark crime. Now you have created a thoughtform which is evil and which continuously controls your mind. If you continue this process life after life, increasing your glamors and illusions, hatreds, revenge, and separatism, you become the embodiment of these glamors, illusions, and vanities. You become them; you become hatred, and so on. *We have people who are not criminal but who are the crimes in themselves.* They are the embodiment of that evil which they created.

In *The Secret Doctrine* it says that apes were created by man. Apes are not evolutionary, even though scientists used to think that man evolved from apes. Apes were created when man had intercourse with animals. Scientists have recently proven that apes did not come before man. They came after him. Apes are a distortion that was formed by the misapplication of man's sexual energy. We must correct the theory of evolution and revise all the textbooks accordingly.

It is not Nature which created evil but man who created evil. We are not so blind that we cannot see that smog was not created by God. The atomic bomb was not created by God. Radioactive waste was not created by Him. Who created these? Revenge created them; greed created them; hatred created them; stupidity created them. We created them. We created evil, and now we are controlled by our own creation. You go to Los Angeles and say, "Yech, what is this? I can't even breathe. God, why did You do this?" And God's reply is, "You stupid person. I didn't do it. You did it yourself." Because we wanted to make more money, to exploit people or politically harm people, we created a mess. God did not create this situation.

We see from these examples that evil is not a principle. It is not God's creation. Evil is a creation of man because of his distorted mind. By considering these ideas, you promote a kind of thinking that will encourage you to live for the Common Good.

An outer force will not attack you unless you have similar elements within you. You attract them by the darkness that you already contain.

There are two kinds of selfishness. One kind is that you want to develop yourself as highly as possible, and that is very good. The other kind is that you want to develop yourself at the expense of others. This is evil. For example, you have land that you want to develop. You cultivate it, and it is very beautiful. You want to be somebody, but then you start taking other people's land, destroying, killing them, and saying, "Now I am growing." This is darkness. It is selfishness, which is evil.

Every time you take an initiation, you pay for your past karma with taxation. For example, in approaching the door of the first initiation, which means victory over your physical nature, everything you did in the past against physical laws, against your body, begins fighting. Now you proceed toward the second initiation. Everything that you did in the past against the emotions of others, for example, using negative emotions such as hatred, fear, anger, revenge, or greed will, from the inside, attract outside forces and turn you into a battlefield until you conquer those negative emotions.

Baptism is the purification of your emotional nature. You purify yourself with the waterfall of love, calmness, and purity. You are clean now. The dark forces of the emotional plane are controlled. Now you are headed toward the Third Initiation. Whatever you have done wrong mentally, such as wrong decisions, wrong thoughts, wrong motives, separatism, destructive plans will start bubbling within you and invite outer forces to make you into a battlefield upon which they will fight continuously. You do not know what to do until you conquer them. And when you finally conquer them, you take the Transfiguration Initiation, which means that you are now totally free from your physical, emotional, and mental evils — from the dark forces.

When we read that Christ went to the top of the mountain, this is symbolic of His climb to the top of His physical, emotional, and mental nature. When He reached the top of that mountain, He was transfigured. At that time, the three disciples who witnessed this occasion bowed down and fell to the earth in front of Him. The three disciples symbolically stand for the physical body, the emotional body, and the mental body. All three of them prostrated themselves before the authority of the Soul that is now radioactive. By conquering these three "evils," Christ was transfigured. Once He was transfigured, He started seeing Celestial Masters and forces. This means that unless we conquer our physical, emotional, and mental natures, we will not be able to establish conscious communication with Supermundane Beings.

The progress, salvation, and victory of the human being is the result of his knowing who and what are his enemy. If you do not know which microbes are in you, you cannot effectively kill those microbes. If you do not know what is misleading you, you cannot overcome it. This point is the beginning and the end of finding our way to the Light.

Suppose a young girl says, "Today I want to go drinking, then go dancing and have sex. Then I will come home and start my homework." Look what has happened. She does not know that she is totally a push button. Different buttons are being pushed, and in her mind she wants to go dancing and waste her energies in drinking and sex. Her Solar Angel tells her, "What about your school lessons?" "I will do them. Don't worry," she rationalizes. Then she goes to a party and drinks until one in the morning, gets pregnant or contracts syphilis, gonorrhea, or AIDS. Then she says, "Let me get on with my school lessons." But it is too late. The dark forces already have her.

We need to teach our children about the dark forces. Our ministers are naïve about these matters. They say, "This is America; let her go and drink a little. So what?" But is it the goal of that young girl to become a prostitute or a beautiful woman? Is she going to have children that will bring honor to the earth and to her family? Will they be dedicated to the cause of Light, or will they produce trash? Which do we want?

A psychiatrist once said to me, "I often advise children who are between the ages of twelve and fourteen to have sex." I told him, "Then you are really serving the forces of destruction." "You are old-fashioned," he insisted. He called me "Mr. Old-Fashioned" for seven years. Then one day I received a letter from him. It read, "Dear Mr. New-Fashioned, will you forgive me? My son has AIDS and my daughter is pregnant and has gonorrhea. I was wrong." I wrote him back, "For seven years I could not make your cabbage into a head. It was only after destroying your children that you have come to your senses. Of course I will forgive you, but karma will take its payment."

Mothers have no training. Women in our modern civilization do not know how to be mothers. They do not know the proper ways to bear children. They do not know how to help their children grow. When a baby is born, the mother does not know how to handle the situation because her life is a mess. She is caught in the mess of radio, television, business, driving the car on the freeway, and modern life in general. She created an evil and now she is caught in it. This chaos comes to bear fruit in her children.

Crime is increasing two hundred percent. Insanity is increasing. The world is becoming insane. Ten years from now, everyone will be afraid to walk the streets. We are already apprehensive about getting on an airplane. Such fears are increasing because we produced bad fruit.

Our teachers and ministers will carry the blame because they did not speak the truth to us. They say, "Go and lay with him. So what? You are sixteen years old now." My Father once said to me, "You are not going to lay with a woman until you are at least twenty-one years old." I said, "Father, because I love you, I will wait until I am twenty-four."

People have taken the wrong course, but it is not too late yet. We can find out that we are going in the wrong direction, restrain ourselves, then find the correct path. I know many mothers who are really trying to do their best under these unfortunate circumstances. They are heroes. But the foundation is wrong. Somewhere the foundation is cracked, and we have built our whole society and life upon a cracked foundation.

How Karma Overcomes Evil

The Great Teacher, in speaking about karma, says that when Christ returns, He will teach us the real meaning of karma and dark forces. We do not know much about karma, but from this statement we can assume that it is a very deep subject. One of the great fundamental laws of Nature is the Law of Karma.

What does karma do? Karma, from my viewpoint, shows you how, when, and where you cooperated with dark forces. Karma teaches you when you have violated the law. It teaches you through pain, suffering, death, internal tension, and crises if you still persist in violating the law. You can avoid pain and suffering by trying to correct the broken law through sacrifice, through paying back all that you have illegally taken from others, or by strengthening the things you have distorted. This is often a Herculean task.

Karma creates balance and equilibrium and tries to put everything in a right condition, in balance. For example, if I walk in a crooked way, karma will make me walk straight. But it does this through the agency of pain and suffering. Let us say that you are feeling depressed. Lots of people get depressed on occasion. Depression is often the result of a misused emotion, the result of doing things wrong emotionally. When your emotional attitudes, emotional actions and negativity increase, they reach a degree which results in depression because these elements sap your energy. Karma brings depression to show you that you were going in the wrong way.

When you mislead people, you distort the facts; you change the truth. All of these activities are translated by the Law of Karma as cooperating with the dark forces. When you start to cooperate with the dark forces, karmic law hits you and causes confusion because you did not use your mind properly. *Confusion is a mental disease which results from the practice of dishonest mental activities.* Karma teaches you that whatever you sow, you reap.

One day a very holy man was caught and beaten by the police. They had mistaken him for another man and so they put him in prison. He asked, "God, what did I do? Why is this happening to me?" While he was in jail, he had a dream. In this dream he saw that ten thousand lives before, he was a policeman who had wronged the same men who were now holding him in jail. He understood and said, "I have paid my karma."

In a situation where these sorts of things happen, remember that nothing will happen unless there is karma to pay. Cooperation with the dark, evil forces is the only means to create karma.

We know that in our current system of law, the Internal Revenue Service can send you a letter which says you did not pay your taxes ten years ago, and that if you do not pay your past due taxes in twenty-four hours your "goose is cooked." So you go and pay it. The same holds true for the Law of Karma. We have the same "computer" in the Universe, a computer that not only records our physical taxes but also our emotional, mental, and spiritual taxes. This is supported by the idea that we live, move, and have our being in God. This means that He is conscious of everything that is happening within us. It is like a super-computer in space. Space is a super-computer.

If you are trying really hard in your life to clean up your karma and become more aware, even though you do the best you can, something from a past life can show up. To explain further, say that I was drinking and doping myself when I became angry at a man, and I beat him up and broke his leg. Then I escaped. The authorities put a five thousand dollar fine on me, but I escaped to another country, which symbolically means that I took another incarnation, and in that country I made a million dollars. Then unexpectedly I receive a bill for five thousand dollars which I have to pay.

If you increase goodness, or good karma, it neutralizes the bad karma and you do not feel it. Once we were traveling on a road from Jordan to Jerusalem. The chauffeur and another man were in the front seat. I was seated in the middle of the back seat, with one man to my right and another to my left. Ahead, a bridge crossing a twenty-five-foot drop was out, but the driver did not have time to stop. Our car fell twenty-five feet and landed in deep mud below. The car began to sink in the mud, so I said, "Come on, let's get out!" But they did not move. "Come on," I said, reaching to shake them. When I touched them, I discovered that they were all dead. I was really horrified. I opened the door and made my way through the mud and escaped. Why did everybody else die, but I did not? A karmic debt was paid.

Karma works against every kind of darkness, evil, and enemy and paves our way to the Light, to perfection, to liberation, and enlightenment. It is not an evil law. Without karma, we do not have a standard, a light to proceed on the Path.

What determines the speed of karma? In other words, how fast must you pay a debt, or if you do not pay it, what is the the result? Karma is a very complicated system. Say, for example, that a father has five children, but in the past he was loaded with karmic debts to pay. In the interest of the five children who are depending upon him, karma waits until his children are grown and everything is beautiful. Then it will catch him. According to the conditions of your life, karma decides what to do.

For example, let us say that a captain of a ship has certain karma to pay. He is transporting five thousand beautiful people, but the time of payment has come and he must die at two-thirty. The Karmic Lords will use the "computer" to review the facts and find the truth. If They determine that if the captain is killed at that moment it may cost the lives of all his passengers, then They may extend his life until the ship has reached a safe harbor.

If the human mind can make a sensitive computer on its level, imagine what kind of computer the Divine Mind could construct. For the sake of the five thousand passengers, the captain is not killed because that would harm everyone else. It is a very sensitive computer which contains an all-inclusive program.

Karma is not punishment. *It is a law which gives you a continuous chance to correct your path by learning discrimination.* We wonder whether karma is not a reward as well. But God is good. We live, move, and have our being in Him — if we do not create artificial walls by living a life that is not in harmony with the higher laws of Nature. There is no "good karma" because we do not earn good karma; it is already ours. To the average consciousness, however, we say that good karma is the result of all that you do that is in harmony with the Laws of Goodness.

The good that we unexpectedly receive at certain times is our heritage. For example, you have ten thousand dollars but you lost five thousand of it. Loss in this example represents karma. The ten thousand dollars was yours to begin with.

Christ did not pay our karma, but He made it possible for us to pay our own karma. He fought against the dark forces so that they would not attack us any more. He cleaned away a dark force cloud so that two thousand years later the sun still shines upon us.

Christ said, "I am the Path, the Truth, and the Life." He opened to the Supermundane Worlds a path, a connecting link, which evil ones try to block. We still have this telecommunication system with the Higher Worlds through our conscience because of Christ. If it is true that He took our sins, why are we still suffering so much? This thinking is due to wrong interpretation. Christ's sacrifice was to prevent Cosmic evil.

Microbes and germs are living entities like us. But they become destructive to us when we have wrong karma. They become instruments of retribution, helping us to correct ourselves. They are agents of karma to straighten us. If a person does not have bad karma, they will never touch him.

There is a secret regarding the immune system. When the immune system is destroyed, AIDS results. This means that your protective energies, your vitality is defeated by your own actions, by the things you spoke, thought, or did. You killed your own vitality and now germs can attack you and do anything they want because you are no longer under the protection of the light. That is why Christ advises us to "live in light and always let your light shine." It is vitality that shines out.

I knew someone who always complained about her mother-in-law. She insisted that her mother-in-law was a very negative person who was always running down her children's friends and her own son, and she wanted to know how to deal with her. "I have news for you," I told her, "but don't be angry with me if I tell you. In past lives, you were just like her. You found the same kind of person in this life so that you could learn why what you did in the past was not good. Your mother-in-law is your reflection. Now you are seeing in the mirror of your mother-in-law the self you were in a past life and learning the lesson that you should not be like her in the coming incarnation."

How can you handle a situation like this? If you resist your mother-in-law, it affects you. But do you just let it go by? The first step is to know exactly what is happening. Try with your reasoning, logic, and analysis to use the situation to develop a contrary point-of-view, and then learn from that situation. Slowly try, through meditation, education, and prayer to transform the situation. It is not wise to fight against it.

There are two ways to fight. One way is to try and destroy the opposite party. The better way to fight, however, is to transform your enemy into a friend. This is what is lacking in our political system today. There is no human being or nation that can really be your enemy because, in essence, we are all God. What can be wrong in them? They may be stupid or ignorant. In that case, enlighten them. When you enlighten them, they become your friends. In essence, they are you. To resist is wrong.

There is a discipline which insists that we learn the science of indifference. For example, if you say three or four really nasty things to me, I may get angry, turn around, and shoot you. I think, "Finished. Now I am rid of this problem." However, I have just created very bad karma. If you curse me and I say, "Who cares?" instead, I am no longer resisting. I become indifferent and say, "That cabbage can say anything he wants." Resistance creates energy in opposing people.

We see in our environment that some people are not particularly active in expanding their consciousness, but they enjoy enormous health right into their old age. My Grandmother, who was a very great esotericist, used to say that karmic law may give them a few years in this life to repent and learn their lessons, but if they do not learn, it will catch them next time.

We sometimes wonder why the general public and individuals who are good people have to pay the karmic debts of politicians and people who have greedy intentions. A very wise man was once asked, "Why is our government so corrupt? Why are the political officials serving their pleasures while the people are suffering?" He answered, "If you were not what you are, those people would not be in power. You are attracting them. You are all collected by the computer of the Universe to suffer together, to pay past karmic debts to each other that you have produced over many thousands of years — whether you like it or not."

This not only applies to our government but also to our friends, neighbors, and family members. If anybody in this nation is doing something wrong, we must pay for it.

For example, I was up one night at eleven o'clock, writing at my table by the window, when I witnessed three cars smash into one another. After I called to inform the authorities of the accident, four fire engines and six police cars arrived on the scene. I went out to the scene of the crash. It had been caused by three teenagers who were really drunk or doped. They were severely crushed. I asked a policeman how much it cost for the fire engines, for their salaries, the gas, and time to take care of this accident. The taxpayers must pay the bill for the stupidity of these boys. This is a good example of how we are connected to the bad things that anyone in this nation or in the world is doing. One man is killed and we mobilize our munitions and send a fleet, and it costs us twenty-five million dollars a day. We are paying for it. This shows that the Law of Karma is universally revealing itself, and that you cannot escape paying the fine for a dirty deed which someone else in the world has committed.

As life advances and the world continues to unite, you will more clearly see this law is in operation everywhere. Two hundred years ago you could not see it, but now you can. You see that a factory which is producing pollution and acid rain is killing the trees everywhere; the trees are sharing the poison we produce, and we are breathing it ourselves.

There is also the good side of this picture. When the Masters meditate, when Great Sages think, when good people send good wishes, they create tremendous happiness within us because we are also sharing in these. Again, in the international, national, group, and individual fields, the forces of darkness and Light are fighting against each other, using us as their battlefield.

Question: *If someone from an international level has digressed to the point where he has lost his soul — he is a terrorist or whatever — are we still one with him? Is our karma still tied to his?*

Answer: The karma is tied, but you are not tied to him. His deeds still continue like ripples in a lake. They go, go, go and hit the shore, then come back, come back and then go again, until they are stilled.

As humanity develops more mentally, they have a greater capacity for creating more karma. Physical actions create less karma than mental actions because mental actions penetrate into higher levels, the deeper levels of existence. For example, an ignorant man or a simple peasant is less dangerous than an atomic scientist who knows how to kill ten million people in one minute. A simple person might take a gun and shoot somebody, but the scientist can destroy an entire continent — or the whole world.

Simple people solve their problems without mixing them with illusions and mental fabrications. They go to the cause. But our politicians take an event and fight against that event without searching any deeper into how the event came into being. They do not seek the facts. We must find out why our enemy is our enemy. We shoot them and they shoot us because we are enemies. But we must sit down and ask, "Why are you my enemy? What did we create in the past that has made us enemies?" We have the mental capacity, the super-logic to solve our problems without war, but because we are brainwashed to use techniques of war, our mind is crooked. We want to go to war to solve our problems, but war never solves any problem. For two million years we have been making war, and it has not solved our problems. It has just become more and more complicated, until humanity is now on the brink of Niagara Falls. It is only half a mile away before

173

the boat goes over the falls, unless we stop it. The world is overequipped with destructive weapons. One insane person can finish us all. We can work against this fate by sitting down together and using new methods, instead of the old methods. The methods of war are methods of evil. If I am wise and you are showing signs of evil, I do not fight against you; I fight the evil in you. For example, when a patient with various infections goes to see a doctor, the doctor fights the infections in order to save the patient. But the way we are thinking, we try to kill the man to save the germs.

We must emphasize principles. If humanity is going to survive, it must not make war. We now recognize this fact. Fifty years ago we did not know this, but now we do. War is destruction; there is no winner. Then why continue this path which leads us to death? On the contrary, we have great technology, great science. We can cure everything in the world and purify the air and water. Why are we not doing it? One atomic bomb costs two billion dollars, while our school children do not have enough to eat. We talk a lot about the problems of hunger in Africa and Asia, but what about our own minority situation? They are suffering to death. If a person goes to the hospital without money, he is rejected. Why isn't the money we are spending to build bombs used for other things? Because we are being controlled by the dark forces!

What happens to those groups or nations which commit crimes against the human race? When they die, their whole spirit is encapsulated in space. They remain in that prison for millions of years. That is what Christ was referring to when He said that He had gone to release the imprisoned souls. Sometimes two or three *manvantaras* go by while that race, that group, waits in space, in darkness, totally frozen — frozen intellectually, frozen spiritually in the refrigerator of space until a time comes when grace is sent from a Higher Command and says, "Give them another chance." This chance sometimes comes after millions of years when a new globe is in formation that is suitable for them, which can speed their evolution through pain and suffering.

We read about "lost souls" in esoteric literature. How do souls get lost? The answer is, they turn to evil. You are going to win yourself. Christ said that the Kingdom of God is taken by violence. What does "violence" mean? It means utmost striving and labor, or else you will never take the Kingdom of God. When asked, "Lord, where is the Kingdom of God?" He replied, "Within you!"

You will never touch your Real Self unless you win the Kingdom of God. If you touch the Atma, the Self within you, you are saved. You are in Nirvana. Nirvana is the highest that exists within you — the Self, the Immortal Bliss that you reach within yourself. But how do you reach there? — with great striving and labor, by paying your karmic debts and not increasing your karma anymore. What is it that cuts down on karma? Having a life based on the five principles decreases your karmic debt. Beauty does not make karma. Be beautiful from A to Z — physically, emotionally, mentally, and spiritually. Goodness does not make karma. Be really good.

One day a poor woman who did not have food for her six children came into my Father's pharmacy for some medicine. He gave her the medicine without charge, along with some money for food. My Mother, who happened to be there commented, "You are always doing this." "Well," my Father replied, "they need it and we have plenty."

Once we were in the pharmacy ready to close and go home for the night, when a tall black man walked in and said, "Doctor, I am hungry." My Father said, "Okay, come and sit here while I fix something for you to take with you." He fixed the man a sandwich with molasses and some very wholesome grains and said, "Take this and go." But the man said, "I would like to eat it here." We wanted to go home, but my Father said, "Well, okay." He was just full of love and always like that, full of goodwill. So we sat down next to the man while he ate. It was the first time I noticed that some people do not have teeth. I enjoyed watching him eating the bread and molasses.

Suddenly, we heard screaming in the streets. My Father went to the door and looked outside to see what had happened. A big bull ox was raging down our dead-end street, and whoever had closed his shop on time to go home had been run down and trampled. There were about fifteen people in the street, dead. My Father closed the door, secured it and sat back down, saying, "Glory to God in Heaven." I looked at my Father's expression and asked him what had happened. He said, "This man and a little bread have saved our lives."

Goodness does not create karma. If you tell this to most people, they will laugh at you. They think it is better to cheat people, to lie to them, to distort them, kidnap them, mislead them, steal from them, and exploit them. They think this is more clever to do. But it is foolish and wrong to do these things to others. You cannot find in any religion where these things are considered right action.

Truth never creates karma. Stay in the truth. "Search for the truth, and it will make you free." What does it mean to be free? *Freedom means that you do not have karma.* You are not free if you have karma because you are ruled by karma. When you are free, you rule karma. Beauty, Goodness, Righteousness, and Joy do not make karma. But your joy must not be at the expense of others. I may steal fifty dollars and enjoy spending it, but this is not real joy. If I give you fifty dollars, then I am really joyful. If I save you from drowning in the lake, if I pull you out and you are alive now, that is joy. If I push you in the river and kill you, this is not joy, even though some people enjoy doing it.

Freedom does not make karma. Do not enslave the minds of others. There was a Christian who came to me and said, "Jesus is the only way, only Jesus, only Jesus." "Dear," I said, "you do not understand Christ. Christ is the embodiment of freedom — total freedom!" It is not real freedom to be evil. Freedom is in light, in beauty, in goodness, and in joy.

Question: *If someone is dying and needs a blood transfusion and you give blood, are you karmically tied to that person?*

Answer: Maybe yes, maybe no. But I will tell you that the Great Sage, in speaking about blood transfusions, says, "No." The medical profession says, "Yes," even though I have read medical reports stating that AIDS and other deadly diseases are transferred through the blood.

Question: *What about a person who is dying?*

Answer: It is better to die honorably than to continue life with degenerative diseases.

Question: *What if someone is dying and you save his life? Are you then responsible for taking care of that person because you saved him and he is alive?*

Answer: Your responsibility is always to express five things: Goodness, Beauty, Righteousness, Joy, and Freedom. There is no karma in these five.

9
Discipleship and Dark Forces

It is my experience that whenever I speak about dark forces, people start building thoughtforms. They are afraid, they hallucinate, they dream, and so on. You should not do these things. Dark forces are very inferior to you. You are more powerful, more beautiful than they, and Divine Light and Divine Beauty live within you. No one can conquer you if you do not allow things to conquer you.

Dark forces are not interested in average people. They are interested in you only when you are becoming a disciple. A disciple is one who increases in light, love, and beauty. When he increases in light, love, and beauty, he radiates many colorful rainbows. This is a signal for dark forces to attack him. Sometimes dark forces are like moths that come and burn their wings when you increase your beauty, your light, and your love.

The greatest lessons in my life have been the result of my friction with the dark forces. If they did not exist, I could not progress. If they did not exist, I would not have written so many books or composed music. All that I do shows them that I am not afraid of them. They are teaching me wonderful things by evoking my creativity, energy, and radioactivity.

Never fear dark forces. Think of them as phenomena creating obstacles and hindrances on our path. We must study intelligently and find ways, first, to make them impotent; second, to use them; and third, to take advantage of them by cultivating more creativity, light, and power within us to stand against them. It is not a matter of fear; it is a matter of growing within yourself to such a degree that you stand above them.

Discipleship is a way of life in which you increase your light, love, and power. Because of this, something occurs in your nature which is under the Law of Nature. As you increase your light, you want to share it. As you increase your beauty, you want to share it. This is how service begins.

Service is an overflow from your barrel, from your Chalice — increasing light, love, and power which you can no longer contain so you give it out. You radiate it through your thoughts and your thinking. When you are giving light, it means that your mind must always think in terms of light. This means no lies, no fabrications, no malice, slander, illusions, or glamor — just clear-cut light.

If someone comes to your door asking for a drink of water, you do not give him gasoline. You find the purest water and give it to him. The first thing you must learn is to organize your mechanism in such a way that it starts to think in terms of light.

The Great Sage says, "Great is darkness." What is that darkness? Darkness is the accumulation of illusions, lies, deceits, vanities, misinformation, hatred, jealousy, malice, slander, and stupidity. Throughout the world, this group of vices is like a thick fog which prevents the rays of wisdom from reaching us. Hence, "Great is darkness."

If you conquer this darkness, you are a son of light. It is easy to talk about, but once you try to be a son of light, your battlefield opens. From then on, you are going to exercise thinking in light.

If you have any doubt about what you are thinking, what you are projecting, stop it. This is a science that cannot be taught. You learn only through the experience of doing it. Thinking, speaking, writing, and acting in light means you are now on the battlefield, and you are fighting against darkness.

Your creative expressions and your life influence must be totally soaked in light, love, and beauty if you want to enter into higher realms of consciousness and be one with the Hierarchy. For example, try to speak beauty, light, and love. It is so difficult, and once you start doing it you will see how many years of training you need to really conquer the darkness in you and in the world. Our minds, our tongues, and our mechanisms are automatically controlled.

Our mental mechanism, etheric and emotional mechanisms (especially the astral mechanism), are built by what and how we lived in the past. If, for example, you were talking in a certain way, mechanically lying and cheating people, you built a mechanism that was totally equal to what you were doing physically, emotionally, and mentally. If you express negative emotions all day, all of your life, your emotional mechanism is built in that way. The mental mechanism is likewise constructed, as is the etheric vehicle. When an influence comes to any of the mechanisms, they react automatically the same way they were previously programmed. To control these mechanisms is not easy, unless you start becoming a disciple. Becoming a disciple means that you are working against your own physical, emotional, and mental nature. This is another definition of discipleship.

181

A disciple is someone who goes against his own mechanical nature. Of course, this creates physical, emotional, and mental problems and crises. But if you want to advance, you must take that action. You must take conscious action against whatever is mechanical within you and stop reacting mechanically to the various stimuli coming from outside you by saying, "I do not want to act or respond until I know what I am doing." If you start pressing on in this way, you will start to be a source of beauty, light, and love.

Have these four things in your mind: Whatever you do, whatever you speak, whatever you think, and whatever your emotional reactions and responses are, they must be charged with light, love, and beauty. Now you are becoming a disciple, and such a life begins to create reactions and responses because your light is increasing. Responses come from your coworkers, from great Teachers, from a Master, from great centers of Light, Love, and Beauty. They encourage you. Their response encourages you and increases your beauty. You feel it. For a while this is unconscious, but as you progress and advance, you even know from where this encouragement and inspiration is coming because your positive development draws positive encouragement and inspiration from wherever they exist in Nature.

The first source of inspiration and encouragement is your Chalice. In your Chalice are many beautiful things that you accumulated throughout ages. Every time you did something beautiful or something charged with light and love, these actions and events were collected as jewels in your Chalice.

When you become a disciple, your light increases, your magnetism increases, and you create a magnetic rapport with the Center within you — the Chalice. You start receiving inspirations, though you do not know yet from where they are coming. For example, you write a poem about something that happened to you ten million years ago; it is there, in the Chalice. Maybe you were watching something glorious fifty lives before; it is there also. When you become a disciple you evoke them, and they start coming into the mirror of your mind.

If that mirror is clean, it will reflect the beauty in your Chalice. And if you are trained, you will be able to receive these impressions from the mirror of your brain and formulate them into talents that you developed throughout ages, such as writing, composing music, singing, dancing, philosophy, art work, psychology, and so on.

What are reactions? Reactions come from your permanent atoms. There are many obnoxious things buried in our nature, such as the times when we hurt people and animals, when we destroyed things and acted violently with hatred, jealousy, revenge, fear, and so on. All of these events are registered in our permanent atoms, and they will react against you on the path of your progress.

There are permanent atoms of etheric, astral, or mental man. There are positively-charged areas and negatively-charged areas around them. Let us say that you are becoming a disciple and your etheric, astral, and mental centers are developing "positivity." The physical permanent atom immediately increases in tension and presses out the negative contents within you. You say, "My goodness, I have started meditation, I am reading good books and trying to behave, but I am becoming worse than before." This is because all of your past trash is coming to the surface. Drugs, alcohol, too much eating, too much sex, hatred, jealousy, revenge, and every other kind of terrible thing is there.

As your Light increases, you throw more trash to the surface. Saint Paul said, "My Lord, save me. I am trying to be a holy man, but I am becoming worse. Save me from

183

this agony, Lord." He was experiencing these things because he was becoming a disciple. A few years after entering into the group, some of you begin acting in strange ways. You start using malice, slander, gossip, and so on. Members come to me and say, "Don't you see what he or she is doing?" And when they see me smiling and hugging that person, they say, "What is he doing? Is he encouraging him?" Of course I am not, but I know what is happening, just as a doctor knows what is happening to his patients.

First, I keep my friendship with them so that with all their obnoxiousness, they do not run away, just as you try not to let a sick person leave the hospital. There is a danger that members directly or indirectly chase such people away when they see all of the hidden trash coming to the surface. I have learned many secrets of human nature by observing how good, long-standing members, with their positivity, draw out the truth from new members who cannot help themselves. The Teaching and increased striving of some members increases the fire of the new members, and the fire throws out all that is bad in them in order to clean them.

If the "good-standing" members are filled with jealousy, revenge, malice, treason, hatred, and so on from the past, they cannot see this process of trash coming to the surface in the newer members. Therefore, many of the long-standing members in the group begin hating the newer people. When this happens, I show sympathy and understanding to them, but sometimes I try to isolate them for their own sake and for the sake of others until they begin to fight against their own weakness and cooperate with their Souls to restore beauty in themselves and be tolerant to newcomers. This sometimes takes years. Not many people can endure it. Some escape after seeing how ugly they are. Some run away because others chase them out. But there are those who, after going through the cleansing period, stay firm in their devotion to the Teaching and become great leaders who understand people and who know how to handle them.

Dark forces can use a person in those moments when his nature is erupting through the evil coming out. The dark forces utilize the evil to create chaos, cleavages, fights, and disintegration in a group. Those who are not attacked or used by dark forces can progress immensely if they begin to see exactly what they are in themselves. Unless one comes face to face with the darkness that is within himself, he cannot progress.

Progress is the result of victory over your own darkness. But if you feel the attack of dark forces trying to use you as a destructive tool, you must be very careful. The only step you can take is to go to your Teacher and ask his advice. Then do exactly as he tells you. Those who are attacked by dark forces often lose their willpower and become machines. Before it is too late, the one who is under attack must ask his Teacher to guide him, until he is able to fight against dark forces.

We attract dark forces in two ways:

1. When we shine our Light

2. When our darkness comes to the surface

Through the help of your Teacher, a moment comes when you see your destructive, ugly actions and their results. You begin hating yourself. This is the moment when the fight begins with yourself. The most precious service of a Teacher is to bring you to such a stage where your fight begins with yourself. Your Teacher stands by. Sometimes he helps, and sometimes he leaves you to fight alone. As you fight, your positivity and your light increase. When you fight against dark forces you develop the most precious wisdom which cannot be attained otherwise.

Now that we understand that there is a sphere of darkness within our nature, why increase it? Let us take action to decrease that sphere and to increase our beauty, love, and light, so that eventually there is no darkness in us. When there is no darkness in us, we become a transfigured personality. This is enlightenment. Enlightenment is not only to increase your light but also to totally annihilate your darkness.

Negative thoughts must be brought to the surface, recognized for what they are exactly, and dismantled. For example, a policemen finds a bomb that is about to explode. Putting it in a safe place, he deactivates it and says, "There, now it is harmless."

I want you to understand that you will never be somebody unless you win the battle. Frequently the enemy is attacking you, and you are yielding by saying, "You want my heart? Take it. You want my possessions? Take them." The enemy takes them, and you become nobody because you are not fighting against him. You are not creating the energy of repulsion.

Question: *What attitude should people take toward the Teaching when their ugliness comes to the surface, or if they serve dark ones?*

Answer: They must leave the Teaching, or else they become the worst enemies of the Teaching. This is why Christ advised us not to give our jewels to swine. The "pigs" will step on these jewels, then devour you.

Throughout centuries it is observed that those people who slandered the Teaching were hit by karma in various ways, and they paid very heavily for their actions.

Question: *What kind of negativity is it when people come into the Teaching to mess things up?*

Answer: Many such people are delegates or agents of the

dark forces. They are wolves in sheepskins, and we must be extremely careful around them.

Question: *Does harmlessness neutralize evil?*

Answer: When one is harmless and full of goodness, his karma fights against evil. Harmlessness is a way to neutralize the attacks of dark forces. It even brings darkness to the surface so that others can see it. Harmlessness is a great protection.

As I mentioned earlier, all negative things which come to the surface in our nature can be used as fertilizer or a source of energy, once we begin to conquer them. We can even use dark forces to destroy darkness. Great Ones refer to this as *tactica adversa*.

We have spoken about ways in which we create reactions from within ourselves, but we also evoke similar reactions from the environment and from our friends. You accumulate forces of aggressiveness, indifference, hatefulness, and insane energies around you because you are positive. Often when you purify yourself, the environment stands against you.

Now you can understand why they crucified Christ. He evoked all of the trash that people had accumulated within themselves throughout ages, and like lightning it hit Him. That was His sacrifice. As you clean yourself, you start cleaning someone else. Imagine the scope of cleaning a nation or humanity.

If you are in this "cleaning" phase, not only do your reactions increase but also your responses increase. For example, humanity hates you but the Hierarchy loves you. Shamballa loves you and the Great Ones help you. You are torn between these two forces. You cannot do any harm because you know the energy that you have. When Jesus was about to enter a village, people from the village told Him that they did not want Him there. Actually, they were smart in one sense because if He came to that village, He would evoke all of the dirty things existing in the people. They felt it, and this is why they asked Him not to visit. People sometimes ask why Masters do not come to the cities. God save us if They did because all of our "trash" would start flowing out into the streets!

When the people of the village rejected Him, one of the disciples said, "Master, why don't you order your angels to attack and destroy them?" He answered, "We did not come to harm anyone." He knew the power available to Him if He wanted to use it. That was His test.

People on the Path evoke reactions from within themselves and from their environment, but as the battle increases, the responses increase. The Great Ones come and encourage you to be more creative and more beautiful. Because of this conflict, you become a genius, an Avatar, a Christ, a Master. This is the conflict that creates that jewel within you. Whoever is ready must enter into that conflict when he enters the Path.

The first reaction is from our own little self, from the hidden, dark corners of our being. The second reaction comes from our environment. The third comes from a source that we call the dark forces, or dark brothers. This was mentioned two thousand years ago in the *New Testament.*

> *Put on the whole armor of God,*
> *that ye may be able to stand against the wiles*
> *of the devil.*
> *For we wrestle not against flesh and blood,*
> *but against principalities, against powers,*
> *against the rulers [world rulers] of the darkness*
> *of this world, against spiritual hosts of wickedness*
> *in high places.*
> *Wherefore take unto you the whole armor of God,*

that ye be able to withstand in the evil day,
and having done all, to stand.
Stand therefore, having your loins gird about
with truth, and having on the breastplate of right-
eousness.
And your feet shod with the preparation of the
gospel of peace.
Above all, taking the shield of faith, wherewith ye
shall be able to quench all the fiery darts of the
wicked.
And take the helmet of salvation, and the sword of
the Spirit, which is the word of God.
Praying always with all prayer and supplication
in the Spirit, and watching thereunto with all
perseverance and supplication for all saints.[1]

Put on the whole armor of God, that ye may be able
to stand against the wiles of the devil. For we wrestle not
against flesh and blood, but against principalities, against
powers, against the rulers [world rulers] of the darkness
of this world, against spiritual hosts of wickedness in high
places. Actually, two thousand years ago, Saint Paul gave
the answer, but no one wanted to analyze it. What is the
armor to which he refers? "Having your loins gird about
with truth. . . ." If you are wrapping yourself with the
truth, no evil reaction will come because you will destroy
it before it reaches you. Dark attacks come to us when
there is untruth in us.

If you lied, mentally, emotionally, and physically with
your bad behavior and expressions, if you were covering
and imitating things, if you were untruthful with every
kind of untruthful thought, action, and word, you create a
window for the darkness to sneak in. Gird yourself! Let the

1. Ephesians 6:11-18

axis of your life be girded with the strong belt of truth. You are the axis; you turn on your axis. The axis symbolizes that wherever you turn, whatever you do, you are the axis; you have the belt.

The breastplate of righteousness. Are you righteous in your thinking, in your conversations, in your judgment and adjustment, in your actions, behaviors, and feelings? Are you really righteous? If you are righteous, no darkness will hit you or can destroy you. Modern philosophers and scientists often ask, "What is this righteousness about which you speak?" The political system and most businesses today are based upon unrighteousness. Unless you are unrighteous, it is difficult to do anything in the world. But the Teaching says, "Stay righteous because eventually you will win." Pay your bills righteously, accept righteously, and speak righteously, in truth.

Take the shield of faith. What is faith? Faith is a real and firm intuitive connection with the Divinity within you. Do you have faith? If you answer, "Yes, I am a Divine Spark" to this question, you have faith. That Divine Spark is unconquerable. It is the source of all beauty, all creativity; that is faith. No one can defeat it; that is faith. I am going to do it; that is faith. I am going to conquer it; that is faith. Faith is the Divinity within you. If you do not have faith, you will be a dry leaf in the mouth of the wind, and the dark forces will dump you.

Take the helmet of salvation. What is salvation? We tend to have a negative feeling about the term "salvation" primarily because people have been asked, "Aren't you saved?" This terrifies you. In truth, salvation is a very beautiful word which means that you have crossed the river of darkness. You have finished with this earthly mess. Briefly, salvation means purification. Because you are in a state of purification, you are saved now. For example, you notice that you have lost a jewel. You search and search, but cannot find it. Finally, you notice that your vacuum cleaner needs emptying. When you empty the bag, you suddenly see your lost jewel in the mess and dirt of the bag. You salvage the jewel. This is salvation because you salvaged your True Self.

The sword of the spirit. This refers to psychic energy or the Holy Spirit. When you have these weapons inside and outside, dark forces cannot defeat you. They may hurt you, and they may create lots of turmoil around you, but you are going to learn one thing: "Blessed be obstacles; through them we grow." Only enemies will create the jewel within you, the jewel toward which you aspire. This is why King Akbar said, "If you do not have enemies, expect them." Enemies will keep you alert.

Walk with the gospel of peace. The gospel of peace does not refer to the *New Testament.* It means to be peaceful outside and inside. Create peace with your thoughts, actions, and feelings. What is peace? Peace is not inertia. Peace is not being dead. Peace is harmonious relationship with the Universe. When harmony is created, you are in peace. Saint Paul adds, "Be sober and vigilant because your adversary, evil, is as a roaring lion walking about, seeing whom he can devour."

Dark forces are recognized in the *New Testament,* and the disciples are warning against these dark ones. You cannot fight them with atomic weapons or machine guns. You fight against dark forces with truth, righteousness, salvation, peace, nobility, solemnity, and soberness. These are greater weapons than ordinary weapons.

Virtues can be kept alive only in using them, practicing them, meditating on them, and by studying their effects.

Question: *Sometimes the names of the virtues do not make sense to many people. Why is this?*

Answer: There are many reasons. One is called subliminal programming. Another is desensitization. Desensitization is a tool of evil which people use to turn you off from great words that embody virtues, visions, and life goals. They use these words in negative context and relate them to ugly events or pictures. They connect them to painful experiences and eventually make you indifferent toward these words.

In the same way, they take bad words and use them in positive contexts and make you love them. Subliminal attacks are desensitization. Subliminal attacks go directly to your subconscious mind and gradually control your life when the image is called out through the Law of Association. This is used now especially in politics and in business. Enjoyable music is played, but behind the music there is a subliminal command which says, for example, "Commit suicide," or "Drink ABC brand of beer." Sooner or later you will obey such commands. For example, they say, "Love is good, but you can catch AIDS, gonorrhea and syphilis." "If you marry, you will have a continuous headache." "You can love a friend, but he will betray and slander you." "They found two lovers dead on the beach." "Poor man. Because of his love to save a man, he was crushed under a truck." When this continues, you start hating love and developing hatred.

There are people who psychologically plan and analyze, using words in such a way that they create desensitization. For example, they did this professionally through the hippies. The hippies were saying, "Love, love, love everybody; hug everybody; lay with everybody. Everything is love; Jesus is love." Through this psychology, millions of young people contracted venereal diseases. When you hear about love, after having gonorrhea, syphilis, and AIDS, you say, "I don't want to hear about love." You are blocked for this life, and for the next fifty lives you will hate love.

There is now a dark corner in you. When your mother says, "I love you," you say, "Mommy, I hate you." "Why? I love you, honey." "I don't know, but I hate you."

When dark corners are open, you think that love is the most obnoxious thing because it is related to gonorrhea, syphilis, and AIDS, as well as punishment, doctors, injections, and the destruction of your life. "Don't tell me about love," you say.

That is why those people who do not love, who cannot love, and who are horrified by love are usually those who were misused by love. A person might say, "Honey, I love you," then steal five thousand dollars from your pocket. You say, "You said you loved me; then you stole money from me. I don't like love anymore." This is how you are programmed and computerized.

How can we clean this stable of Hercules? In the labor of Hercules, the manure from the animals had been collecting for ages, until no one could enter. Hercules was needed to clean the stables. He saw the mess and said, "How can we clean this?" He diverted two rivers and released them into the stables. The rivers rushed through the stables and cleaned them. These two rivers are Light and Love. The same stables are within us, and they must be cleaned from all the manure of our animal behavior. Great virtues and ideas cannot enter into the mind when it is in such a rotten condition.

Question: *Is the projection of dark forces telepathic?*

Answer: Yes, it is. It can also be stimulation, energy, and force. With their remote control, the dark forces push the buttons within your mind that are connected with these dark corners of your subconscious. But why blame the dark forces? You must be blamed for inviting them to do these things. That is why Christ says, "Be awake and sober."

We must dwell on three words: watchfulness, soberness, and awakeness. They are very important.

Question: *What is the Christian meaning of salvation?*

Answer: If you search for the real meaning, you will discover that only a pure Soul can be with Christ, with the Hierarchy, or in the Father's Home. Purification, cleanliness, and taking yourself out of the mess of the world is salvation.

Question: *Christians believe in repentance. Is this the first initiation?*

Answer: For the last two thousand years, Christians have been the most terrible killers. In Spain, they burned thirty-three thousand so-called witches in one night. These "witches" were those who did not believe as the Church believed. Is this what love is? In Christ's name, people died and others continue to do many obnoxious things. Many monsters were created to destroy humanity in the name of great principles. But the real principle behind most all of this destruction was money, ego, and self-interest. In my opinion, the one that must repent is the Christian Church, which has preached the words of Christ, but which has crucified Him in actual life.

Question: *Do dark forces tempt us at certain times? Do they make suggestions and actually manipulate people?*

Answer: Yes. They actually send people to you and make you excited. You are going to have control over yourself. Dark forces use remote control and suggestion. Let us say that your subconscious mind is like a computer. The various lettered keys represent dark corners in your mind. These dark corners are the accumulations of dark events. The dark ones see this, so they stimulate the "B" key, or the "N" key to put you in contact with that dark corner. When this happens, you go into action. This is remote control.

In *The Science of Becoming Oneself* and *Cosmos in Man,* I emphasized strongly that man is a machine until he surpasses his mechanical way of living. Whatever we do is sixty to seventy percent mechanical, but do not get discouraged.

Consciousness acts only when you start suffering. If you work harder, you immediately understand these principles. It is the greatest fun. For example, many pages of *Challenge for Discipleship* and other books were written only because I had such fights and experiences. It is a fantastic psychological treasure to see how these kinds of things operate.

Question: *How are they aware of all of the critical moments in your life?*

Answer: We think we are a sealed and bottled soul, and that no one can see our minds, our emotions, our feelings. On the contrary, on the astral plane dark ones see everything you do and everything you think. You are an open book. It does not take a genius to see what you are. If you are a little clairvoyant, you can see the centers working. For example, if someone is excited, the color red shows up, making different forms. Then suddenly, a white light hits these forms and they disappear. This means the person has come to his senses. These things are easily seen, if one develops that eye.

Occupy your mind with these thoughts so that the alchemical change starts within your nature.

Question: *How do these dark forces operate through a person? What are the signals that they are starting?*

Answer: Remember that you have protection. Your Solar Angel is your protection. The Divinity within you is protection. Your light, love, and righteousness are protection, but do not open windows and invite the dark forces inside.

195

1. *They program your mind in such a way that you attach to transient objects.* "This is my jewelry, my yard, my tree, my house, my country; this piece of meat belongs to me, and so on." You are hooked now on transient objects, and you run day and night after these objects. Like a mouse in a cage, your life is over and you are never satisfied unless you can have these objects — and then when you get them, you still are not satisfied.

There was an eighteenth century poet named Ashughchivan who said, "The world is like a hotel and people in it are the guests. This is the state of the world; people come and go."

Through attachment, the dark forces will sap your psychic energy and not let you go forward to the greater path. Of course, the Teaching does not say that you cannot have property or objects such as money, savings, and so on, but have them without attachment. Do not let them control you. You must control them.

When superficial objects and superficial values continuously limit your freedom and expansion, you cannot belong to yourself. I remember seeing a very comical incident in the Middle East. There was a beautiful medical doctor. One day he become very angry with the goose that lived in his backyard. Early one morning I said, "Good morning, Doctor. How are you?" "I am fine," he replied. "What are you going to do today?" I asked. "I will see a few patients, write some prescriptions, and so on." We talked briefly, then the goose appeared, and he started cursing and chasing the goose. He chased that goose off and on from eight in the morning until three in the afternoon, but it was impossible to catch. I was laughing so hard. Finally, he sat down and said, "I will have a heart attack over that goose." "Good," I said, "then the goose can write prescriptions for you."

I realized that humanity has its own goose which it runs after day and night — the sex goose, money goose, property goose, ego goose, vanity goose, and so on. Many people chase the sex goose day and night until they are crazy. They want to catch that goose. When it is too late in the afternoon of their lives, when they are in their eighties or nineties, they feel very bad. You cannot catch those geese; you can only chase them! Disciples must know these things and handle them accordingly.

2. The second attack is vanity. Dark forces develop vanity within you. They develop ego and separative tendencies. Separatism comes from evil, from dark forces. Vanity is to create some type of thinking in which you assume that you know everything, have everything, can do everything, and are the best of everything. If this comes to your mind, you are hooked to the radio station of evil. All jazz that comes from that station is from the dark forces. Rock 'n' roll and disco come from there.

Ego is a tendency to use everything for your own behalf. Ego rejects advice. See how dark forces are encapsulating you? You do not listen to your teachers or your friends; you have ego. If you start touching his ego, a man will scream. People think that an injection into your skin is painful, but the most painful injection is when you touch the ego of others. They not only feel pain, but they prepare to take revenge on you. Do not build the painful capsule of ego around you. It comes from evil.

Humbleness means lack of ego. One day a man went to a very holy man and said, "You are dirty. You are this and that." The man smiled and did not reply. Then the accuser furiously asked, "Why aren't you answering?" The holy man replied, "Because you are right." "If I am right, then why do people think that you are a holy man?" "Well, I did things five thousand years ago that were very obnoxious. I remembered them when you were telling me how dirty I was."

You are holy today, but what about yesterday or two years ago or five lives ago? Why are you angry if someone says that you are obnoxious? The holy man in the story did not have an ego. Ego covers your shortcomings and failures and says, "You are the best. You are the holiest. You are really saved and already living in the heart of God." Are you really?

3. Evil forces develop the tendency toward malice, slander, and treason in you. For example, a person who gives our secrets to another nation is a traitor. The Great Sage says that traitors will not find salvation for millions of years. Treason is the greatest sin. Treason to your friends, wives, husbands, fathers, mothers, students, teachers is forbidden because treason is the darkest poison that is injected in you by dark forces. Do not allow it to come to you.

Sometimes you use very foul language to slander and malign people. Because of slander, malice, and treason, you are blind to your own condition. Dark forces create blindness in you, and once you are blinded, you start searching for the errors of others and you do not see exactly what you are.

4. Dark forces also prevent your spiritual progress and expansion of consciousness by force or by bribery. For example, let us say that you are studying for a major exam being given tomorrow. Suddenly you hear a knock on your door and there stands your girlfriend. This is bribery. Until morning you make love; then you fail the exam.

A boxer was going to have a great match. Two days before the match, his girlfriend came over, and she was impossible to resist. In the third round, he was beaten nearly to death. The girl said to him, "Honey, I love you so much." "Get lost!" he said. "I don't want your love."

This is how evil operates. You must know how it operates. You must know their techniques, where and how they hide, and from where they attack. Because you are becoming disciples, you are going to know the tactics of the enemy. If not, they will delay your progress.

What are attacks? Attacks are the stimulation of those things that suddenly come into your consciousness, making you feel very depressed and unable to do anything in your life. They flood your carburetor. They say, "Life is no good; money is no good; I have no job; I have no friends; no one loves me; my life is this; my husband is that; my children are that," and so on. Finally you say, "I want to die." When this occurs, the dark forces have been successful. You must learn their techniques.

5. The dark forces want you to be separative and non-inclusive. When you talk about religion, you immediately have a feeling that your religion is better than others. Be careful now. When you speak about your nation or your race, you feel that yours is better. "Me, my tradition, my religion, my country, my philosophy, my tomatoes, my potatoes." This is a sign that you are under the influence of separatism. They want to create non-inclusiveness.

Dark forces are separative and separatism helps their business. This is their duty. They are coming from unity to diversity; that is their duty, their tendency. We are going from diversity to unity. These two opposing paths conflict with each other. If we follow darkness, we are reversing our evolution. Instead of evolving ourselves, we are coming under the influence of involution, toward matter. We must oppose this. As much as they try to make us separative, we are going to make ourselves inclusive. But being inclusive does not mean to empty a trash can into your home. There is a hint here.

6. The sixth method the dark forces use is to cause people to become victims of marijuana, hallucinogenic drugs, and alcohol. This is a very subtle technique which the dark forces use more and more these days. Alcohol is the first arrow. If they hit you with it, then they will lead you into other things. How will you see these things? When you use these drugs, you will immediately see the hopelessness of whatever you want to build, construct, and organize.

My Mother used to say, "Evil enters like a needle and after it enters, it becomes an elephant that cannot find any hole large enough to exit from." Let us say that a bad thought comes to you. Then you nourish that bad thought. It becomes a camel or an elephant. As much as you try to throw it out, it is impossible because it is growing and eating you.

Discipleship is not easy, but we are going to do it.

10
The Dark Lodge

The Great Teacher states that the dark brothers are far more advanced in their externalization than is the Hierarchy. To help the Hierarchy externalize, disciples of the world must increase and try to help humanity enter onto the Path leading to light, love, and beauty. This is hard labor, labor which must be carried on day and night.

The evil lodge externalizes through those who have no heart, those who are greedy and eager to exploit, deceive, and manipulate people for their pleasures, those who enjoy crime and murder, those who are ugly and are engaged in destroying the morality and sanity of people, and those who are lazy and occupied with their own pleasures and comfort. And because the numbers of these agents are in the billions, the dark lodge has a greater facility to externalize.

The work of the disciple is not easy. He must fight on three fronts:
- against the lethargy and ignorance of people
- against the stupidities of those on the path
- against the dark forces

The more disciples we have, the more light will penetrate into the world, and the greater the chance will be for the Hierarchy to manifest.

We are told in the Ageless Wisdom that every human being is a ray of light projected from the Central Fire, from the Central Spiritual Sun.

Let us study the following diagram which symbolizes the seven Cosmic Planes and the source of life, the mystic Sun.

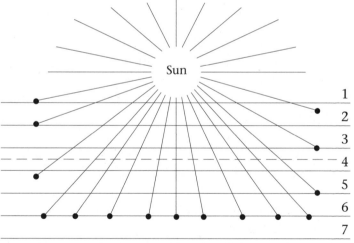

Diagram 1. The Seven Cosmic Planes and the Source of Life

This is the Sun, the storehouse of Light, Power, Beauty — God Almighty. A Spark is sent forth into space, ever-descending until it reaches the lowest plane and becomes an atom. Actually, living here on earth, you are still tied in your essence to your Source. There is no division between you and the Source; you are Him in your higher essence. It is only in your physical consciousness that you think you are separate.

As this light descends into denser and denser matter, it eventually reaches the mental plane (4). Here is the Cosmic Mental Plane. The Cosmic Mental Plane is divided into two sections: the lower mental plane and the higher mental plane. In the lower Cosmic Mental Plane the light becomes really dense. At this point of "condensation," the ray begins to feel its separation from the Source because it is condensed there.

According to Cosmic Law, the Spark must descend to the lowest and then climb back to reach the Source and become Itself, a supreme Spirit. It must pass through all the stages in school. In the lower mental plane, the Spark develops the consciousness of separation. When it descends further, into the Cosmic Astral Plane, the dark forces try to inflame it and gain the Spark for their side, or at least create in it an intense desire for matter. When the Spark enters the Cosmic Physical Plane, there its light dims more and more until it collects a shell of matter around itself. Here it becomes helpless, unless it has contact with the Forces of Light.

THE DARK LODGE

The Great Teacher says that the headquarters of Cosmic evil is in the Cosmic Astral Plane. In explaining the Great Invocation, He says that the stanza which reads, "and may it seal the door where evil dwells," does not refer to the evil existing in humanity but to the Cosmic evil existing in the Cosmic Astral Plane. This is the headquarters of all spirits who have disobeyed Divine Will. Their intention is to oppose, by all ways and means, those who are trying to return to the Source.

The Prodigal Son went deep into matter, to the last station, and then he wanted to return Home. And he did. The intention of the dark forces is to prevent every human being from returning Home, to his Source. The dark ones try to prevent our salvation, our liberation, and our freedom. Thus, a great headquarters of evil has been established on the Cosmic Astral Plane. One is also found on the astral plane of the Cosmic Physical Plane.

We have seven Cosmic Planes: Divine, Monadic, Atmic, Intuitional, Mental, Astral, and Physical. Each of these planes also has seven subdivisions of each plane. For example, the Cosmic Physical Plane has a Divine Plane, a Monadic Plane, an Atmic Plane, an Intuitional Plane, a mental plane, an astral plane, and a physical plane. These are the subplanes of the Cosmic Physical Plane.

The dark lodge is a rebellion clique in God's government. It has no roots and is doomed to destruction, but it tries to further its goals because of vanity and Cosmic glamor, thinking that it can resist the Will of the Supreme. This evil lodge does not exist on higher planes. It is rootless, and its success brings us all closer to destruction. We must understand clearly that evil is self-destructive and that nothing can destroy good which is rooted in the Supreme Source.

The headquarters of evil on the Cosmic Astral Plane stand against the Will of God. When Christ was ready to be crucified, He said, "Thy Will, not mine, be done." Whoever works against the Supreme Will, which means against Goodness, Light, Beauty, and Freedom, is evil. These evil entities work to prevent people from climbing the ladder of evolution to reach perfection.

People may wonder why the dark lodge stands against evolution and perfection. The answer is very clear. The dark lodge wants to perpetuate its own position and expand its power by gaining control over humanity and preventing people from reaching the Cosmic Astral Plane. Each soldier of Light is a danger to the dark lodge and to its servants. Because of their glamor, they do not see the future, and they blindly force their will on whomever they can.

The dark lodge in the Cosmic Astral Plane is not composed of human beings. They are entities on the arc of involution. Their bodies are composed of the substance of the Cosmic Astral Plane. They are extremely powerful compared to human beings. Only the Hierarchy as a group and certain high-level Initiates can cope with them.

Certain situations on earth allow such Cosmic evil entities to approach the Cosmic Physical Plane and work on the astral plane. Some of them even incarnate to spread evil all over the world. But this is not easily done. The Hierarchy of Masters is expert in the ways of the dark lodge. It often fights against the dark lodge not only on the subtle planes but also here on the physical plane. History has many records about these incarnated evil ones who brought death and destruction to earth.

To counteract evil on earth, some Great Ones Who are in incarnation try to break evil's power and make it fail. Actually, every time a Great One comes to earth, it is because evil has taken incarnation. The *Bhagavad Gita* states this very clearly in the following:

> *Whenever men become indifferent toward their*
> *duties and responsibilities, and whenever*
> *unrighteousness and disorder increase,*
> *then, indeed, I manifest Myself.*
> *To protect the virtuous, to destroy the wicked,*
> *and to re-establish the sense of duty and*
> *responsibility, thus I manifest Myself*
> *age after age.*[1]

---

1. *Bhagavad Gita* 4:7-8, translated by Torkom Saraydarian.

The Hierarchy, the group of great Masters and Great Ones, sent Jesus, Moses, Krishna, Mohammed, and many other Great Workers to tell people that there is darkness and there is light, and that they need to awaken and work out their salvation. The dark forces also send their agents, people like Hitler, Nero, and those who are destructive and inhuman. For example, Sultan Hamid was a Turkish king who had no conscience at all. He massacred four hundred thousand Armenians and enjoyed seeing them die. He ordered five hundred young girls to dance naked before him while gasoline was poured upon them to burn them to death. A human being can only do such a thing if he becomes a slave to the dark forces.

The dark lodge communicates with its agents mentally, by telepathy. It has agents and stations on every plane. Even here on earth, it has main centers of activity through which people are trained in its ways. These people are then promoted into higher positions and made more effective. Through these trained individuals, the dark lodge obsesses churches, religious institutions, governments, and nations, making these organizations completely their slaves.

The White Lodge, or the Hierarchy, does not work this way. It leaves human beings free to choose. The Hierarchy does not impose its will upon human beings but tries to educate them and inspire freedom from the dark ones.

Once a person is obsessed by the dark forces, he no longer thinks freely, and he turns into an automaton, into a sheep. The same holds true for a nation. Those who rule lead their sheep toward Niagara Falls. The destination of every person or nation which is possessed by evil is total destruction. *Remember, evil destroys itself.*

Dark forces cannot influence you unless you develop illusion, glamor, ego, and vanity in the lower planes. The moment you develop these, they can contact you. If they have a frequency of five hundred, they cannot communicate with you until you share the same frequency. Then they can key in, and you become their slave. They manifest through you.

The dark lodge has strength and power because, essentially, its members have Divine Origin, and because of their plane they are charged with greater energy. Saint Paul, in speaking about the dark lodge, says, "We are not fighting against humans, but against principalities, against kingdoms of darkness." We need to know more about who they are.

The dark forces have their kings, their queens, their lower-ranked officers, and armies. The least ones come among us to talk and whisper to us telepathically, emotionally, and symbolically so that they take us from Light to darkness. For example, one of them may put a wrong sign on the freeway; you were going east, and now suddenly you are heading west because you did not really discriminate and see that it was a false sign put there by the dark forces.

Christ said that the children of darkness are smarter than the children of Light. They are so smart. For example, they make the price of gasoline jump from twenty-five cents a gallon to one dollar forty-five cents a gallon.

We may wonder why it is that an evil person who commits an unpardonable crime on the physical plane against human beings is doomed to be annihilated and become a part of chaos, while these Cosmic Astral entities remain unpunished by the Law for a great cycle and are not annihilated. Every entity in heaven and on earth is bestowed with free will. One can obey Divine Will or not obey it. Some learn to resign their wills by breaking the law. Others resign their wills by obeying the Law.

Divine Providence gives the dark forces a chance to follow the Path and come to the Cosmic Physical Plane, eventually to the earthly plane, where they will come under judgment. In the Cosmic Astral Plane, they are mindless. They cannot think, but they can follow the dictates of their urges. They are separative. All evil that erupts on every plane is the fruit of separatism. All vices, crimes, violence, hatred, and revenge are fruits of separatism.

Divine Providence makes them take incarnation on lower planes and develop the mental principle. Thus, they are given a chance to consciously choose either the path of liberation or destruction. Many human beings have incarnated from the dark lodge. A great percentage of them are ready for liberation because of the help of spiritual education and various worldly experiences. Let us remember that earth is a purgatory, a school from which every soul must graduate with honors.

Humanity, especially disciples in all departments of human endeavor, must study the ways of the evil forces — not necessarily to fight against them but to bypass them if possible, to frustrate their efforts and make them fail. We are advised to "resist not evil," but the One Who gave us this advice was the Greatest Hero Who resisted evil, even until death. What is the purpose of saviors who come to earth other than to resist evil and protect humanity from evil?

Let us say that we received a message from space that aliens from another world were going to attack us. We would learn here what their techniques were, what their ways and means would be to stop our evolution. We would learn and study so that we could frustrate their efforts and make them fail in what they were doing because their success is guaranteed only if we have those elements in our bodies which enable them to contact us.

For example, let us say that I have a machine that can hurt you if you contain any iron. If you do not contain iron, my machine cannot harm you. But if you contain iron, a beam from my machine will hit and kill you.

Symbolically, iron is when you have karma, when you are guilty, polluted, hateful, jealous, revengeful, and separative. These elements draw the energy and attention of the dark forces to reach you, to manipulate and control you.

To fight against the dark forces we need

— to know their ways and means

— to be karmically pure

— to be ready to fight

Let us elaborate on the third point. Being unready to fight is a transgression. If a person sleeps in a time of danger and runs after his pleasures, he cannot prepare himself to face and overcome danger. One must be ready at every moment, which means to be

* alert, and to make others alert

* conscious, and to make others conscious

* in control of his nature

* educated

* discriminative

* decisive

* daring

Dark forces fight you even in your dreams if you are on the astral plane, especially on the lower levels of the astral plane while you are sleeping. How do they fight you?

• They hypnotize you in a certain direction so that you turn into their slave on the physical plane.

• They inject ugly and obnoxious thoughtforms into your mind and inspire you to express them in your speech, art, movies, and so on.

- They connect you with the wrong people, awakening certain desires in you.

- They stimulate your vanity, ego, and illusions.

- They transfer heavy glamors into your aura.

They are not restricted to playing only in dreams. They play in the astral, mental, and even the higher mental planes.

We must be very careful not to call people evil unless we are absolutely sure that they are. For example, to most Christians, anyone who is not a Christian is evil and cannot be saved unless he follows Christ. Other religions hold similar views, that their religion is the only religion. Nationalism, self-interest, and hatred force us to call others evil. Many people we think are evil are not. Perhaps in our judgment they are evil, but God's judgment may be different. For all these reasons, we must be very careful in our judgment as well as very sharp to see the signs of evil.

11
The Existence of Good & Evil

The originating source of many human tendencies is not in the human psyche but in space. Many sicknesses, moral distortions, and degenerative tendencies have their source in planets, systems, and constellations that are in the process of decay and disintegration. Black magic tends toward destructive and criminal activities of many kinds and is the result of the response to such processes of disintegration.

The disintegrating planet, solar system, or galaxy affects "bodies" which are found in the field of their influence. On the other hand, those planets, systems, and galaxies that are in the process of regeneration and vitality produce all the movements on earth which are progressive, unfolding, creative, and constructive.

The influence of these sources in space is gradual and translated in the world by all life forms which are either on the path of disintegration or on the path of regeneration. Those life forms which carry a decaying process in their physical, emotional, and mental bodies become the threefold channels of the decaying influences in space.

Those life forms which carry a regenerative process in their physical, emotional, and mental realms, or are spiritually unfolding and radiating, become the transmitters of creative, constructive, and progressive influences coming from radioactive sources in space.

The two key words, "decay and regeneration," have very esoteric meanings.

The decaying process takes place when the ensouling energy with all its activities, plans, and purpose withdraws into higher realms, just as a human soul leaves the body and departs.

The body that is left disintegrates, causing disintegrating effects on all that is found in the field of its influence. This means also that such a body no longer carries an advancing, unfolding influence in harmony with the Greater Entity from whose body it is in the process of being eliminated.

On the other hand, a regenerative process takes place when a unit of consciousness takes hold of a form or creates a form and tries to express through it the purpose and the plan it has in its Core. Through this form, it unfolds its plan and purpose, in the meantime causing the form to flourish and expand to be able to express the directions of the expanding consciousness.

But how are two such tendencies — decay and regeneration — translated into evil and good?

Evil is related to all those processes which are not in harmony with the advancing, developing, and unfolding plan and stay as a hindrances to all movements leading to the purpose of the entity using a form. Thus, evil is against the unfolding of the purpose existing in the Core of the life animating the form.

The good is related to all those tendencies, activities, and processes which assist the purpose of the unit of consciousness existing in a form (man, planet, or a system). All those activities on all planes that promote the purpose of a unit of consciousness are termed "good" because they are in harmony with the good of all.

The question here becomes, "Doesn't the decaying process also play a part in promoting the regenerative process?" The answer is "yes" and "no."

If the decay is the result of a failure of a unit of consciousness, or the result of "abortion," it is not a part of the regenerative process. But if the decay is the result of maturity, it is a part of the regenerative process. Maturity here means that the ensouling unit of awareness in the form made all the atoms of the form reach the limit of their evolution, and it releases them in a radioactive process to go and be parts of other units to continue their evolution.

In the other case, the atoms of the decaying forms are aborted and are left to the chaotic forces of Nature to put them back into their original substance to start again their evolutionary cycles with advancing units of consciousness.

Thus, evil and good are translated and broadcast in the world by their agents who have either decaying centers and bodies or regenerating centers and bodies.

Good promotes the Purpose of the Most High. Evil creates hindrances on the path of all creative processes. Of course, agents are promoted or discarded according to the karma they create through their life activities.

The decaying process in space and the regenerative process in space both have their chains, or networks, in the field of their influence. This is why an "evil" person has such power supported by the network. Also, this is why a good person who "walks with God" is invulnerable and unconquerable, even if it appears that the evil temporarily conquers him. Dark forces in the Universe are agents of decay. The Hierarchy of Light is the agent of regenerative processes in the whole Universe.

The Great Teacher says in *A Treatise on Cosmic Fire*, "There is one such [disintegrating] constellation, situated between the lesser Dipper and our system, and another, interrelated with the Pleiades and our system. . . ."[1] One wonders if, in the future, the science of astronomy will have a chance to deal with the subtle influence that such bodies have upon human culture and civilizations!

It is true that God does not create either good or evil, but people discover that good is the right way to do things, and evil is the way which leads to self-destruction. Those who discover this truth, life after life, become the Teachers of humanity and cyclically come to the world to teach humanity how to live, how to relate, and how to strive toward perfection. It is these Great Ones Who establish the doctrine of good and oppose the doctrine of evil.

Evil and good do not exist. It is we that make them exist by responding or reacting to the existence as a whole.

Good is when we are healthy and make others healthy, are happy and make others happy, are successful and make others successful, progressively unfolding our potentials and helping others to do so. Then we say that evil is from those people who prevent other people from being healthy, happy, successful, and progressively unfolding. Such people, age after age, will form the group of evils who will perpetuate disease, pain, suffering, failure, and defeat. Thus man himself creates evil, and he creates good. Evil ones enjoy the suffering of others. Good ones enjoy the health, happiness, success, and progress of others.

Good or evil is temporary. When you transcend the levels in which human measures dominate, you do not see

---

1. Bailey, Alice A., *A Treatise on Cosmic Fire*, p. 837.

the existence of either good or evil. You see only an increasing love within you, which accepts all that is.

God did not create either evil or good. If He did, He
would be guilty for all conditions that evil creates and for
all hatred and separatism that good holds against evil.

*God is not responsible for our concepts and assump-
tions. We must create our own path in our Universe.*

People reason and say, "If there is no evil, then whatever I do to hurt people is neither good nor evil." Such a
reasoning could be used if we did not have the Law of
Karma which says, "Whatever you sow, that also will you
reap." It does not say what to sow. You are free to sow anything you want, but know that you *will* sow its consequences.

Does the Law of Karma work for the good? You may
think so, but the truth is that the Law of Karma exactly
shows the result of your actions. Then you may choose a
path that you name, for example, "good." Thus it is you
who creates the good, and then you create a long list of laws
of how to perpetuate the good because it appears to you that
increasing the good is more profitable in the long run.

All our values are created by us, and if we research into
the depth of values, we discover that all values are based
upon one reality — the unity and oneness of all that exists.

Does evil exist in the world? Of course, it exists. But
who created evil? The answer is man.

Evil in the world now appears in the form of

- greed
- exploitation
- hatred
- totalitarianism
- pollution

215

- diseases

- separatism

- ignorance

- egoism

- vanity

- fear

- and all those thoughts, emotions, and actions related to the above elements

Of course the evil exists, because we created evil. Of course good also exists, because some of us created it.

We are just discovering that it is through goodness that we can enjoy all creation. With evil we destroy the creation and ourselves too. So evil is not prosurvival; good is. But in reality, good and evil were not created by the Absolute Source. We created them because they were not created originally.

It is interesting also to know that our relation to good or to evil makes a difference. A certain attitude toward evil creates good. A certain attitude toward good creates evil. The most subtle evil is one that appears in the form of goodness.

People have many such experiences. We cover all our evil motives and actions with colorful blankets of legality and good intentions. This is such a poisonous action that its effects last many generations.

We are told that God shines His Sun over good and evil because there is no original idea in His Mind about good and evil. But the interesting thing is that the rays of His Sun multiply the evil as well as the good, and the effect on life of such an increase of good and evil depends on the existing quality of good and evil.

One may ask, "Is it good to annihilate evil, if possible?" How can one be good in annihilating evil? This is why in the Great Invocation we are told to pray, "May it seal the door where evil dwells." With the intention to annihilate evil, we organize many games and eventually create all weapons of evil to annihilate evil. What a smart way to do things!

Then how will we get rid of evil? By teaching humanity to get rid of evil

      — thoughts

      — emotions

      — actions

No one in the world is good or evil without you being good or evil with them. Also, the good on a lower level turns into an evil on a higher level. The same is true with evil. Sometimes good comes out of evil. But people follow the path of their nature and interests.

We do not absolutely know what is good and what is evil. We have our own good and evil. Though it is true that humanity created an organized evil and beside it an organized good. It is also interesting to know that it is easier for a good to turn evil than an evil to turn into good.

Evil is created when a person seeks more for his benefit than for the benefit of others. Even thinking only for your own salvation leads you into evil. Any virtue that is used only on the behalf of yourself turns into a vice.

Thus the search for evil and good leads us to one principle: *the principle of living the life for the benefit of all that exists.* This is the highest good as far as can be seen.

When people think that bad things will happen to good people, they prove their ignorance, believing that there is no justice in God's creation. In assuming that bad things happen to good people, we fail to discover the reasons why the bad things happen to good people. We fail also to see the evil hidden in so-called good people. Thus we cannot find a solution because we deceive ourselves.

If you do not know about the law of "whatever you sow, that is what you reap," then every time something unpleasant or drastic happens to you, you say, "Bad things happen to good people." And if you have the faith that God is righteous, you fall into confusion.

People also talk about ugliness and beauty. God created things as we see them. Some of them are called ugly, some of them beautiful. Ugliness is the creation of man. God never created ugliness, but man had the free will to create ugliness. Ugliness is not the opposite of beauty but the degeneration of beauty or that which Nature created. There is not only physical ugliness, but also emotional and mental ugliness created or generated by man.

When we choose beauty, we see how beauty brings integrity and health to us. Something is beautiful to us when it inspires us to strive, to serve, to love, to forgive, to understand ourselves, and to have closer contact with the reality within us. Beauty also evokes gratitude and patience.

Ugliness causes cleavages in our nature gives us fear, hatred, anger. Under ugliness we gossip, we slander, we steal, we cheat, we go into depression.

So we can create ugliness or beauty.

Beauty and ugliness, evil and good did not exist for twenty million years. It is the experience accumulated in the human being, age after age, incarnation after incarnation, that certain things were considered prosurvival and certain things were considered antisurvival, or beautiful and ugly, good and evil.

All religions of the world are the voices of those who graduated from the wheel of incarnation and were able to speak about their experiences of evil and good.

12 The Origin of Evil

The Teaching says that our solar system comes into existence three times. The first solar system came into being billions of years ago, and then gradually disappeared. Then the formation of the second solar system, our present one, began after an interlude of millions of years. Eventually, this solar system will disintegrate, and the formation of the third solar system will begin.

The first solar system, we are told, developed Light — or intellect — to such a degree that light and consciousness even penetrated into each atom, molecule, and form. The second solar system is developing the Love principle. Eventually, unity and compassion will be created in every living atom and form through the Law of Attraction. The third solar system, to be formed in the future, will develop the principle of Will.

In these solar systems, the three principles of Light, Love, and Will are present, but one predominates over the others. For example, in the first solar system the goal was to develop the intelligence principle, but toward the end, fifteen percent of the people began to develop love, and two percent began to develop willpower. In this solar system, the goal is to develop love-wisdom, but a small percentage of the people have begun to develop willpower. The numbers of such people will increase toward the end of this solar system; these are the seedlings for the next solar system.

When the Monads were traveling from higher Cosmic Planes toward denser and denser substance, They felt in Their Cores that They were departing from the ocean of homogeneity and unity and entering a state of heterogeneity. When They reached the Cosmic Mental Plane, They were actually separate beings, but glorious in Their beauty and radiation. In the lower levels of the Cosmic Mental Plane, the Monads on both the evolutionary and involutionary arc faced the massive illusion of the "imperfect gods."[1] Their ideas and thoughtforms seemed like absolute truth to the Monads. Some of these Monads were trapped by these illusions, making both the descending and ascending paths very difficult for the Monads. Some of Them lost eons of time wandering in these most glorious illusions. Some of Them made it and continued to follow the path from the higher levels of the Cosmic Mental Plane to the Cosmic Astral Plane — the plane of Cosmic glamor.

With Their innate sense of direction, certain Monads eventually conquered Their illusions and continued Their path. The difference between Monads began to accumulate during the course of involution which became the

---

1. NOTE: "Imperfect gods" are the souls of planets, solar systems, and even galaxies, which are on the path of perfection. They are still imperfect in relation to their Source, and they have glamors and illusions at their own level. Just as certain actions of a human soul, which is not perfect, hurt the cells or atoms of his bodies, the "imperfect gods" similarly may take certain actions that are harmful to their "cells."

decisive factor in Their future orientation. On the lower levels of the Cosmic Mental Plane, this difference played the decisive role.

The next plane of descent was the Cosmic Astral Plane, where the Monads developed a tendency *to have* and hesitated to follow the path of descent. It is very interesting to note that the Cosmic Astral Plane is a sphere which is flooded by the glamors of the "imperfect gods," or Planetary and Solar Logoi on the path of perfection, Cosmic service, or incarnation. When the Monads reached the Cosmic Astral Plane, They were faced with an entirely new phenomenon — the existence of other planes. The atmosphere was thick and patches of glamor were everywhere. They began to fight, to adjust Themselves to the existing glamors or oppose them with instinctive and spontaneous discrimination. It is at this point that Cosmic evil came into being.

Some of the Monads began to identify with the glamors and refused the course of descent into matter, where They were to have further training and experience to further the cycle of spirit and matter and develop those properties offered by the Cosmic Physical Plane. They refused to descend to the physical plane. To remain in the Cosmic Astral Plane, They created a situation which, in many religions, is referred to as the *rebellion*.

The rebels gradually separated themselves from the Monads on the involutionary path and established a headquarters and kingdom on the Cosmic Astral Plane. They stood against those who were journeying to the Cosmic Physical Plane and those who, after graduating from the Cosmic Physical Plane entered the Cosmic Astral Plane on the ascent. Great Sages say that those Great Ones who graduate from the Cosmic Physical Plane enter the Cosmic Astral Plane as Warriors against these rebels. This is why every disciple and Initiate must be trained as a warrior and be ready for the conditions found on the Cosmic Astral Plane.

Some of the rebels on the Cosmic Astral Plane managed to incarnate in the Cosmic Physical Plane. They organized the dark lodge in the astral plane of the Cosmic Physical Plane and on the physical plane itself with those who followed evil in their physical life and entered the astral plane with all their maya, glamors, illusions, and crimes.

Not every rebel remains on the Cosmic Astral Plane. Armed with the spirit of rebellion against the Law, they descend to the Cosmic Physical Plane to spread the spirit of evil into people's hearts and mislead them in all their undertakings and endeavors. As the rebel lives and incarnates, his ego, glamors, illusions, and sense of separatism increase and, life after life, he builds a reactionary and conflicting mechanism against all principles of oneness.

Of course, karma follows his every step to bring him into the line of Divine Principles by presenting pain and suffering. But sometimes, the inflow of energy coming to him from the dark lodge is so powerful that the agent or soldier of the dark lodge endures all suffering without giving up his destructive separatism and dark motives. When people are born with such a mechanism, it obliterates or rejects any light that is in their hearts — and conscious evil comes into being. Such beings incarnate life after life to perpetuate evil in all its forms, until the cup of karma is full.

The dark forces not only have a Cosmic origin but also originate from earthly humanity. A few examples are

- real criminals
- those who are continuously occupied with evil thoughts
- those who are soaked with negative emotions and imagination
- those who are under hypnotic suggestions

• those human beings who live in the astral plane and who are dedicated to evil

1. Criminals. People sometimes become criminal because of certain adverse social conditions or because of self-interest, hatred, anger, jealousy, and so on. Once they are caught in this network, they automatically lean toward criminal paths. Year after year, hatred, revenge, lies, crimes, anger, greed, and jealousy increase in them and their spiritual nature eventually dies.

When such a person passes away, he takes with him all his pollution and vices, and he is born again with similar tendencies. If such lives are repeated for centuries and centuries, the person becomes an evil one himself, an enemy of humanity. Of course, during his many incarnations he may become obsessed by evil forces. He may even become possessed or sell his soul to them.

Such criminals are not only the products of our social conditions but also are reactions to the injustices done to them over many years and lives. It is also possible that they are the products of fanaticism, when in the name of religion or national interests they became criminals and remain forever in crime. Many religions create such criminals in the name of their saviors, dogmas, and doctrines. One must read the stories of the Spanish Inquisition to gain a broader understanding of this point.

Thus, many soldiers of the dark forces come from humanity itself. Hypocrisy leads many people to enlist in the army of the dark forces. Dictators like Hitler fashioned many soldiers for the dark forces by forcing them to commit crimes.

One path that leads to the army of the dark ones is sexual abuse, especially the rape of women. Such conduct creates heavy guilt feelings in the abuser, from which he can seldom recover. The only way he feels safe is to join the dark army.

Once a rapist was asked, "What will you do when you are released from prison?" He replied, "I will do again what I did in the past." Another man who was found guilty of kidnapping, abusing, and then murdering children never showed any regret for his crimes. The souls of such people are dead; their vices run their lives.

Some people are not criminal in their true nature, but circumstances, the influence of certain people, and temporary obsession may lead them to failure. But they do not continue in their crimes. They awaken and feel terribly sorry for their failure and take every precaution not to fail again.

People who have experiences of temptation, failure, pain, and suffering often regenerate themselves and stand as leaders who can help thousands who need help in those moments of life crisis.

Another door leading to the camp of the dark forces is treason to one's country. Such an act leaves a mark like a stamp on the forehead which cannot be hidden either on earth or in the Subtle Worlds. This forces the criminal to join the army of evil.

Greed is another door to evil. People become so identified with their possessions that they almost become one with them. To protect and perpetuate their possessions, they exercise many forms of crime. Havingness is a bottomless barrel which can never be filled. All those who are contaminated with greed try to exploit people and use illogical ways to obtain more. Eventually, they find themselves active in the field of evil.

Terrorism leads many people to the army of darkness. People use terrorism for revenge, to obtain what they have lost, or to force their will upon others. All terrorism is proof of the failure of intellectual and higher principles. Righteousness must be pursued. Terrorism undermines future success and creates unending karma.

2. *Evil thoughts.* People have a few bad or evil thoughts. Often they do not feel the least bit bad about them, and then just forget about them. But the fact is that every bad thought creates a vehicle for a dark entity to incarnate in our mental plane.

If evil thoughts accumulate all over the world, you will see a long-lasting, huge cloud overcasting our planet, thus giving the dark forces a chance to have access to human life.

3. *Negative emotions formulated through imagination.* Negative imagination, criminal, separative, and destructive imagination controlled by dark feelings provide another vehicle for evil forces to come closer to us. They use those forms created by our imagination as their vehicles, giving them an opportunity to control our emotional life. Every bad feeling or emotion can become a channel through which evil forces, from both Cosmic and human sources, can control you and your environment.

4. *Hypnotic suggestions.* The human mind can lose its independence and direction as it is continuously bombarded by hypnotic suggestions which have accumulated at the time of pain and distress. Hypnotic suggestions are also accumulated within us while we are in the womb. We are also under the hypnotic attack of dark forces during our sleep, when we are generally unconscious in the higher planes. This is a serious matter, and many people are subject to astral suggestion.

5. *Evil entities living in the astral plane.* These evil entities are those who have graduated from the universities of crime in the world. Such universities have many names, but one discovers the names by himself. Evil entities are also those who came from the Cosmic Astral Plane and are active in the astral plane of the Cosmic Physical Plane. They do great damage to those who are halfway criminals in the astral plane, programming them to incarnate with evil, posthypnotic suggestions.

Fortunately, human evil cannot penetrate into the higher levels of the mental plane. If such evil ones try, they burn. Even before they make such an attempt, they are often annihilated, if their "high-water mark" is already achieved.

These five factors together form Cosmic evil which works against the Forces of Light and Compassion.

Question: *How can you define the Universe and what the evil is?*

Answer: The Universe is the organism of the Cosmic Mind or Intellect, just as our body is for the awareness unit which we call man. Man is the book on our level to study about the Universe because the Universe is reflected in the constitution of man.

Evil is an act of ignoring such a wholeness and is an effort to manipulate the whole for the interest of the *part*. There is no "part" in reality. That is why living for a "part" or as a "part" is evil.

There is no evil in the process of involution (which is the process of materialization or multiplication of the one energy) except if the separated units reject each other and try to manipulate or control each other for their separate interests.

Question: *How did evil come into being if it is not inherent in the whole?*

Answer: As the whole becomes multiple and fragmentation takes place, the separate units lose the consciousness or sense of unity of the whole and feel that they are the whole. These fragmentary units reject the existence of "others" and develop ways and means to eliminate them or use them for their own self-interested existence. This is what evil is, the root of which is *ignorance*. In esoteric language ignorance means lack of awareness of the wholeness.

The formation of the dark lodge on the Cosmic Physical Plane and in the fourth globe of our fourth chain started when humanity passed from the third globe to the fourth globe, when the involutionary path was terminated and evolution toward higher planes began. The dark lodge opposed evolution — the path of perfection or the path leading to Higher Worlds. As the formation of the dark lodge proceeded, the White Lodge also came into being through the assistance of those Great Ones Who had graduated from the Cosmic Physical Plane and were continuing Their training on higher Cosmic Planes.

The dark lodge cyclically increases its attack on the fourth globe, our earth, and on humanity, to prevent humanity from proceeding further toward perfection, unity, and synthesis. On the other hand the White Lodge, the Hierarchy, has done everything possible for humanity to advance.

Evil on the Cosmic Physical Plane is under the command of Satanic forces which are stationed on the Cosmic Astral Plane. The higher counterpart of the dark lodge is found in the lower Cosmic Physical Plane. It is this lodge that uses the forces of Nature destructively in the solar system.

There is a lodge of evil on earth which carries on the plan of Cosmic evil. We are told that human beings who serve evil have the same freedom as those who act under the banner of the White Lodge. But when nonhuman entities from the Cosmic Astral Plane attack humanity, the Hierarchy of Light immediately fights against them, as was the case in 1942.

Planetary evil is the result of the relation between our Planetary Logos and another Planetary Logos Who are not yet in good and perfect relationship. This condition creates a tremendous tension between our Logos and the other Logos, and the tension creates all painful conditions and destructive activities of certain people who respond to this situation.

We are told that this relationship between the Logoi eventually will be corrected and adjusted by the help of another Logos, Who will create balance and harmony between Them.

A long time ago, H.P. Blavatsky wrote about imperfect gods, referring to the Planetary Logoi Who, on Their own plane of achievement, have Their own failures, defeats, and victories.

As far as Cosmic evil is concerned, the Great Teacher gave certain information. He says that the Cosmic evil related to our planet is the result of the relationship existing between One of the Rishis of the Great Bear and one of the Pleiads of the Pleiades. Such a relationship creates a Cosmic tension in space which affects our globe because the Great Rishi is the prototype of our Planetary Logos.

We are told that this situation also will eventually be corrected when the energy circulates through the Great Bear, the Pleiades, and our Planetary Logos, creating a readjustment between their relationship.

Knowing this condition, the dark forces utilize the situation and bring to our earth their distorted vibrations, which are translated as hatred, fear, anger, exploitation, totalitarianism, and so on.

As the Planetary Logos and Rishis and Pleiads reach perfection, evil will slowly vanish, and right human relations will be established on earth.

There is another source of evil which is mentioned by the Great Teacher. He says that there are lots of decaying bodies in space, such as the moon, or moons, and they affect our planetary life very strongly. As the moon disintegrates toward the seventh round of the earth, its influence will totally vanish.

Terror, genocide, slaughterings are all because of the influence of the dying moon through those who, because of their decaying nature, respond to the moon influence, corresponding to the malefic force of the moon. There are disintegrating constellations which pollute the space and create negative and destructive effects on our planet and other spatial bodies.

The Great Teacher says, "There is one such constellation, situated between the lesser Dipper and our system, and another, interrelated with the Pleiades and our system which still have a profound effect upon the physical body of the solar Logos."[2]

These two constellations are dissolving, but "some of their life force and energy has been transferred to our solar system, just as the lunar life force was transferred to our earth, and this it is that is the cause of much cyclic evil."[3]

The only way that human beings can escape these malefic influences is by increasing their spiritual fire and psychic energy through meditation and selfless, sacrificial service.

People devoid of the fire cyclically fall into the influence of such disintegrating bodies and commit various kinds of crime, becoming causes of suffering and pain. We must not forget that these are Cosmic entities who are nourished by their sources of decaying and disintegrating bodies. They have their agents on earth who, being dedicated to evil activities, draw force from these entities and turn into agents of pain and suffering on the planet. This evil is nourished from space and from the earth.

The Teaching given by Great Ones is mostly related to the evil and how to protect ourselves and humanity by following their Teaching of

---

2. Bailey, Alice A., *A Treatise on Cosmic Fire*, p. 837.
3. *Ibid.*, pp. 837-838.

- purity

- unfoldment

- meditation

- sacrificial service

- and invoking the "Light, Love, and Power to seal the door where evil dwells"

The Great Teacher explains further that some of the evil existing within the human kingdom can be eliminated by creating right relationships between the fifth kingdom, human kingdom, and animal kingdom. The human kingdom will play a great role in eradicating evil by rejecting the magnetic forces of animal, vegetable, and mineral kingdoms. The human kingdom will be used by the fifth kingdom to do the job.

Similarly, much evil comes into existence in human life when the atoms and organs in the human body begin to disintegrate, creating irritation and imperil and poisoning all the bodies.

Most of the negative and destructive activities of certain leaders are influenced by such decaying organs in their physical-etheric bodies or by decaying thoughtforms in their mental bodies. Such decaying forms not only affect people physically but also psychologically and nourish these entities who live in decay. Certain illnesses are the result of such obsessions and possessions.

The macrocosm also has similar problems on a bigger scale.

Cosmic and planetary evil existed since the creation of this chain, but it is only in the fourth root race — the Atlantean race — that some people consciously offered themselves to the planetary and Cosmic evils.

This is the reason why the whole continent of Atlantis was submerged in the ocean. As evil activities extinguished the fire in the human family, the fires of space withdrew, letting Atlantis sink.

Atlantean dark adepts still have their influence through the thoughtforms which they built in space and through those who followed them and incarnated in various countries. It is the followers of the Atlantean dark lodge that still exist on this earth in various nations who are demonstrating inhuman cruelty, exploitation, and totalitarianism.

The Great Teacher, referring to those who are engaged in serving, helping the creative and constructive forces of Nature, says that they must be armed with purity, high aspiration, and healthy vehicles because if these conditions are not present, they will be stimulated by Higher Forces to such a degree that one or two of their vehicles will disintegrate and this will set back the progress of the human soul for ages. If these conditions are not present and the server is not firmly established in right motives, he will destroy himself when his power is increased by relating to these creative forces of the Universe.

The Great Teacher says,

> . . . *Knowledge of the laws of magic puts into the hands of the student powers which enable him to create, to acquire, and to control. Such powers are fraught with menace to the unprepared and unready, for the student can, in this case, turn them to selfish ends, use them for his own temporal material advancement, and acquire in this way that which will feed the desires of the lower nature. He takes, therefore, the first step towards the left hand path, and each life may see him progressing towards it with greater readiness, until (almost unconsciously) he will find himself in the ranks of the black masters. Such a state of affairs can only be offset through the*

cultivation of altruism, sincere love of man, and a steady negation of all lower desire.[4]

The Great Teacher suggests to have

— physical purity

— astral stability

— mental poise

Hierarchy, time after time, sent Its Masters of Wisdom not only to educate humanity but also to protect them in certain cycles when the aggressiveness of the dark lodge was planned for humanity. Those who follow the Masters of Wisdom, such as Christ and Buddha, will eventually free themselves from any influence of evil and shine as sources of Beauty, Goodness, and Righteousness.

Dark forces on earth have various ways to channel their force through their agents. One of the most popular methods is to imitate those who are serving humanity in various ways. They dress like them. They use various symbols and books like them and play a reversed role. Instead of playing the role of the sacrificial servers, they play the role of the enemies of sacrificial servers in such an ugly and criminal way that they try to destroy the image of the sacrificial server in the minds of the public.

Often such images are destroyed by the police force so that the public both hates the police and hates the sacrificial image. Once the sacred images are destroyed in the public's mind, people have no more standards to follow and are in danger of following those who are working to bring corruption and crime upon the earth.

The agents of Cosmic evil are very intelligent and ugly. They are heartless, destructive, and always lead to anarchy.

---

4. *Ibid.*, pp. 993-994.

It is deplorable that many innocent people fall into their traps without knowing the future that awaits such people.

Once a person falls into the hands of evil and is bribed by money, sex, position, he slowly prepares to sell his soul. In reality, a ceremony of selling the soul does not exist, but the fact is that the moment a person enters into the path of evil, his Solar Angel prepares to leave him if Its warnings are not heard.

After the Solar Angel leaves, a person is in dire danger of disintegration. This happens two ways — either the human soul leaves his personality, destroying the three permanent atoms, or the human soul cuts his relation with the Monad and disintegrates in the chaotic forces of Nature after he dies. The Teaching says that the disintegration of the human soul creates those pains and sufferings that are unimaginable.

Beauty, Goodness, Righteousness, Joy, and Freedom are the five gates leading to health, happiness, prosperity, power, and enlightenment.

PART 2

THE BATTLE

13 Fear

People think that fear is an emotion, but it would be better to say that fear is a reaction to an enormous power who rules on this planet — who is, in reality, a dark entity, one of the elders who rebelled against the Command and had his light taken from him. This entity was sent from the Cosmic Astral Plane to our earth to veil the souls of men, to prevent them from seeing the Path, the future, the reality. This entity penetrated not only into the earth and the physical body of mankind but also into the astral and mental bodies of mankind, conditioning its actions, emotions, and thoughts.

Our worship is often backed by fear. Our agreements are generated through fear. As long as fear dominates our feelings, thinking, and actions, we will not have clear direction, which is inspired by the Higher Forces. It is very true that fear is our number one enemy. At present, fear permeates all human beings.

The dark lodge realized that fear would prevent

- the increase of light
- the progress of humanity toward unity, synthesis
- an understanding of each other
- clear knowledge about life in general
- clear vision about the afterlife
- trust
- abundance
- freedom to radiate our light, our pure ideas, and our visions
- freedom from the imposition of those who exploit in various levels
- living without the pressure of negative emotions, actions, and thoughts
- sincerity, frankness, and openheartedness
- joy and health
- the opening of eyes that see

Thus fear, like a universal, black, overcasting cloud, builds a barrier between humanity and the Source of Light. It permeates each human being and causes spiritual paralysis. It is through this force of darkness that people hate each other, exploit each other, hide from each other, kill each other, lie to each other, and are jealous of each other. It is through fear that we violate the Laws of Nature. Fear fills us with an insatiable greed and spiritual ignorance. It is through fear that mankind mobilized the forces of Nature to destroy Nature itself.

Life on this planet is propelled in physical, emotional, and mental fields by the winds of fear. It is through fear that people deceive themselves and others. Fear rules in politics and in education. Fear increasingly controls the media, especially at this time. Fear is the motivating force behind our modern day sciences. Fear already controls most religions, especially Christianity, which should be a philosophy of fearlessness and love. Fear controls the economy of the world. It obscures the eyes of humanity so that humanity cannot see the presence and influence of fear.

Fear has obsessed almost all human beings. There are still those in whose hearts the flame of fearlessness burns. This flame must be kept alive by all means. The hope of humanity is fearlessness.

Some people ask, "How can one be corrected without injecting fear in him?" Of course, fear is used on many occasions to correct people. Punishment, pain, and suffering bring correction to the person because pain and suffering become associated with their wrongdoings or evil acts. But in both cases, the person does not go through a real change; he is inhibited. True correction comes when the person understands that if he changes his actions, greater joy, happiness, and wealth will be on the way.

He can also be taught that actions taken against light, love, and beauty, in any form, upon any field, prevent him from reaching harmony with the creative forces of Nature, which guarantee his conscious immortality and spiritual actualization. We do not need to show a person the abyss and warn him. We can show him the summit of a mountain and help guide his steps toward the summit.

In the near future, philosophers and psychologists will mobilize a war against fear. A new technique will be developed to educate people in fearlessness and harmony with the principles of Nature. Thus, one more device of evil will be exposed.

14
Speed

Evil has another way to destroy humanity. In this age, people are fascinated with speed. They think that speed is the main factor for success and development. Because of this false idea, they have created a lie which imposes increasing speed upon us. In a very short time, man will lose control over his time and turn into a wheel in a great machine — and those who push the buttons will determine his speed and make him run until he is useless.

In an advanced age, people will live in the idea of Infinity. They will not force their bodies to run faster than they are capable of. In our age, life is scheduled in such a way that every hour is planned for something. Very soon, no one will have any private time which is not loaded with something to be done.

Forced speed has many disadvantages. For example, children are forced to act as adults. Man is forced to pace himself and live by the speed of machines. Speed can turn into a disintegrating factor; it can load our minds and hearts and make them machines.

We are receiving three hundred times more knowledge than the average student was two hundred years ago, yet our brain is almost the same brain. We are receiving five hundred times more emotions than an average person received one hundred years ago. Our daily papers, television, and news load us and bring emotions to us from all around the world. Our bodies are under more pressure every day, loaded with radioactivity, short waves, telephone calls, and increasing daily obligations.

One hundred years ago, under normal conditions, a child had only a few emotional shocks in his life. But in these days, a child has, in one day, an equivalent number of emotional shocks to those of the entire life of a child in the past. If he watches a violent or criminal movie, if he hears news of war, crime, terrorism, and earthquakes, his emotional body goes through intense pressure. When he hears that "respectable" people deceive the government, or that a president is impeached or assassinated, or that the police are selling drugs, he undergoes immense mental and emotional shocks. These shocks are responsible for the way he acts at school, the attitude he has toward his parents, the relations that he has in his community, the crimes he will commit in using drugs and alcohol, and his evasion of duty and responsibility.

Why do we load our children's hearts and minds with images of crime, terrorism, destruction, dishonesty, and failure? All of these images will affect their education, behavior, and health. Satan knows this and will make every effort to create more violent, criminal movies, news, and events in order to produce an insane world.

The speed imposed upon our systems is dangerous not only to our physical health but also to our sanity and moral life. We collect information and knowledge in our minds, and fifty percent of that information and knowledge has no use for us or for others. Like junk, we collect information in the backyards of our minds and thus lose precious space in the clutter. Many people cannot store more appropriate data because of the junk that occupies all their space.

We are forced to speedily collect data, emotions, and information. We are forced to do things in a mechanical way. One day we will become only an operator of that machine which we created to do all our jobs and, if the machine goes wrong, we will lose our heads.

We speed our vegetables in growing. We demand that our children grow up sooner. We want immediate responses, rewards, and solutions to our problems. We have lost the state of timelessness. Timelessness is health, relaxation, and tuning in with Infinity. Timelessness originates not from knowledge but from liberation.

We are imposing such a speed upon our mechanisms that we will end the life of humanity on this planet. We must slow down. Speed leads to insanity if it is not controlled with patience. Patience is a feeling of Infinity.

When merchants brought big clocks to certain eastern countries for the first time, they were examined and considered a tool of Satan. They attacked the merchants and destroyed the clocks with hammers. My grandparents used to tell us this story again and again to make us aware of how ignorant those people were who thought clocks were the tool of Satan. But on closer analysis, there was an intuitive perception in the actions of those people. We have turned life into a machine through clocks, watches, and speedometers.

We force ourselves every year with greater and greater speed, paying for it through our ill health and insanity. Our consciousness is wrapped in the concept of time in such a way that we do not have a period of ten minutes of timelessness. Even the periods of "rest" are flooded with thoughts of what will be done after that short period of "rest." It is only in a state of timelessness that the health of the body, the heart, and the mind can be restored.

Certain people are already machines. They run by a speed imposed upon them because speed has become equal to survival. To survive, one must continually increase his speed of thinking, feeling, acting, and even speaking and writing.

One day a garage mechanic told me that he could change a tire every five minutes. "What is your purpose in doing that?" I asked. "More money," he said. Months later, I went back to have a tire changed. He was sitting on an old battery. "What is the matter?" I asked him. "I was in the hospital for three months. They changed my tires, but my engine is not running very well and I cannot work for a while." One can "change tires" but if his engine is worn out, new tires will not help. We pay for violating the principle of timelessness.

The whole concept of time and speed is an illusion fabricated by dark forces to exterminate human existence from this planet. How can we isolate ourselves from such a mechanical life based on time and speed? The only way that still presents hope lies in the moments of meditation in which we may enter the domain of timelessness and feel a deep relaxation from the imposed pressures and demands of time and speed. There is no cure except through a catastrophic explosion or through a well-organized plan to decrease the demands of time and speed and give people an opportunity to relax and live in ease, at least for a few moments, in the joy of timelessness. Ecstasy, concentration, and contemplation are moments of timelessness.

To make the idea of speed more clear, we can give the following explanation. Let us imagine a clock that can give us the real time. It has twenty small wheels which are geared to each other. They must move with their standard speed, or else we will have neither the right time nor a working clock.

The solar system is a clock. Many kinds of "wheels" are geared to each other by invisible energy fields. The speed of the wheels is relative to the timing for which this big clock is set. Every wheel in this Universe will adapt itself to the speed of the other wheels, which must run at the standard speed. If any wheel is slow, there will be problems in the clock. If any wheel is speeding, there will again be problems in the clock. To remove this problem, the slow wheels must speed up to reach the standard speed, and the speedy wheels must slow down to the standard speed.

Satan's intention is to distort the standard speed and make humanity, which is one of the wheels in the big clock, slow down or speed up or do both at different times, creating chaos. This chaos is already evident. Some nations are speeding, while others are retarded. Both of these conditions contribute to world problems.

The clock may be tuned up by creating a standard speed. We do this superficially sometimes when we say, "By the time the child is twelve, he must finish elementary school; by the time he is eighteen, he must graduate from high school." Or we say, "By the year 2000, this computer system must be in operation."

We already have a sense of speed, but it is related to outer phenomena based on greed, pride, vanity, and ego. Since our greed, pride, vanity, and ego are operated by the dark forces, they can make us speed to fulfill our greed, pride, vanity, and ego in order to create difficult and sometimes unsolvable problems in the "big clock."

We are going faster and faster, disturbing our health and happiness — even the weather — and polluting the air, water, oceans, and earth. We are traveling at such a speed that if we realize the danger into which we are propelling ourselves and suddenly try to stop, we will end in final destruction.

We want to fill the gas tanks of our brains with knowledge in faster and faster ways. We want to feel excited and reach more excitement in faster ways. We eat faster; we eliminate faster; we live faster and die faster. We want to be rich faster; we want to make others run faster. Eventually, we foul up both the universal clock and the clock within us and end in the abyss.

A laborer used to work eight hours, then come home and rest, eat, and enjoy himself with his wife and children. You can find very few people today who live in such a state. Most people travel one or two hours on the freeway or use various means of public transportation to reach their factory or office. They eat their lunch in haste and end up working overtime. They come home nervous and exhausted to find that their husbands and wives are not home yet because they are in the same shoes. Or they come home to a dinner that has been made in speed, and then eat it in a hurry to fulfill a self-made program of previously established obligations. We are even sleeping faster because in our sleep we imitate what we do in our waking states of consciousness. If our speed is fifty times faster than it was fifty years ago, what will be the speed of the population living two hundred years from now in a world that is polluted, radioactive, and devastated? The greatest assistants of Satan are not devils but those who speed.

Even our sexual excitement is faster. In the past, men and women had fewer chances to become excited, and they followed their normal speed. But now pornographic literature, movies, and theaters make their excitement one hundred times faster. To satisfy the speed of their excitement, they need more fuel to burn, and very often they end up burning out their engines. In a certain nightclub, fifteen hundred women watch nude male dancers. Then the next week, men watch nude women dancers. Such vehicles of excitement speed the secretion of their glands beyond imagination, and they go out of their way to find other vehicles capable of carrying them at that speed of excitement. People do many insane things to satisfy the speed inspired by the dark forces, to "enjoy" life and collect money to disturb the standard rhythm of life.

One day a great genius will come and calculate the speed of our solar system and find the ratio between its speed and the speed of each kingdom, and then the speed of each individual in each kingdom. This will be the beginning of a great tune-up of the life on this planet. The proper speed will not only be set for our cars, airplanes, and rockets but also will clearly set the speed of our learning, the speed of our emotional experiences, and the speed of our spiritual development. It may be necessary to retard the speed of some and increase the speed of others. This will be possible if a genius comes and if leaders and rulers are free from Satanic influences.

We have inner and outer speed. Outer speed is what we do with our body, actions, and machines. Inner speed is related to the progress of our spiritual unfoldment and the expansion of our consciousness. If we synchronize these two speeds in some way and set our timing to the standard, then we will enjoy immensely our lives and play our role in the Great Movement.

People think that knowledge is always good. This is not true. Knowledge is not good if you are not ready to use it in the right way, if you have wrong motives and selfish or destructive intentions, or if it is premature for you. Premature knowledge hinders your future progress. Knowledge and light are energies. They are like medicine which must be given to people with the wisdom of a specialist in medicine.

Most children do not even have a childhood. They are fertilized to grow up as soon as possible to enter the competition of life. Some children are forced by religion or by cults to live a life of heaven, to dream about hell or paradise before they learn how to put on their shoes. Their mental mechanisms are forever ruined, and they live an abnormal life.

We expect our children to know everything and to behave like adults. Television and movies make them prematurely play like they are adults, and when they pretend they are adults, either we are pleased or we think that something is wrong with them. We also fail in thinking that to make children behave like children, they must do whatever they want.

Speed fascinates us. We want to learn a language in one month or read a five-hundred page volume in two hours. Of course, this is possible by speed methods. Why are speed methods bad, when they apparently save time, energy, and money and make us successful?

Our mechanism must be ready for the increasing speed. We must have right direction and a field in which to share the result of our speed. All of these things can be possible if we consider speed to be progress only when we synchronize it with the speed at which our consciousness can expand.

I have seen in the Far East a great Teacher cooking, gardening, and making a pair of shoes with his own hands. From the western or modern approach, the Teacher is wasting his time because he is not using the speedy methods of modern inventions. But if you ask him about it, he will say, "Speed and time have no value except if, through your labor, you are trying to transform yourself."

Outer action and labor must have in mind the transformation of consciousness. The speed of transformation of consciousness must be parallel with the speed of labor.

If the speed of labor is faster than the speed of expansion of consciousness, soon your consciousness will retard and degenerate and become a slave of your mechanical speed.

Humanity did not expand its consciousness in spite of sending spaceships to other planets. The proof of this is that we have

- more separatism

- more terrorism

- more crimes

- more danger of planetary annihilation

- more poison and pollution

- more racism and nationalism

- more totalitarianism

- more pornography and exploitation

- more fear

If our spiritual progress were parallel to our mechanical progress, we would already have

- a united world

- peace

- more love and understanding

- more opportunities

- more freedom

- unpolluted and contamination-free water, air, oceans, and earth

To synchronize our outer speed with our inner speed means to progress neither too quickly nor too slowly but to be in synchronization with the heartbeat of Nature.

When leaders understand the philosophy of speed, they will attempt to speed the evolution of those who are going too slowly and to slow the evolution of those who are going too quickly. Christ once said something very mysterious, "Those who are first will be last, and those who are last will be first." Another time He said, "The greatest one among you must be the servant of all."

When mechanical speed is controlled by spiritual speed, you have happiness, joy, and health. When mechanical speed increases in velocity without spiritual speed, the world enters into crises and heads toward destruction. When mechanical speed is controlled by those who are fast in their spiritual speed, they become the "servants of all," the "last ones" who serve humanity before themselves. Those who benefit from such a service become the vanguards of humanity.

The Great Ones are thousands of years ahead of us in Their spiritual evolution, but They are not ahead of time. They are Those Who entered into the stream of Divine timing and steadily kept pace with that timing. The rest of us must speed our spiritual evolution. The only chance to do this lies in freeing ourselves from mechanical speed, which not only obscures our progress and wastes our real time but also makes us incapable of responding to the standard speed of Nature. Mechanical speed retards our spiritual speed and prevents us from synchronizing ourselves with the clock of the Universe.

One may ask how can we combat the speed at which germs are increasing, how can we combat rockets that move faster than the speed of sound, how can we combat the speed of lies, terrorism, and insanity? Do we fight speed with greater speed? This is the logic of one who thinks that blood can be washed away with blood, that hatred can be eliminated through hatred.

An Oriental proverb says, "Haste is inspired by Satan." Why don't we stop the *causes* of those things that are against our survival? Why should we create giants and then mobilize all our powers to fight against them? Why should we create pollution and then organize all our resources to fight pollution? Why create criminals and then build prisons in which to house them? There are also other questions which demand answers.

We are cells in the body of Nature. Nature has its regular cycles. Nature is a cell in the body of the galaxy, which has its own regular cycles synchronized to the cycles of even greater wholes. An individual or humanity itself can become a tumor on the body of the planet by imposing upon itself an unnatural speed of growth. Nature will eventually destroy the tumor as a hindrance on its path. Harmony with Nature is achieved in synchronizing our outer and inner speed with the cycles of Nature. Outer speed is the speed of machinery; inner speed is the effort to negate time and space and enter the domain of timelessness and spacelessness.

The greatest killer in this century is speed. Man will use speed to annihilate his existence. Nature burns away all the trash and junk in space by accelerating their motion. Karma does the same thing. Accumulated karma evokes a concept of speed in the minds of those who must pay. Such a person wants to know everything all at once, and he becomes insane. He wants to be rich all at once and turns into a criminal. He wants to achieve a great position of power and becomes a professional exploiter. He wants to be "somebody" in the shortest length of time and becomes a nobody. He wants to solve his problems and turns into a problem. He wants to drink the wealth of an ocean and becomes a fish out of water.

251

The following two questions arise:

- Don't we need to do things at a certain speed?

- Can we forget time in our current society and culture?

The answer is that we are victims of the concept of time and speed. A whole generation must be educated in the concept of timelessness if we want future human beings to live on this planet.

We are not speaking against speed but against speediness and speed which are imposed upon us. We are not speaking against the concept of time but against the *imposition* of time. At present, we must accept the illusion of time as a reality, but at the same time understand the reality of timelessness.

Average people are victims of time and speed. Disciples are those who have control over time and speed. Initiates are those who are beyond time and space.

Speed must not violate the ratio of time and space as follows:

$$\frac{T}{S} = \text{Speed, where T = time and S = space}$$

Speed is the effort of time to conquer space. Space can never be conquered by people who are bound in time and speed. Space is conquered by being space, which negates speed and time.

Our conclusions then are these:

- Do not give great value to speed. Seek quality.

- Do not speed at the expense of your health or failure.

- On occasion, forget about time when you are engaged in something very important.

- Those who are not forced to speed produce and create a better life.

- Learn patience. Know that patience is not negligence or indifference but, rather, an intuitive sense of timing.

- Try on occasion to live, for a period of time, in a feeling of timelessness.

- When things are forced to run more and more quickly, watch to see if the fingers of Satan are at work.

Slow down and follow your own rhythm. Once a tightrope walker said to me, "I can keep my balance and equilibrium and do things safely on the rope only when I do not think about time."

People like to buy carpets that are made by hand, such as Persian, Native American, Chinese, and Armenian carpets. Machine-made carpets are cheaper. Anything which is made by machine or grown in hothouses has less value. The secret to value is in time and speed. The less speed and more time that is taken makes the product better. Machines gave us speed, but they took away from us the flower, the quality, which is a combination of emotions, thoughts, and love going into the product.

15 Motives

The ancients gave much attention to the process of thinking. They used thinking to discover those means by which a person could be healthy, happy, prosperous, and enlightened. They did not waste their lives creating poison, pollution, destructive devices, insecticides, and pesticides.

The great ancient thinkers tried to formulate a way for humanity to walk toward greater enlightenment and beingness. They taught the science of right thinking, knowing that the energy of man follows the direction of his thought. If a thought is destructive, the energy will do destruction. If the thought is creative, the energy will do the work of creativity.

The main disciplines in the science of thought were

- how to control the mind

- how to create right thought

- how to make right thought influential or effective through deeds

To control the mind, many forms of concentration exercises were given to the neophyte.

To create right thought, to make the neophyte learn how to think, meditation disciplines were given to him.

To make right thought influential or effective through deeds in a neophyte's life, the science of motives was explained and observed in every labor.

Students were trained to sustain the purity of their thoughts in abiding continuity within their right motives.

A right motive should be

- selfless

- prosurvival

- in harmony with the principles of Beauty, Goodness Righteousness, Joy, and Freedom

- sacrificial

- all-inclusive

To explain the importance of the motive behind thought, a Chinese sage wrote the following story:

There was a powerful king who had two sons. Feeling that his years were numbered, the king called the younger prince to him and gave him his title. But the younger son rejected the title, saying that the future king must be his elder brother. The elder prince was unhappy, seeing that his younger brother was daring enough to reject the decision of his father. He urged his brother to accept the throne, but the younger prince would not change his mind.

The two princes left the kingdom to serve in the army of a king in another country, but this king was attacked by his enemies and killed. This king had a son who immediately organized an army to attack the enemies who had killed his father. The two princes advised him to mourn his father for three years, according to their national tradition, before starting a war against the enemy because starting a war after his father's death would bring dishonor to the dead king. The son agreed and waited, deciding to also kill the two princes when the time came. But they escaped and lived in the wilderness, surviving on bracken.

One day a person who was passing by asked them, "Why are you hiding in this wilderness?" They told the man their story, and the man informed them that the bracken upon which they fed belonged to the son of the dead king. Hearing this, the two brothers decided not to eat the bracken anymore, as it was not honorable.

One day they came upon a white deer, who allowed them to milk her, and they drank her milk. After the deer went away, one of the brothers said, "Since the milk of the deer is so delicious, how much more delicious would be her meat. Let us kill her." The other brother tried to silence him, but the angels had already heard his words and the brothers were abandoned. The two princes died without food, as the deer never returned. She had been an angel in disguise to test their true motives and thoughts.

In this story we see how the two brothers acted nobly and respected each other enough to leave their kingdom. They also acted nobly when they stopped eating bracken because it belonged to a person who was not noble. But when the final test came to see if they would act in a selfish way or be grateful for what they were given, they failed the test because they wanted to kill the deer who had given her milk to them. The moment their motive and thought became selfish, they lost their life.

We are told that one can easily control the actions of his hands or feet. One can even control his emotional reactions or responses. But the most difficult things to control are our motives and the thoughts following those motives.

A change in thought can affect our emotions and deeds in no time, creating conditions which either lead to progress or to destruction.

16

Eliminating Traitors

Esoteric groups demonstrate a very interesting phenomenon. Certain members, for various reasons, are eliminated from the groups because they show negative signs. For example:

- They do not pay their dues regularly.

- They do not study or meditate.

- They show signs of jealousy and revenge.

- They gossip and bring in various kinds of problems.

- They use belittling criticism.

- They are periodically absent from the meetings.

- They form cliques, act antagonistically and depressed.

- They avoid sacrificial service.

- They develop hatred toward the Teacher.

- They associate themselves with people of doubtful character.

- They seek self-interest.

- They become lazy.

An experienced leader sees these signs and tries to warn them *indirectly* because he does not want to interfere with the plans of those forces that handle such people properly. These forces, in subjective levels, see the dangers in which the member may fall and take precautionary steps.

The process of eliminating such people is very interesting. For example, some of these people leave the group because they hate others. Some of them suddenly are caught in another interest. Some of them fall in love with someone outside the group and leave the group because of their relationship or marriage. Some of them become pregnant or make someone else pregnant, which creates complications in their life. Others leave the group because they move far away for no apparent reason. Others leave the group because someone talks badly or slanders the leader or another group member. Still others leave the group because of hurt feelings or even guilt feelings.

I have seen such people leave because they feel that they are ugly, or that they cannot cope with the standards presented in the group. Suddenly some people even feel extremely holy or superhuman and do not want to have anything to do with the group. These "holy" people, not remembering their past, heavily attack others, use ugly criticism, and resign.

It is interesting that the eliminating force, which is actually the group's Guardian Angel using various means, eliminates such people and liberates the group from their pollution, just as the ocean eliminates corpses and throws them onto the shore.

It has been noticed that after such people are thrown out, progress takes place in the group because such people act as gophers under the roots of the group tree or as short circuits in the wiring system of the group.

Of course, this does not mean that a group is always immaculate in itself. Those who continue to be part of the group are those who

- strive and serve continually in spite of their weaknesses

- fail but stand up because of their right motives

- make mistakes and cause certain damage to the group but sincerely regret their misdeeds

- are honest and sincere, even in their shortcomings or faults

- have no hidden plans

- do not let treason cross their minds

- are absent from meetings but support the group, solve their own problems, and come back

- have clashes with other members, but seek sincerely to reconcile with them

- have different viewpoints but make sincere efforts to increase or expand their viewpoints

- may feel superior sometimes but then develop the spirit of humility

The Guardian Angel of the esoteric groups is the reporter to Great Ones who watch anxiously to see the unfoldment of group consciousness, so that they use the group as a vehicle of service for humanity.

People may have various problems in their group. One such problem is related to sex. We had severe problems at least ten times from certain young men who were brought to the group by our female members as their boyfriends. Three of these young men left their girlfriends pregnant. They did not marry them, and we had many headaches trying to solve their problems or trying to avoid problems. Four young men tried steadily to involve themselves with other young women in the group, causing jealousy, rejection, and hatred. Another three were real problems. One of the young men was a drug addict. One was sick with a contagious disease, and the third one was a criminal.

It cost the leader a great amount of energy and time to finally make them quit the group before greater damage was done and without developing hatred toward the leader.

These young women were involved with young men without a sense of responsibility. One by one they left the group with hatred against the group.

The leader watched the group members. Most of them tried not to become involved; they did not participate in gossip and criticism but observed the situation. The members were hated because they were able to stay uninvolved.

The young men disappeared as fast as they came. They did not have any interest in the Teaching, though they pretended that they did. Some took away very promising young women and polluted their lives. Some young women did the same. But the group as a whole adhered to the Teaching with devotion and a sense of responsibility.

Those who attacked the group also gossiped. For example, when a promising person came to the group, these people, whose secret duty was to create problems, surrounded the person and spoke badly about certain members and increased weekly the dosage of gossip. The victim, thus filled with negative images, gradually withdrew, not wanting to be a part of such a group where everyone was bad, according to the gossips.

But the strange thing was that these attackers became slowly involved in their own personal and family problems to such a degree that eventually they eliminated themselves from the group. For example, there was a woman who worked in one of our offices. Whenever we brought in a new worker, she filled the worker's mind with dirty gossip to such a degree that the new person disappeared. This woman was also eliminated from the group with some mysterious disease.

We had members also whose hobby was to collect the trash, the weaknesses, and the shortcomings of others and spread them to others or use it for blackmail. It was rewarding to see how all these people operated by involving and damaging people and then disappeared mysteriously.

Attackers hate those members who have great possibilities for leadership.

We noticed that all devoted workers were attacked in various ways to make them quit. The leadership thought it was wiser not to warn workers of such attacks directly, so that members had a chance to see the real worth of the worker and also to observe the technique of the attackers in order to protect themselves in the future.

Good members followed their common sense and spiritual principles, and from the beginning rejected such people who were contaminated by evil motives. Such members who demonstrated group changes in their character and developed spiritual maturity became healthier, happier, and more joyful.

In the leadership meeting, while considering such attacks and attackers, there was always an atmosphere of serenity and joy. The leadership never condemned those who used malice and slander or even treason. The leadership observed events and let the forces work as they should.

Often in leadership meetings there was a feeling of

gratitude about unhappy events and unhappy attackers because the leadership felt that unhappy events and unhappy attackers taught them the most precious lessons they could have. Because of such trouble-people, the leadership became more informed, more strengthened, more solid.

It was felt that in order to carry out greater combat against dark forces in the future, such experiences and training were a precious gift to them.

The leadership also took another step. They tried to communicate with the souls of traitors and kindle their love nature. We saw certain results in the lives of these many enemies when, ten to fifteen years later, they became the friends of the group or sincerely attempted to change their lives . . . or forever disappeared into their miseries.

There is a rule in esoteric groups which states that when a member backslides, leaves the group, or commits treason against the group for any reason, the other members of the group withdraw their relationship with that member, though they maintain loving understanding and noncriticism toward him. This is done for various reasons: to protect the group from psychic attack, from personality conflict, gossip, and other disturbances; to protect members from the influence of resigned members; to prevent contamination by their hatred and malice; to avoid justifying the action of the departed one. Many esoteric groups were disbanded when group members did not observe these rules.

Members of the group slowly see how subtle techniques are used by traitors to undermine the group activities. Esoteric groups are trained to recognize the cases of obsession and possession, to recognize those who have darkness in their hearts, and to recognize those who are commissioned by dark forces to do destructive work. All these provide important lessons for the group members, if they are kept awake and observant.

In such a group the traitor reveals his face or finds it impossible to breathe and leaves the group. Karma takes him away. This is why integrity and unity are the most important characteristics of a group.

In a unified group those who have separative interests and cleavages in their nature cannot survive, and the Group Soul eliminates them. One of my Teachers wrote, "The elimination process goes on until there remains a tried and tested, conscious, integrated, and strong group which can go forward together under any and all conditions."

All of the elimination process is carried out under the Law and, when observed and understood correctly, it turns into a source of wisdom for the guiding disciple and for his coworkers.

A group provides an opportunity to solve past problems. This is why if the members are sincere in their striving toward perfection, they must try by all means to solve their problems with self-forgetfulness, harmlessness, and right speech.

The group teaching can give them enough devices to solve their problems and create right relationships and unity. But if such an opportunity is disregarded by a short vision and personality fever, then the one who rejects solving his problems puts himself in grave danger. He builds antagonism and hatred, which appear in his mental body as a tumor. For many lives this tumor turns into a source of physical, emotional, and mental problems, suffering, and pain.

This is why, when the opportunity to dissolve past karma presents itself, one must not reject, escape, or neglect such an opportunity with a stubborn and arrogant spirit. Of course, this does not apply to traitors who follow every Teacher, making it their official business to disturb their work. The karma of such people will not be easy.

The Group Soul eliminates people when their tie is broken subjectively from the group. It is not the Group Soul that severs this tie but the individual. After the individual breaks the tie, the Group Soul finds the best way to eliminate that individual with the least damage to the group body.

Some leaders carefully watch those who were eliminated from the group. Most of the cases present a very sad picture. Some of them fall into a very ugly form of life loaded with the most offensive vices. Others go deep into inertia and fall into glamors. Others engage themselves in treason. Their health degenerates. They fail in their business. Some of them commit suicide. Some of them go to prisons or asylums. Misfortune follows their steps.

Of course, not everyone who leaves an esoteric group is subjected to such calamities, if the reason for their departure is karmic or guided by their Soul or Teacher. Such people depart from an esoteric group with gracefulness and deep gratitude after asking for the blessing of the leader.

Those who are eliminated show the signs of treason, malice, slander, and hate. It is not difficult to discriminate between these two types.

Often those who gracefully depart become subjective friends of the group and occasionally show their gratitude in various ways. They understand how hard it is to keep the integrity of the group and how much suffering and sacrifice is needed to create a unity through which spiritual forces can have an anchorage in the three worlds of human endeavor.

Leaders in esoteric groups must put their faith in those who are subjectively watching the group.

We are told that any group which is formed to help humanity in various fields is very dear to the Hierarchy because through such groups the liberation of humanity will be achieved. This is why special observers are appointed to watch the groups and protect and help them to grow in Beauty, Goodness, Righteousness, Joy, and Freedom.

17

The Battle

Once we learn the ways of the dark forces and enemies, we can use their existence to create results that are diametrically opposed to their expectations and goals. This can be explained in the following story:

Noah was resting inside the ark contemplating the flood and the future of mankind when he suddenly noticed that the ark was going zigzag and turning around in its course. He was surprised about this and wanted to know the reason for the erratic movements. After walking through the rooms of the ark, he reached the stern and came upon Satan who was playing with a piece of wood, using it as a rudder to change the course of the ark. He was amazed at Satan's game and watched how he manipulated the wood to change the course of the ark. Finally after learning his tricks, he cast Satan into the ocean — but not before he had learned how to make a rudder and control the course of the ark.

If you have power over the forces of darkness, you can use their existence for your own benefit. Enemies keep the Forces of Light awake, alert, and in line with higher principles. The strength of the enemy originates from the weakness and moral failure of the servants of light. The presence of the enemy urges servants of light to remain alert.

Enemies challenge the servants of light to surpass their level and find new states of consciousness by which they can defeat the forces of darkness. Enemies reveal the beauty, the integrity, and the philosophy of the Forces of Light to those who have never before heard about the Forces of Light.

A new precipitation of ideas and energies is raining upon humanity. These energies will either destroy our crystallizations or help certain people become more concrete in their crystallizations. The conflict between these two opposing camps is an opportunity for the Forces of Light to help the cracking of crystallizations to proceed more speedily than it was supposed to happen, or to help the other camp become more rigid in its attitudes, dogmas, and doctrines, thus intensifying the tension between the two camps and leading them to possible destructive conflicts.

The Forces of Light always "make haste slowly" and teach leaders not to force the release of the soul from its prison until it learns how to manage itself in a freer environment.

There is also the advice that if a progressive unit breaks the speed limit for which his vehicles are ready, he attracts the attention of evil, which mobilizes its forces to attack the vehicles of the progressive unit and harm him greatly.

Once you learn the art of fighting with the enemy, you will enjoy it. You will even anticipate it and, if you do not feel the attack of the enemy, you will feel bored.

Enemies help exercise your spiritual muscles. Eventually, you will feel that you can use the intelligence of your enemy to sharpen your psychic energy, just as you sharpen a sword with a whetstone.

One of the virtues that all advanced Initiates must eventually possess in order to combat Cosmic evil is fearlessness. This virtue is developed and cultivated in our worldly existence only by confronting evil in its various forms. When fear vanishes completely, the Great Ones accept you as one of Their warriors.

Fearlessness grows only in a heart that has pure motive, is harmless, and is dedicated to the service of all. But the blade of the sword is sharpened only through confrontation with the enemy.

On the path of combat, there are significant events which one must clearly notice. Sometimes your best friends or teachers disguise themselves as your enemies to give you an opportunity to practice the art of fighting and to learn a few more secrets of the art. But some people do not recognize this, demonstrate violence, and break the rules of noble battle until, one day, they realize that they were hurting magnificent friends. This is the test for the discriminative faculty of the warrior. He must recognize the true enemy and respect those who come disguised and with the intention of training him in the subtle techniques of combat.

Some young warriors declare that enemies and dark forces must be destroyed all at once. Curiously enough, an experienced warrior knows that when the annihilation of the enemy is carried out too soon, it creates various complicated problems for the Forces of Light. This is a mystery to those who are new to the Army of the Lord, but when they reach maturity, they will understand how much caution and time are needed to slowly and gradually annihilate the dark forces.

271

People think that negative and positive energies of Nature are conflicting forces and that evil is equal to the negative force. In reality, evil has no polarity, although it identifies itself with one or the other according to its intentions. This means that it can even work with positive forces to reach certain ends. When it is using the positive force, people fall into confusion and cannot see why it is using the positive force. Actually, the positive and negative forces of Nature, like the forces of attraction and repulsion, are *impersonal*. One is as good as the other because nothing can exist without both forces. Evil is not the force of repulsion or attraction; it can, however, use both for certain ends.

Every progressive movement needs opposition. Opposition is not necessarily evil or an enemy. However, evil can side itself with the opposition to disturb the real duty of opposition.

True opposition is the limitation which the evolving Monad faces on Its path. It is Its own shell. It must break Its own ignorance and weakness, Its own limitation in order to grow. But often evil uses opposition to reach certain ends.

After passing to the Cosmic Mental Plane, the growing Monad will still face opposition from chaotic forces, electrical and solar storms, and the winds of chaos, which are neither evil nor good. Rather they are like great oceanic waves, running rivers, gales, or tornadoes. On the lower planes, the dark forces use these forces of chaos to reach certain ends.

Some people think that spirit is good and matter is bad but, in reality, both are good. Each serves the other to bring manifestation into existence. However, evil may use matter to make people identify with it and fight against spirit. In reality, spirit and matter are like two sides of your hand. Matter is spirit; spirit is matter in various states of existence.

My Father once told me the story of a village which was sunk in inertia, sex, alcohol, and indifference. After seeing this lamentable condition, a few advanced thinkers found a way to revive the village from its stupor. They decided to take a risk which might hurt a certain number of people in order to save the whole village.

They grouped together and bought some guns and began to attack people and steal from them, day and night. They even kidnapped a few children and trained them in the art of fighting. A few months later, the elders of the village held a conference and came to the conclusion that if they did not mobilize, sooner or later the "bandits" would kill everyone in the village. The village elders formed small groups of fighters and trained them. Eventually, all the youth were forced to join the army. As they organized more, the bandits increased their surprise attacks until everyone came to their senses and began to shape up.

In three years the schools, businesses, and all fields of the village were organized. People felt joy and prosperity. At last, revitalizing the village successfully to the standards they had desired, the "bandits" entered the village as merchants and opened a school to educate the children in science and mathematics. Thus, disguised as the enemy, the Forces of Light transformed the village.

All religions present various techniques to combat evil. To fight dark forces one needs to develop certain principal virtues such as

— the sense of unity

— attentiveness

— the sense of renunciation

The sense of unity raises you up from any situation which evokes self-interest. Attentiveness makes you see any symptoms introduced by dark forces and keeps you alert. The sense of renunciation makes the mechanisms of evil forces impotent. From early childhood, people must be trained to combat evil, whether visible or invisible.

LIGHT VS. DARK

It is very important to know that man's bodies are *solar* and *lunar*. Solar bodies respond to progressive currents of the Cosmic Magnet and lead the Pilgrim onto the Path of Glory. Lunar bodies respond to the forces of disintegration and involution — to matter, ego, vanity, glamor, and illusion.

Solar bodies respond to those organized forces in the Cosmos which act as transmitters of the Plan and the Purpose. Lunar bodies respond to those organized forces which inspire crime, violence, terror, and degeneration. This being so, our existence is the field of battle on which these two organized forces fight against each other.

The human soul is like Arjuna, in the *Bhagavad Gita*, who stands in the battlefield between these two armies. His success or failure on the Path depends upon his choice as to which army he will join.

Aspirants on the Path pass through various stages. For example:

- They are too slow in responding to both of these forces and serve neither good nor evil but their own existence.

- They serve alternately the forces of evil or the Forces of Light.

- They commit themselves either to the Forces of Light or to darkness.

It is very important to discover which forces use our existence to fight against each other on the personality battlefield, the family battlefield, the group battlefield, the national battlefield, and the global battlefield. The duty of the disciple is to awaken humanity to the existence of these forces and battlefields and to expose the activities of the dark forces.

On the personality battlefield we have

The Army of Darkness and *The Army of Light*

which manifest as

The Army of Darkness	The Army of Light
1. all those germs, microbes, and other tiny lives which serve for disintegration, death, and degeneration or which produce pain and suffering	1. all those tiny lives which serve to bring health, happiness, release, orderliness, growth, harmony, vitality, and vigor
2. all those events which prematurely destroy, prevent progress, create chaos and confusion, and lead to self-destruction	2. all those events which help in construction according to the Plan, which inspire progress and create rhythm, progressive harmony, clarity of vision, and self-actualization
3. all those chemicals, poisons, pollutants, drugs, gases, and herbs which lead the body into disease, inertia, and death	3. all those elements which give the body health, nourishment, beauty, and energy and enrich it with vitality
4. all those sexual relationships which drain or waste energy, pollute the body, and lead it into various diseases	4. all those relationships which build closer unity, integrity, health, creativity, cooperation, striving, happiness, and joy

5. all those negative emotions. . . fear, anger, hatred, greed, jealousy, and revenge, which turn the emotional body into a sphere of poisonous arrows and eventually make it a painful robe

5. all those positive emotions. . . fearlessness, enthusiasm, love, generosity, sharing, self-giving, solemnity, gratitude, and so on, which make the emotional body a sensitive sphere for refined impressions and a source of love and joy

6. all those words which poison, divide, belittle, destroy, pollute, misdirect, misinform, lie, bribe, flatter, curse, seduce; all those words which inspire fear and slavery and kill hope and faith, which dissolve unity, cooperation, and friendship

6. all those words which nourish, unite, glorify, build, clear, direct, inform, and create trust, honesty, nobility and light; which enlighten, bless, establish confidence, make us fearless and free, give hope, increase our faith and lead to unity, cooperation, and friendship

7. all those thoughts which limit, distort, cover, separate, impose, confuse, and complicate

7. all those thoughts which expand, restore, release, unite and synthesize, clarify, evoke, and simplify

8. all those efforts which distort, degenerate, lead us into darkness, debase, and defame us

8. all those efforts which transform, sublimate, transfigure, and glorify

Every action, emotion, thought, motive, and effort may belong either to darkness or to light. Inaction produces action when the opposing forces act because of your inaction. Discrimination is the ability to recognize the nature of the forces you are transmitting or for which you are serving as an agent. This is the path of the *razor's edge*, which you must cross if you want to commit yourself to the Army of Light and advance on the path of perfection.

On the family battlefield, the fight intensifies. The forces that fight on this battlefield are generally known as follows:

indifference	sense of responsibility
egotism	selflessness
sensuality	purity
separation	unity
waste	economy
lust	love
domination	freedom
imposition	leadership
license	tolerance
isolation	inclusiveness
inertia	striving
individuality	group sense
pleasure	joy
laziness	education

The family which dedicates itself to the Forces of Light becomes a cornerstone in whatever group captures its interest.

On the group battlefield we see the following forces active:

self-interest	group interest
personal goals	group goals
use of group resources	resources supplied to the group
bad example of thinking, speaking, and acting	good example to society
bringing shame	bringing honor
scattered	punctual
selfish	sacrificial
indiscriminate	discriminative
irresponsible	responsible
inconsistent	constant
possessive	giving
personality relations	soul relations
unorganized	organized

Those who graduate from the group battlefield enter the national battlefield and appear there as Knights of Light, as leaders of Beauty, Goodness, Righteousness, Joy, and Freedom.

There are many who function on the national battlefield without having graduated from a group discipline. Also, there are many who dropped from the group battlefield who want to work on the national battlefield. There are also those who enter the national battlefield with the intention of carrying group interests into the national battlefield.

All of these people will create more conflict and more waste of energy, time, and money and will eventually vanish, until they graduate with honors from a group whose main purpose is to serve, uplift, transform, heal, and make people free and dedicated to the Common Good of all.

National Battlefield

national interest	group interest
separatism	inclusiveness
single viewpoint	multiple viewpoints
one way	many ways
sectarian	sense of synthesis
greedy, self-centered, narrowly defined group interests	sacrificial and indifferent to personality and group interests
imposition	freedom
anarchy	organization
military power	spiritual, moral power

Spiritual help to heal a really sick person endangers his life or can even kill him. One of the games of the dark ones is to offer panaceas to make people lose time and focus and forget to search for those principles which will give them everlasting help. Once a secret enemy in the army of a king offered the king an herb which relieved the pain of his wounds, but which was addictive. The king refused real help from those who were truly qualified to help him, which would have saved time and energy, but instead accepted the addictive herb.

Political tranquilizers are given for other reasons, too. Sometimes the most deadly enemy works under the cover of the peace initiative. The most godless one introduces the notion of universal prayer and preaches from *his* holy book as loudly as possible in order to carry on his destructive work. Those who prepare for war speak about peace. Those who fight day and night in their homes go forth and try to promote right relations with their neighbors with various motives. Be careful of such charlatans who carry their prayers to the streets.

When the planet is sick, fundamental cures are needed. Peace cannot be achieved because a few million people are hypnotized by peace merchants. *Peace is the result of transformation.* This is exactly the object of hatred of those who propose peace with superficial activities and hidden motives.

Accumulated karma must be destroyed. People cannot offer peace until they pay back what they have taken from others. Peace is built only upon the foundation of righteousness. How can God create peace or even offer peace if mankind is building karma?

Is peace the absence of war? If this is what peace is, war would be better than peace. When there is injustice, when there is exploitation, when there is totalitarianism, when there is slavery, when the planet is in serious danger of total pollution, when people hate one another and terrorism and crime are rampant, we must pray to God to give us some kind of war in order to terminate all of these conditions, and then bring us peace.

Some people who work under the disguise of peace are already preparing a great destruction for those who know their aims. At this time, the merchants of "peace" are using the idea of peace to drug or dope the multitudes, so that they have an opportunity to continue playing their games.

Of course, peace is a most desirable condition. It is like the health of the body. But true health is impossible to achieve as long as the body is polluted with separatism, exploitation, and totalitarianism.

In the Great Invocation there is no appeal for peace but for the fulfillment of the Plan. Humanity and its karma will decide how it will reach the fulfillment of the Plan.

Sometimes dark forces and their agents do not directly attack a leader. Instead they make the dark agents friends of the leader, while attacking the coworkers of the leader. In this way their operation works in two directions: one party observes and slanders the coworkers; the other party keeps the leader informed and pretends to protect the leader. But in a critical time, this dark agent exposes the coworkers to the leader in such a way that the leader, for the sake of the agent, fires his coworkers.

After the leader fires his coworkers, the dark agents, who worked closely with the leader, try to replace them. For a while they use the authority and wisdom of the leader correctly, then they attack him and finally replace him with one of their evil agents.

It was recorded that the prophet Mohammed never allowed anyone to slander any of his coworkers. Those who dared to slander were put to death without question. He knew that when any of his coworkers were under attack, subjectively the attack was aimed at him. A wise man once said, "The foundation cannot feel safe if, for its protection, the walls and roof are attacked."

> . . . The dark forces work also through the intensifcation or stimulation of the psychic mechanism, so that the lower psychic powers become abnormally developed and prematurely assume proportions which are almost uncontrollable.[1]

1. Bailey, Alice A., *Esoteric Psychology*, Vol. II, p. 578.

This is just like putting a child on the back of a wild horse or handing him a loaded gun. He will not only damage or destroy himself but also will mislead millions with his false statements, prophecies, and warnings.

Many political leaders and influential people are the slaves of such psychics, and they follow them literally. Once the dark forces have such leaders in their grasp, the leaders will be led to create cleavages and separatism, and fight against those forces which work for peace and right relationships between nations. Observe those who are led by psychics, and be careful of their actions.

Sometimes the agents of darkness play complicated games to hide their faces. They always try to take the side of public opinion in order to gain strength and power over various leaders. If the leader of the people takes disciplinary action and tries to create greater striving for a better moral life, for better unity and service, the agents of darkness try to attack him in various ways under the guise of protecting the interests of the public. They create dislike, tension, and cleavages between the leader and the people.

If a leader follows the crowd and encourages them to live for their pleasures, individual interests, and vices, the agents of darkness divide. One part attacks the leader for his weak leadership, the other part praises him in order to perpetuate the indifference of the leader to the real interests of the public. When this conflict begins, the agents of evil always become victorious, no matter who wins the game — the public or the leader.

If the public elects good leaders, the agents of darkness immediately praise the philosophy and values of those who lost their positions. In all of their approaches, they try to create cleavages and to remove from their positions all those who are really dedicated to the Common Good.

If there is a certain misunderstanding between the public and its leader, the dark forces try further to expand

and complicate the issue so that understanding between them becomes impossible. They do not always attack; they also praise people in order to destroy them. For example, if they want to hurt a leader, they praise him to such a degree that they invite strong jealousy against him and create heavy fear of him. Once fear and jealousy are created, the rest becomes easy for them.

They also know how to involve people with their competitors. If two people are in competition for an office, the agents of darkness try to create conflict between them after the election is over. Some of these agents dig out all the past words that the two people used against each other. Other agents advertise the outcome of the conflict, encouraging both sides to continue their fight.

Real leaders are careful not to become trapped in the net of the dark ones. The best way to combat them is to pursue a path of honesty and sincerity, to show support for those who are elected, to try always to create greater harmony between leaders and the public and, for the good of the whole nation, never to walk under the banner of the dark ones.

Dark forces encourage the public to follow their vices and low-level pleasures. They degenerate the morality of the public by providing them with every kind of pleasure that suits its animal instinct: alcohol, drugs, prostitution, nightclubs, pornography, crime, terror, and so on.

The dark forces have another form of activity which bypasses the attention of many citizens. This form of activity is called, "there are wolves outside." When there are "wolves outside," people will give their money, possessions, and lives to protect the world from these "wolves." After the "wolves" are destroyed, intelligent people finally discover that the actual wolves were in the ranks of those who were screaming about other "wolves." Many "wolves" will be created, each time in a different form or color, so that people can be cheated.

An intelligent public must be very alert to find out if these "wolves" really exist or not before sacrificing their lives for the benefit of the deceivers. "Wolf" psychology is corrupt.

For example, a boy asks to use his father's gun to practice target shooting. The father says, "No," so a few weeks later the boy creates a story about a "wolf," and the father then allows him to use the gun. Then in a moment of anger, the boy shoots and kills his friend.

Many people create "wolves" which are inspired by the dark forces. We created hell, the Last Judgment, seven deadly sins, fears of various kinds just to control the masses and make them stupid. We created human enemies. We have nuclear weapons. And tomorrow, we can create Technicolor "wolves" upon which to use those weapons.

Man is very sensitive to the whispers of the dark ones the moment he stands apart from the shield of truth, righteousness, and justice. He runs after "wolves" to justify the many crimes he wants to commit. Try to see how "wolves" are created, who creates them, and why.

Dark forces have other agents who have a very great talent for fabricating things and making them appear real. These talented people are often specialists trained in distorting and forging facts. They are often well-paid and do their job with pleasure because their hearts are dead. These are the people who serve those who create stories about "wolves."

We must begin to accustom ourselves to the idea that there is not one single nation, race, or party that is acting against human progress but many groups, nations, and religions that act against its progress. All criminals, terrorists, and totalitarians, big or small, vibrate on the same wavelength. They form one group, ornamented with many different feathers to hide their identities.

It is not a single race or nation that produces criminals and terrorists. They are everywhere, in every nation.
But because they are everywhere in different forms, it is
impossible to annihilate them using our current ways and
techniques. Sometimes those who are criminals execute
those who work for the benefit of all humanity.

The only hope we have is a nation or government
which is free from crimes and terrorism, which stands for
the rights of people everywhere in the world. If a nation
really demonstrates such an image, the rest of humanity
will join with that nation to clean out criminals and terrorists. But because there is no nation like this in existence,
it is impossible to uproot crime and terrorism.

Justice in the world can be achieved only by those
whose records of life show that they were righteous, compassionate, and free from crime. Because no nation can
meet this standard, people of the world who have a clear
conscience and clean life records must form the spiritual
government and make their voices heard everywhere.
They will be called the servers of humanity. They will
have a terrible time with official and unofficial crimes and
terrorists everywhere because such criminals will think
that the activities of such a group will create an international barrier to crime and the condemnation of crime on
all levels. This will be the reason to persecute these servers and lose the best hope for the elimination of crime.
But the servers will finally succeed in raising the consciousness of all and mobilizing everyone to join the re-
demptive movement for all humanity. Their activities will
eventually make all instruments of war, crime, and terrorism obsolete.

Ideas and visions are stronger than weapons. They
are stronger than armies. The power of ideas is the only
power which leads humanity on the path of progress. If
enough people transmit this idea and spread it all over the

world, in all languages, one day the servers of humanity will make their voices heard. They will talk, write, and labor for all humanity — not for any nation, religion, or political ideology. Their aim will be to create the brotherhood of one humanity and one world.

Every group of people may cultivate their culture, not to minimize the value of the cultures of others, but to enrich the culture of humanity, to make humanity prosperous and free from crime, terrorism, materialism, and totalitarianism.

18
Slander & Slanderers

Dark forces are very advanced in the black art of slander. One of their occupations is to inject the spirit of slander into the psyche of their victim. Often they achieve greater devastation through slander than by any other means.

Slander has two powers over its victims:

1. *When people are attacked by slander they give up and slowly change into the image built by the slanderers.* This is the destiny of an average man. He becomes the victim and slave of slanderers, and his animal nature begins to reveal itself.

2. *It creates tremendous striving in advanced individuals, and their influence spreads all over their environment.* Slander opens new connections between people and the victim. If the victim is loaded with new ideas, thoughts, and creative activities, people come in contact with his ideas and thoughts and begin to share them and assimilate them. Thus, the slanderers work for free to spread the ideas and visions of a person who is attacked by them. This is why, we are told, that our enemies are our best advertisers.

But it is interesting to know that the effect of slander on the slanderers is the same — self-destruction. Slander builds a living entity that, year after year, life after life, haunts its source, continually bringing misfortune of various kinds on its path.

Slandering is the most wasteful and failing business, and it leads eventually to complete self-defeat.

Slander is not determined by the facts but by the motives, by the negative emotions, and by the desire to destroy its victim and take revenge on him.

The slanderer not only eventually falls into various nervous troubles but also may fall into the malady called *sleeplessness*. He gradually loses his sleep because the astral guardians do not let him enter into the astral or higher worlds, as the subtle bodies of a slanderer are in a state of decomposition and spread a noxious smell in the Subtle Worlds.

Many of those who have sleepless nights and are subject to insomnia in various degrees are victims of their own past slander. Their tax is often very heavy because insomnia is a sign of coming storms.

Slander spreads poison in the place where it originated and was nurtured. For example, a mother or father engaged in slandering labor soon see the process of degeneration going on within their bodies, families, and friends. The poison spreads through their contact and subtle emanation; even their breath and voice become contagious.

In olden times elders used to advise their children by saying, "Do not engage yourself in slander. It is like falling into quicksand. Eventually you will lose all that you are. Change your life, engaging yourself in the labor of doing good for others, especially those whom you hate."

From my own study I watched the lives of those people who were very intelligent in their slandering profession. One of them suffered with cancer and divorce. The next one abused drugs and alcohol and lost all his business, family, and friends. Another one fell under heavy psychic attacks and obsession and committed suicide.

Keep an eye on those who slander others, and do not involve yourself with them. If you were involved in various ways with a slanderer, immediately withdraw yourself from his companionship. Often, escape is equal to a victory.

No leader must engage himself in practicing slander of any kind. People are like books, which a true leader studies. By observing them without criticism, he learns the true laws of Nature and the psychology of people.

In observing people's responses, reactions, their destructive or constructive actions, the events revolving around their lives, and so on, the leader learns precious lessons of the living Teaching. He has no time to slander anyone. He can protect his friends and his group from dangerous people by raising their standards so high that they immediately see those who are sources of problems, those who are traitors or agents of destructive forces.

For some leaders it is relatively easy not to slander people, but there is a form of slander into which they fall very easily and joyfully. This kind of slander is directed toward the Great Ones in the form of telling anecdotes, jokes, stories, or remarks.

For example, some leaders tell funny stories about Saint Peter, Saint Paul, Moses, Jesus, or Mohammed to entertain people without knowing that this is a deeply slanderous action. Playing with the name of a Great One is recorded as a heavy slander because it denotes a lack of respect and devotion and the presence of light-mindedness and vanity. Another form of slander is to use sacred words such as the Hierarchy or Shamballa as jokes or in stories. Examples must not be mentioned here, but one can easily see and hear many such kinds of slander.

Holy and sacred names must always be pronounced with the highest respect, spoken softly, and with great devotion. In my many years of service, I have noticed that those students who made jokes with sacred names were eventually thrown out from the field of service, and misfortune followed their steps. Solemnity is an act of highest respect to Those in higher realms and to the Holy Ones and sacred names related to spiritual centers and locations. Lack of respect to Holy Ones and holy places is a sign of inner degeneration. Leaders must be careful to be examples of solemnity, nobility, and simplicity.

One must also be careful not to slander his own inner Divinity or his Teacher. Those who slander their inner Divinity and their Teacher pay heavy taxation in coming years and lives.

Some people, when they feel the uselessness of their life with an awareness of failure, maliciously attack others, slander them and try to destroy their reputation and life. They do this just to make themselves feel that they still have value, that they still exist, and that they still can operate and draw attention from people. But in such an effort to prove to themselves that they still exist, they find themselves in deeper and deeper despair and emptiness. For a while the fight against their victim keeps them alive, but as the victim is knocked down or annihilated or not even moved by their attack, they feel that they have totally lost their existence. This leads them to depression and suicide.

The awareness of your existence cannot be restored by the destruction of others but by the affirmation of the existence of others. Attacking others slowly reduces your existence. Recognizing the value of others builds your awareness about your own existence.

People destroy themselves by trying to destroy others for the sake of their hatred, anger, jealousy, and fear.

Man is created in such a way that he can regenerate and vivify himself only in regenerating and vivifying others. This is the most mystic law.

People slowly become like vacant and abandoned houses in trying to stop others from their value and beauty. They wait anxiously to see an error in others or, out of malice, attack them. Such an attack is like a thief who takes away furniture from your home and carries the furniture to another home whose owners you hate.

Our individuality is built only by the moments of recognition of the values of others or in the moments when we try to help others overcome their errors. By giving light, you increase your light. By giving your love, you increase your love. By trying to make people beautiful, you increase the resources of your beauty.

FOREBODING

Slander has a very peculiar function. It draws out the psychic energy of the victim, fuses with it, and impresses the aura of the victim with its ugly image. Such a mixture of psychic energy and the current of slander acts as a poison in the aura of the victim, and soon the victim slows down his striving and gradually falls into activities which are against his highest interests and survival.

You can see in the victim's life a pursuit of low pleasures and interests which slowly degenerate his whole character. Once such a poison is allowed to damage the aura, it takes years of aspiration and dedicated work to regenerate it with psychic energy.

It is also interesting to know that some people have the capability of deceiving and damaging themselves through slandering someone to themselves and building on it. They do this because of envy, jealousy, or hatred when the victim did not satisfy the cravings of the slanderer. This is one of the greatest crimes that a person can do to himself: deceiving and hypnotizing himself in this way to take revenge on the victim.

Such behavior is called a "double-edged black sword." He hurts himself not only with the venom from his slander but also from the arrows that he releases through his slander toward the victim; they come back and pierce his aura.

Closely watch the health, family life, business, and other relationships of the slanderer and you will notice not only a slow or fast degeneration in them but also will see a slow process of darkening in their intellect, reason, and logic. This is why in the Far East a slanderer is called a self-devouring wolf.

Those who poison their own aura by slandering someone to themselves show signs of decomposition of their morality, though they are built in such a way that until their whole body has sunk into the mire, they boast about their high morality and integrity.

There are ways to save oneself from the evil of slander. One way is sincere confession to one whom he slandered, asking forgiveness and blessings and even paying in some way for the damage the slanderer caused the victim. Another way for the slanderers to help themselves is to pray continuously. This is done by those who still carry a grain of nobility in their hearts.

Some of the slanderers are either obsessed ones or hypnotized ones. They do not have real evil in them but are victims of their environment and their examples. There are those who still have some nobility, and it can give energy in certain crises and help them to turn back from their evil paths.

Slanderers and traitors usually create for themselves a kind of hell which people call *foreboding*. They increasingly feel that something awful is going to happen to them in the future, something that is unavoidable. In their conversations and in their actions, they continuously stimulate the feeling of foreboding.

Foreboding happens because of associations. Association comes into being when there are things in our mind that associate themselves with what we read or hear. Usually association with an event is linked with fear and anxiety. One must closely observe what words, sentences, or even voices create the foreboding. If these words, sentences, and voices are identified, then one must search for how they formed initially in the mind of the person.

The fear obscures the person's consciousness, and he cannot see the reality of events. Through his imagination, he projects his fear into the future.

There is another side to foreboding. If for karmic reasons some calamity is going to come to that person and he is not aware of it, the words, sentences, and voices heard by him act as warnings for the future calamity. We call this maturity of karma which forces itself to manifest.

What can we do about this? There are five things we can do:

1. The best way to take away the sense of foreboding is to help the person face the consequences of his past wrongdoing.

2. If possible, dissolve them by paying back the debt.

3. Make the person understand that his wrongdoing was controlled by his bodies under a posthypnotic suggestion.

4. Make him strive toward Beauty, Goodness, Righteousness, Joy, and Freedom.

5. Every week suggest that he isolate himself, read, and meditate. Read about the higher Teaching. Meditate on the One Self.

Through these five steps it is possible to disintegrate the circuit formed by karma. If the foreboding continues, the person develops an acute degree of irritability and fear, which eventually appears as diseases in his bodies.

Foreboding persons must be watched very carefully, as they involve people around them in their feelings and gradually make them a part of the circuit causing the foreboding. This may create heavier problems and waste time.

People having experiences of foreboding must see that they do not engage themselves in gossip, slander, treason, and in acts of betrayal. These are the most common causes that make them have the experience of foreboding.

Whatever a person does to hurt others creates a resistance from his own heart or conscience. It is this resistance that offers the needed pressure to build the cloud, the device, the cause of foreboding. Some people do not have such a warning device in them because they do not have a sensitive heart or conscience or because their heart and consciousness are petrified.

Another factor which helps to decrease the tension of the foreboding is to avoid those persons who trigger the mechanism of foreboding. Sometimes a boss, friend, or any person around the subject acts as a switch for the feeling of foreboding. Sometimes a good vacation in Nature helps, especially if the vacation is taken on an isolated island near waterfalls.

Sometimes it happens that a person does not feel any foreboding for himself but feels it for others. In this case, the solar plexus of the subject is overstimulated. The cure is to massage daily the solar plexus. The use of wormwood oil and eucalyptus oil brings relief. This can also be a sign that the person lacks a certain chemical in his blood, which can be corrected by medical help.

It is possible also to recover from such an oversensitivity by dedicating oneself to a sacrificial service.

There is another step that the subject can take. Whenever he experiences foreboding for others, he can bless them, pray for them, and visualize a blue light around them. This also helps him to detach himself from psychic involvement with the victim.

Foreboding does not happen without a reason. To avoid such experiences, one must dedicate oneself not to the forces of destruction but to the forces of construction, which serve the Common Good.

SLANDERERS

There are many kinds of slanderers. For example, a mother is jealous of her daughter because a young boy or a man is interested in the daughter instead of herself. The mother, out of jealousy, slanders the man to keep him away from her daughter. When the man is kept away from the daughter, the mother uses all tactics of slander to convince the daughter that the man was not good.

The other type of slander comes from young girls. For example, a girl will flirt and write letters to a man and if the man makes a move, she slanders him for his immoral conduct. This is very prevalent. Such girls want attention. It is a great honor for them to slander a man to gain attention and make people think that they are something. Such girls often come from families who were alcoholics, drug users, or even prostitutes.

Another kind of slander that is prevalent is generated by husbands and boyfriends. Out of their jealousy they slander those who show any kind of affection toward their wife or girlfriend and imagine various kinds of situations in which they see their wife or girlfriend in a relation with their opponent. Such people not only cause grief to other people but also bring suffering to themselves, their families, and their friends.

Slandering others because of your jealousy or because of your failure to attack your victim is a sign of an inferiority complex and even a mental disorder. Often such slanderers are from broken homes or are people who had very unsuccessful friendships or an unhappy family life. Happy families do not engage in slander. One must be terribly unhappy and lack self-esteem to slander people because of one's fear and jealousy.

I remember a woman of fifty-one years who wanted to have a relationship with the boyfriend of her daughter. Eventually she succeeded in her plan. After the experience she let her daughter know about it, and her daughter left her boyfriend. The mother tried very hard to grab the boy for herself, but the boy refused. The woman used all kinds of slander to hurt the boy.

Especially dangerous are women who are jealous toward the girlfriend or wife of their son. They very scientifically prepare the poison of slander and inject it into the brain of their son so that eventually the son hates his wife or his girlfriend. Such a mother will have a hard time with her conscience and, in the Subtle World, will pay a high price for her jealousy.

Jealousy devastates friendships, families, groups, and even churches.

Jealousy is not only a feeling but also the most convenient vehicle for dark forces. The dark forces easily use this vehicle to carry on their destructive work because jealousy begets hatred, revenge, pride, vanity, and ego. With all these devices of darkness the entity brings devastation, if one is not alert and smart enough to stop his jealousy.

The slanderer has a very complex and disturbed psyche. He slanders for some of the following reasons:

- He slanders because he has many hidden crimes in his life, has a rebellious consciousness, was hurt by his parents or friends or by those who once loved him, is possessed or in the past failed in controlling people for his own advantage.

- He slanders because he wants to hide himself and his past.

- He slanders because he wants to take revenge using another person as his tool.

Whenever a person comes to you and slanders a third person, know that he most probably slandered you previously to that third person. He wants to create cleavages between you and the third person so that you do not hear from the third person whatever he told him about you. Whenever a person slanders a third person to you, go and find that third person and ask if that slanderer said the same thing about you to him. The slanderer would never engage himself in that dirty job if he did not feel guilty in his heart against the one whom he slanders.

Slandering is an ugly way to get rid of the puss accumulated in your nature. But a slanderer does not know that projecting his own ugliness on others is the easiest way to weaken his immune system, to cut his relation between himself and his heart, to destroy his psychic energy, and to expose himself to the attacks of dark forces.

Slanderers force you to build an image about a third person. Your pain and suffering depend on how many images you build in your mind. Each image will be a heavy debt on your shoulders, which occasionally will demand payment with a heavy penalty.

Those who encourage slanderers share their karma

and contaminate their own soul.

When slanderers see that they cannot hurt their victims to the degree that they want, they collect followers by infecting them with poison. They say, for example, to their friends, "He (or she) not only did this or that thing, but he said very bad things about you such as. . . ," and on and on. Thus, they create a group who hates the victim and tries to take revenge on him. The slanderer contaminates the lives of others and involves people in his dirty job.

It is noticed that some slanderers play smart. They imply more than they say. They hint more than they reveal to keep the curiosity of people alive. But this game accumulates and suddenly, like lightning, it hits them in various painful ways. Those who join slanderers share their karma.

The pain and suffering caused by the cruelty of slander sometimes takes centuries to heal. Beware of slandering people.

The shortest way to get away from such an association is to talk directly with the victim. This often saves time and energy and protects you from the dirty consequences of involvement.

The Great Sage says,

". . . *Enemies are the source of tension of energy. Nothing can so greatly increase the energy as counterattack. Therefore, why invent artificial obstacles when the dark ones attempt with all their strength to increase our energy?*"[1]

---

1. Agni Yoga Society, *Hierarchy,* para. 319.

Dark forces attack those who try to bring

- Beauty
- Goodness
- Righteousness
- Joy
- Freedom

But the Cosmic law is that such principles increase

- by actualizing them in our life
- by teaching the masses the benefit of such principles for all their life
- by experiencing organized attacks on these principles

Higher principles are like burning fires, and counter-attacks are like fuel oils. The more fuel added to a fire, the more explosions we will have. This is why the servants of darkness cannot understand why their attacks are increasing the energy and success of their victims.

The dark wolves are also able to play their roles in sheepskin. All their undercover activities eventually lead them to defeat in the following three general forms:

1. They inspire sincere people with greater enthusiasm to devote themselves to those principles against which they are supposed to fight.

2. They increase the energy of the devotee of Light.

3. They create conflict within their own being which makes them either withdraw from their ugly occupation, or makes them bring other people closer to the principles of the Teaching and perhaps eventually making them converts to those principles.

Dark ones know also that they have many in their army who do not believe their dark principles. They keep an eye on them because they know that, though they serve them for various kinds of self-interest and expectation, they may leave the dark ones and pass into the ranks of the other party at any time. To keep such "lukewarm" people in their ranks, dark forces try to involve them in those kinds of activities which exhaust their time and energy and develop their dependency on the dark forces.

Often dark forces manipulate such "lukewarm" people by playing on their "virtues." For example, suppose a lukewarm dark agent is working in a political committee which is planning something very important for the safety of an entire nation. Dark forces help their agent to see, for example, that one of the committee members smokes cigarettes or has illicit relations with a woman or drinks beer. Dark forces then play on the "virtues" of their agent and make him a zealot or a puritan. They say, "That fellow member is no good because he smokes, he has illicit relations with women, he drinks alcohol, and you know that these are terrible vices. So you must attack him, gossip about him, slander him, and try to throw him out of the committee for the sake of the success of the committee!"

And the "virtuous" one attacks the victim, his fellow committee member, and eventually succeeds in making others less respectful, less trusting toward that member. This is how dark forces use our virtues to create most obnoxious situations and temporarily paralyzes certain benevolent activities. But their success is temporary because the committee as a whole becomes more experienced, more determined, and more enthusiastic in trying to actualize their plans in spite of problems.

Thus, the attacks of dark forces may bring temporary success but prepare those heroes who will be invincible in greater tasks and responsibilities.

Most of the destructive work is carried on in the world by so-called honest, virtuous people — people who are self-righteous puritans. Great Teachers advise us not to give chances to such people by our indulgence and weakness, especially when we are engaged in sensitive duties. It is possible that we are wholeheartedly devoted to our vision and duties but have certain personality weaknesses. The more we advance on the ladder of greater responsibilities and duties, the greater measure of control we must exercise over our personality so as not to yield to its weaknesses and give a chance to dark agents to waste our time.

I remember one day a man came to our monastery to stay and work there. Our Teacher had an interview with him. In the conversation the man said, "I am *really pure.* I do not lie. I do not do bad things *as others do.* I *obey* my superiors. I *hate* those who fall into certain moral weaknesses. . . ."

While he was talking like a tape recorder, my Teacher walked toward him and took his arm very politely and led him to the gate. When the man realized that the Teacher wanted to get rid of him, he became furious and said, "But why didn't you accept me with all these good qualities I have?"

"We do not need you."

"Of course, you don't need me because I know what is going on in this monastery; all rotten people are here for secret reasons. . . ." The Teacher closed the gate and walked away.

For at least five minutes he did not talk, then he said to me, "Were you impressed by that man while he was counting his virtues?"

"No," I said.

"Why not?"

"Because. . . ."

"Because why?"

301

"I don't know, but my heart rejected him."

"Well, that is good, but in the future be careful of those who advertise themselves and try to knock your coworkers down."

We had many troubles later with that "virtuous" man. He organized many attacks against the monastery and even stole a few goods. Fortunately, the students were alerted not to listen to his dark slander about our Teacher.

In the last graduation ceremony our Teacher gave a message. "Today we have forty-seven graduates. This is the result of continuous attacks organized against our principles. Each of you will go out in the world and spread Beauty, Goodness, Righteousness, Joy, and Freedom and be examples of sacrificial service, gratitude, and striving. Do not be afraid of attacks. Use them as sources of vitamins."

Ambitious people who want to climb upon the shoulders of others are used by dark forces. To reach their goal such people surrender into the hands of destructive forces to secure themselves and to succeed in their job. Of course dark forces benefit from such fools. They help them climb toward the goals of their ambitions, wiping away as much as possible those who were working in constructive labor.

Ambition is the result of a poison in the brain which increases as it manifests, leading the ambitious person to take nonsurvival and self-destructive steps.

Ambition must not be confused with the spirit of progress and striving toward higher usefulness. A person should strive, have great goals, try to have better positions, better knowledge, better relationships. But all these must be done not at the expense of others but to fill a vacancy in the chain of coworkers and to help others to climb on the ladder of their service. When the spirit of striving is captive of the ego, vanity, and separatism, it turns into the poison of ambition.

An ambitious person demonstrates from childhood

the existence of this poison in his nature. For example:

- In gatherings, they push away others to have a better place to stand or sit.
- They are the first in line to eat.
- They decorate themselves with the plumage of others.
- They show off.
- They answer questions not directed at them.
- They put their nose in the business of others.
- They appear that they are defending the rights of others.
- They protest against anything that they think hurts their interest.
- They use bribery and flattery to advance.
- In their character, they have various phobias, but they show off as if they do not have fear.
- They attack people when they are sure they cannot be detected.
- Before they take your position they pretend they respect you, but after they take your position they insult you.
- They are very smart in not losing any opportunity to occupy new territories.

Ambition sometimes appears as enthusiasm. The difference can be seen when you realize that enthusiasm is inclusive, selfless, and sacrificial, but ambition is separative, selfish, and demanding or imposing.

When ambition increases, it creates mental imbalance which shows itself through various defects of character. Such people fall into cyclic depression, hopelessness, and suicidal moods. The only thing that helps them temporarily is the poison created from exercising slander and treason. This poison eventually unites with the poison of ambition, leading the body and psyche of the person into disaster. It is this period of degeneration that is the most dangerous moment in the life of such people. They become revengeful, destructive, and malicious.

Ambition ends in self-destruction.

19 Attacks

We are told that in difficult times, in crises and tribulations, during attacks of various sorts, our true nature comes to the surface. On such occasions we see how people put their wisdom into practice, put the Teaching into practice, reveal their hidden hatred, jealousy, and fear in words of criticism, slander, and gossip, or reveal their dignity, sense of brotherliness, sacrificial nature, and various talents to help the situation and people under attack.

Some people can do nothing but escape. Others observe and take a neutral attitude. Others stand as warriors to save whatever they can.

Many times in an individual's family or group life such hard times occur and reveal enemies and friends. During good times, all are friends, especially those who have expectations or profit to gain. But when difficult times come, in which these so-called friends must sacrifice and risk, they reveal their true colors.

Friends are tested during difficult times, and their true nature comes to the surface. In advanced work, a leader must trust important work only to those who have been tested in times of trouble and are found to be faithful, stable, focused, and sincere, just as in the olden days when a king would collect the best warriors and make them guards in his palace.

Those who leave you in the midst of difficulties are traitors who can never be trusted in the future until they are tempered by life and tested again and again. An old saying is, "Never use a cracked boat while sailing on the ocean of life."

A good leader will sometimes create artificial crises and try to find out how his friends and coworkers will act. Once a leader told his coworkers that he was in danger, that certain people were following him for certain reasons. A few days later he noticed that some of his coworkers had disappeared, while others were guarding his property and secretly following him to various places, watching over him. This continued for one month. The leader finally gathered those who were on guard and promoted them to higher responsibilities and offices. Then the ones who had departed returned and asked if all was well. The leader told them that the danger had passed and that there was no further need to worry. Those followers, upon hearing the good news began to justify their absence saying that suddenly they had had other things to do and that they were sorry for their absence. The next day they found out that they had been released from their offices.

The leadership must exercise forgiveness for personal weakness but not for those who take it easy in their responsibilities and fail to protect the foundation of the work. For example, a leader can forgive a coworker if he occasionally falls into the traps of sex, liquor, smoking, or eating too much. But he will think twice before he forgives one who slanders the leader, his work, and his coworkers, or overlooks his duties and responsibilities for his pleasures and acts against the leader, influenced by slander, gossip, malice, and the evil plans of the enemies of the leader.

Of course, it is possible that under certain conditions a leader will manifest certain weaknesses and failures. But the coworkers' first step is to come in direct contact with the leader and receive firsthand information about the issue and stand by his side to assist him in overcoming the situation.

Traitors wait until they see a weakness in the leader. Then they attack. Most traitors work very closely with the leader and appear very obedient and cooperative, but their intention is to find an opportunity to hurt the leader — even to take over his position.

Sometimes people have the opinion that a leader is perfect in all his nature. This is not true. Every leader is a progressing light, an expanding beauty. In every step of progress and expansion, he confronts difficulties and passes through tests and crises, sometimes temporarily falling into difficulties and traps.

When people realize that a leader needs his coworkers' help under certain conditions, they are not as likely to exercise a critical attitude toward him. On the contrary, they rush in to help him during the crisis.

There are times that a leader needs to fight alone. There are also times in which a single word of encouragement and cheer helps him overcome a dark hour in his life. Coworkers not only help to carry on the plan presented by the leader but also they are there to stand by the leader at times of attack and difficulty. As coworkers cooperate, the leader finally understands that a group of servers is like a body — it either stands or falls together.

The field of labor of a group is a field of creative

learning. Every day one is tested physically, emotionally, mentally, and spiritually to prove that he is ready to graduate from that field and enter another field of service where he lives in higher responsibility and labor. Those who fail in group work lose two or three lifetimes until another opportunity is given to them to cooperate with certain people in the spirit of self-forgetfulness, harmlessness, and right speech.

There are three kinds of people who are related to the Teaching:

1. Those who accept and try to live according to the Teaching

2. Those who, after accepting the Teaching, teach and propagate the Teaching

3. Those who, after accepting the Teaching, defend the Teaching

Every disciple of the Teaching must have records in the book of his life reflecting these three stages.

Without defending the Teaching a disciple cannot be accepted into the Hierarchy. It is only when you risk your life for the Teaching, suffer, and go through various kinds of pain and sacrifice for the Teaching — or even die for the Teaching — that you prove your merit and become accepted by the Hierarchy. But you begin your association with the Teaching by learning about it, reading about it, listening to it, meditating on it, and demonstrating the Teaching in your life in solemnity, beauty, and devotion.

Then you begin to teach the Teaching first in silence, making your life so beautiful and magnetic that you draw people to yourself as a living embodiment of the Teaching. Then you teach the Teaching on a gradient scale, according to the *level* of the people, the *conditions* of society, and according to the *time* you can put into it without neglecting your karmic responsibilities and duties.

Then the third stage follows when the enemies of the Teaching begin to appear, one by one. Some of them are from your own family or group. Some of them are unknown to you, often working with authorities. Some of them attack you through invisible means, directing currents of thought-force and emotional force toward you. These groups individually or collectively attack you to distract your work and hinder your activities, trying to prevent you from spreading the Teaching.

They use five methods to accomplish this end:

1. They approach you as friends, servants, assistants, secretaries, coworkers, and so on.

2. They approach you with sweet words, flattery, or bribery, as ones who highly love you and are ready to protect you.

3. They appear as enemies who use slander, malice, and treason.

4. They appear in violence, using physical force, weapons, and other means to try and destroy your work.

5. They appear as orders to stop your work, to persecute you, to put you in prison or to death.

Graduation into the Hierarchy goes through the three major stages previously mentioned and eventually through these five doors of ordeal. These five methods have been used throughout ages against the Teachers of the Law. Once a Great One said, "Times came when We did not have a place to pass the night."

Those who pass through these five doors prove themselves as warriors. Nothing can stop their progress. Greater resistance from evil is a sign that they are destined to be victorious. Actually, their usefulness and influence increase with every attack. In the Teaching it is known that the best propagators of the Teaching are its enemies. They do such a job that the Teaching penetrates into every layer of society without resistance.

Besides spreading the Teaching, the enemies of the Teaching

- help devotees deepen their faith

- make weak ones quit

- expose weakness in the character of the leaders, which helps them strengthen themselves

- help leaders to develop new facilities and make themselves up-to-date against the attackers

- make hypocrites leave the Teaching and encourage those who are in the Teaching for self-interest to disappear

Attackers often do a better job for the Teaching than the Teachers themselves. It is during a period of attack that the destiny of the survival of the group is determined. If the group is unworthy, it is dispersed. If it is worthy, it is strengthened immensely with each attack.

There are other kinds of attacks which are more difficult for the leader to control or eradicate. For example, attackers use a technique to create confusion in the minds of group members. They try to introduce similar Teachings with slight variations. Such attacks sometimes are very successful if the devotees of the Teaching do not have a sense of pure discrimination. The few seeds that the attackers plant in the minds of the weak ones soon become bushy plants which obstruct the true harvest.

Attackers try to introduce into the group certain kinds of social activities and pleasure events that eventually consume the time of the group members, involve them in various problems, tasks, and expenditures so that they gradually feel that they do not have time for their true spiritual studies, meditations, and meetings. Once a member is caught in such a trap, he goes rapidly in the current toward the falls. Many well-intentioned students fall easily under such attacks because of a lack of discrimination and because their roots in the Teaching are weak.

A leader must watch especially those who are eager to make friends and establish ties with various members. Such people are often traitors who

- make friends

- take their telephone numbers and addresses

- visit

- have fun together

- take trips together

- organize parties to involve others and disperse their focus of dedication and service

- involve them with various business

- eventually involve them in slander, malice, and treason

These are some of the steps the enemies of the Teaching take to devour the sheep.

No leader in the Teaching, no disciple of the world attacks any teaching or any religion but carefully studies them to find ideas and meanings.

Disciples are inclusive. They accept similarities not differences. Differences for them create the power of discrimination. Negative talk about any religion or teaching deprives those people who profit spiritually from them or urges people to attack them in fanaticism. Ways and means to approach the Presence can be different — but most of them seek the same ultimate goal.

The Teaching has various elements

- intention, goal, purpose
- method, discipline
- knowledge
- information
- tests
- experience
- revelations
- history
- principles
- open doors

Those teachings which make claims humiliate the truth and make themselves the "only way to fly." Such teachings have lost their purity and are used for certain interests. The teaching that guides people to discover truths on their own level and in their own time witness that that teaching is one of the many which attracts thinking people.

To be possessive and fanatical means ignorance and, if the clergy of a church say all discoveries start, grow, and end only by the knowledge of their particular faith, they deny all who contribute to discoveries all over the world.

Inclusiveness brings people closer to their goals and ends their sectarianism.

A building contractor hired fifteen subcontractors to finish a job. The owner asked why there were fifteen kinds of contractors. He wanted only builders. The builder said, "If you need only carpenters, you will not have electricity, plumbing, heating, a foundation, a roof, and so on. To build your house, I need people who are specialized in different fields to cooperate in building the house you need."

Let people follow a teaching the way they want if that teaching is making them

* noble
* intelligent
* law-abiding
* sacrificial
* pure
* cooperative
* loving
* forgiving
* honest
* intuitive

Those who build dogma, doctrines, cleavages, and fanaticism are the enemies of human progress and the enemies of the expansion of consciousness of humanity.

Disciples of the world discriminate between the teachings that are for beginners and those which are for advanced students, but they do not belittle the teachings of various teachers. Those who engage in attacking other teachings prove that they do not live the teaching they practice. If any teaching creates cleavages between people who are on the spiritual path, that is not a true Teaching. If they see differences in the teachings, they try to bring them closer to each other. Sometimes different teachings are given to people of different temperaments. To fight, trying to disprove things that are above your capacity, makes you look ridiculous.

But how can people be led to synthesis if the purpose of the Teaching is to build an individuality which will guide them later to synthesis?

People need universal unity, but if they do not have independence and unity within themselves how can they be part of the universal unity? Teaching people to have independence is not against a teaching that teaches renunciation of self and universal unity. Teaching a youth to be pure does not contradict teaching him to be a good father. In every phase, we need a teaching. When the phase changes, the teaching is obsolete for that phase.

This does not mean that there are no false teachings. A false teaching is against the Common Good of humanity and especially against

- perfection
- cooperation
- purity
- law and order
- responsibility
- freedom
- righteousness
- forgiveness
- striving
- sacrificial service
- synthesis
- unity

"Brother will not censure brother, for he knows that condemnation is dissolution."[1] Those who walk on the path of self-perfection and service are considered brothers, and spiritual brothers are not allowed to criticize each other's religion or teaching.

Fanaticism is not encouraged by any great Teacher or disciple.

Question: *Is it fanaticism to have firm beliefs for which one can sacrifice even his life?*

Answer: It is not fanaticism if your belief is based on many viewpoints, not on one viewpoint. It is not fanatisicm if you do not force your belief on others by fear or bribery. It is not fanaticism if your belief is not used for your income, personal gratification, and pride. Fanaticism is bigotry if turned into separatism. After fanaticism, your belief becomes your own coffin.

Suppose a man only admires one flower and neglects to see ten thousand of them. The concept of beauty forms in our mind when we love all flowers, in all shapes and fragrances. Beauty prevents us from falling into fanaticism.

INNER ATTACKS

It is very important that one does not allow his self-image to disintegrate. Disintegration of the self-image is caused by outer and inner attacks.

Outer attacks are vicious criticism, gossip, slander, hatred, jealousy. Such currents of force slowly penetrate into your sacred self-image and begin to destroy it like termites. To protect yourself and your self-image from such intruders, you must also keep yourself identified with the image of the Lord in your heart.

---

1. Agni Yoga Society, *Brotherhood*, para. 424.

Inner attacks come from your subconscious mind or when you identify yourself with outer attacks and begin to change your self-image to the image that your attackers are presenting to you.

Subconscious attacks are recordings of the moments of failure, defeat, embarrassment, and guilt feelings registered in your subconscious while you were swayed by your lower nature. Inner attacks also are built of crystallized thoughtforms which were built during the moments when low opinions were expressed about you, comparing you with others.

Some attacks are very frequent, and they cooperate with outer attacks to defeat the self-image. Here I am referring to your self-image built by the highest assimilation of your ideal, built with the moments when you really believed that "you are that Self — the most radiant. . . ." Such a self-image must be kept in your heart at all times as your safest refuge.

You must not let the enemies penetrate into the sanctuary of your Self and cause decay because that sanctuary will protect your integrity, your identity, the diamond of yourself.

Your inner sanctuary can protect you from all evil, from all possible attacks, if you let your Inner Watch be vigilant.

The downfall of nations, groups, families, and individuals starts when they allow their true self-image to be distorted, decayed, and degenerated. All ills of life start from such decay. Health, happiness, prosperity, and power are all signs of the integrity of the self-image.

The self-image must stay within your heart, solid and radiant like a diamond, even if the muddy waters of inner and outer enemies attack you. Realize that you are "more radiant than the Sun."

All your failures are caused by your elementals who are under your training. Do not identify yourself with them during their failure, but observe them. Through such an observation you keep the integrity of your self-image which is the reflection in you of the image of the All-Self.[2]

OUTER ATTACKS

Entities that attack from the outside have seven goals. If you study them you can easily see what kind of techniques they are using to reach their goals.

1. *They want to stop your evolution or retard it by keeping you busy with transient objects, by increasing your karmic debts, by forcing you to engage in your self-interest.*[3] This is a heavy attack, and dark forces use various methods to stop your meditation, your study, your observation, your interest in your future and make you sink into inertia. Whenever you observe such a downfall in your behavior, know that you are under attack. Those who retard your progress fall into very painful traps.

2. *They try to stop your service to others, creating various complications in your relationships with people.* They put certain thoughts and feelings in you and you begin to think, "I am not paid for this service. No one is praising me. Why work if there is no income? I feel people do not appreciate me. I serve them and I feel they are very indifferent to my labor."

They also make you greedy. You want to pursue physical pleasures so that you avoid any service that does not pay, or you fall into pleasures and forget about service.

---

2. First published in *The Mystery of Self-Image*, pp. 152-153.
3. See *The Science of Meditation*, Ch. 28, "The Problem of Evil."

3. *They stop your future plans.* This is done by encouraging people to frustrate you through slander, gossip, or by stimulating your greed, sex, and hatred to such a degree that you involve yourself with unending court cases or pass through deep humiliation. They also try to make your friends turn against you, stimulating their touchiness or personality interests and making them find weaknesses in you. They try to make you and your coworkers fall into fear because fear makes people selfish, self-important, aggressive, stubborn, uncooperative, suspicious, and untrustworthy. They also try to destroy your income and the prosperity of your coworkers or divert their interest into different fields so that you depend on your small income and forget about your great dream.

When people are trapped in such poisonous elements, they resign from their plans and search for security to protect their pitiful self-interest.

4. *They create cleavages within your family members and coworkers and destroy unity.* They want to destroy unity wherever it exists. They spread gossip, slander, and lies through their agents.

They stimulate ego, self-interest, and showing off. They stimulate the tendency toward nosiness and superiority and create conflicts.

During such attacks they create various psychological attitudes within your coworkers which hurt their health and they withdraw from helping you. They make people threaten you by letters, by blackmail so that you fall into worry and waste your energies.

Every time disunity appears in a family or group, the dark forces deeply rejoice for their success because they know that disunity is the root of many evils.

By all means possible they try to destroy your joy and happiness because they know that joy is the best communication line between the Higher Worlds and the

Hierarchy. Once they take your joy away, you no longer can receive help from Higher Sources. This is why Great Ones try to tell us to stay in joy no matter what happens.

The Great Sage says, "Without joy you cannot enter into Our spheres."

Leaders must see that the unity in the group and in coworkers is kept healthy. Leaders must try by all means to prevent cleavages between nations because the intention of dark forces is to see our planet as lifeless as the moon. Actually, the moon is there to warn us of the future danger for our planet.

5. *They try to create a feeling of superiority, ego, and vanity in you.* When you see people acting with superiority feelings, demonstrating ego and vanity, know that they are under very subtle attacks and your first step is to exercise extreme caution in your relationship with them.

Ego, vanity, and superiority feelings among your coworkers prevent every effort toward cooperation, and instead they seek self-interest to increase their greed and create unending conflicts between coworkers. When leaders are contaminated by ego and vanity, they stop the evolution of their coworkers and destroy future possibilities of service. It is important that you watch closely and not tolerate such symptoms of vanity, ego, and superiority and find the roots in your family and group.

6. *They try to stimulate your weakness to show off.* When a leader is contaminated by such a vice he slowly loses his roots, his depth, his devotion to the Teaching, to the Hierarchy, and floats on the surface of life. He becomes a prime example and serves the causes of dark forces.

Buddha used to expel any disciple who was contaminated by the sickness of showing-off.

Dark forces greatly enjoy people who fall into such a trap because they then become precious instruments in their hands to promote superficiality. Superficiality is a disease in society. It becomes more dangerous if it operates in the ranks of those who have high positions.

One thing we must know is that evil never discriminates between methods. It uses beauty or ugliness, truth or falsehood, health or disease, sanity or insanity. It uses all and everything in such a way that its purpose of destruction is reached.

Once my Father said, "Do not be trapped when evil smiles at you or saves your life. It does all to achieve its goal."

Evil uses right things for wrong purposes. It hides its intentions and goals behind its cosmetics and then traps many people. Evil is the expert in setting traps. It destroys you by either using your beauty and your talents or your ugliness and your weaknesses.

7. *They make you crave praise.* Dark forces stimulate your desire for praise to such a degree that you do various ugly things to make people praise you. This not only increases the size of your ego but also creates rejection from everyone around you. Craving praise makes you lose the essentials of life and your true purpose in life.

Dark forces create those conditions in which you are praised constantly and then create conditions in which you are criticized constantly. Between these two states of consciousness they develop in you a huge ego and a sick ego, which is useless in any constructive work.

Watch for those who praise you. Often your enemies are found in their ranks.

With all these goals, dark forces generally use a method which is called "inflammation of the sex urge," and they stimulate the sex centers in families, in groups, in nations to such a degree that people lose their control and catch various diseases, hate each other, are jealous of each other, and eventually fall into cleavages and endless problems.

Again, we say that you can fight against evil by standing on your principles and reminding yourself of the "words of power." Through such a method you may avoid many attacks in your life. Also, you must communicate closely with your Teacher so that He illuminates you about the situation.

Sometimes within a group people fight for right and wrong, destroying friendships and the spirit of cooperation. If the "right and wrong" destroys cooperation, you are lost.

Once two brothers fought to prove to each other that one was right and the other was wrong about the type of fish they saw in the river. This fight grew to such a dimension that eventually they both killed each other.

Sometimes the "rights" belong to our vanity, ego, and self-interest or even to the level of our consciousness. The important thing is to hold the unity and cooperation. Tolerance, broadmindedness, forgiveness, understanding, inclusiveness are the steps leading to the temple of cooperation and group consciousness.

Sometimes people exercise many vices to prove that they were right in something. The ego is a negative fighter; it fights for its self-interest. Also, there are people who do not fight for the sake of right but for the sake of hidden interests.

We must also learn to differentiate between those who are agents of dark forces and those who are agents of their inner posthypnotic suggestions or of their subconscious mind. In group or family life, the first step is to isolate such agents, cutting all possible relationship. Sometimes agents, feeling that they are destructive, isolate themselves from the group so that their harm does not spread into the group or family. These agents sometimes are then forsaken by their lords because of their uselessness.

Some entities attack your life thread, some your consciousness thread. When they attack your consciousness thread, you lose consciousness for a few minutes, a few hours, or even days. During this period all that is stored in your subconscious mind surfaces, but because the consciousness is not there you remain unaware of it. Later, when your consciousness reinstalls itself, you see a very complicated situation in your mind with forces, thought-forms, memories — all in a state of chaos. The intention of the dark forces is to create confusion and storms within you, thus weakening you so that they take over.

Another form of attack is an attack on your life thread, which extends from the Monad to the heart center. Sometimes such attacks are fatal. Sometimes the life thread restores itself, and life energy flows again.

It is known that people do not easily survive such attacks. It is the intention of the dark forces to make you vacate your body. They make you move out so that they can occupy it. Some people, after they die for a few minutes or hours may regain their life, but they are no longer the real owners of their bodies. Certain entities have replaced them. You see in such individuals a different personality with new ways of living, with new directions, tastes, and relationships which are sometimes evil and sometimes average. Sometimes the real owner returns if there is a karmic relationship with the possessing entity. They live in the same body. This is the cause of a split personality, or multiple personalities if other intruders are present.

The reason that such attacks become possible are found within the person. *Those who attack the lives of others invite attacks upon themselves.* Those who try to obsess, damage, or kill the consciousness of other human beings are led by life into situations in which they are obsessed, damaged, and dulled in their consciousness. The law is this: What we do unto others we force others to do to us.

Even people who are law-abiding in their current life, cannot escape their past serious transgressions and find themselves attacked by dark forces or faced with their own karma. Attacks of this kind can be handled only by the power of the spiritual shield.

Question: *You mentioned that dark forces use the sex center to distort plans, progress, and unity. Can you say something further on this?*

Answer: The sex center is one of the main lines on which dark forces work, at present, increasing sexually transmittable diseases, divorce, hatred, court cases, waste of money and time. All these are enough to destroy an entire civilization. They use the sexual images collected in your subconscious mind from movies, from magazines, from stories and excite you to such a degree that you can no longer control yourself.

It sometimes happens that when your sex center is open they channel into it many currents of sexual thoughts and make it an ever-burning fire. Many earthbound entities can possess you and destroy your future, if you do not save yourself as early as possible.

It is possible to hide from the traps of dark forces. It is also possible to come to your senses and use your energy to help solve the problems of humanity. If you notice overstimulation in yourself and in others, first try to find the source and then exercise control over yourself.

Question: *Is marriage wrong?*

Answer: Not at all. It is the best school for wisdom and discipline if there is love and dedication in it. Of course you must exercise moderation, not extremes, to meet the needs of each other without being pressured by each other.

Question: *What are astral entities?*

Answer: Astral entities are those who left their physical bodies and live in their astral vehicles. They may live in the astral plane for a long time until the time comes for them to go to the mental plane, leaving their astral vehicle behind. When they leave their astral bodies, they never come back and inhabit their astral bodies again because the door is closed for them. Their bodies either evaporated or were consumed in fire or began to decompose.

Only those who live in the etheric plane or are caught there can possess mediums. The etheric plane inhabitants have an etheric body until their physical body is cremated or until it decomposes. Then they live in their astral body in the etheric plane. It is possible that an astral entity attacks you if you enter into the astral plane and contaminate your astral body. But he does not come to the physical plane and possess you unless he is of a very low order and trapped in the etheric plane.

Question: *What is Transfiguration?*

Answer: Transfiguration is a state of beingness. When your intuitional substance descends into your etheric, astral, and mental bodies and its light radiates through them, you have achieved Transfiguration. Consciousness is the awareness of possibilities. Beingness is the actualization and the experience of these possibilities.

Question: *How can we help subjectively someone who needs help?*

Answer: If you are referring to some entities who are in the etheric, astral, or mental plane, then the answer is that you must have an organized etheric, astral, and mental body and be trained to step out of your physical body and be active on the proper plane. If you do not have proper bodies, such subjective help is impossible.

If by "subjective" you mean your astral and mental bodies, sending good feelings and lofty, noble thoughts to someone who is emotionally and mentally troubled helps.

You can affect telepathically or emotionally the aura of one who is in need. If you know how to get out of your body on the emotional or mental planes, you can become an invisible server and help many people in the astral and mental planes. To do this you must develop your astral and mental bodies. You must learn how to get out of your bodies, and you must build your continuity of consciousness or the Antahkarana.

Those who serve on the physical plane can be candidates for subjective service. But do not hurry to help subjectively until you are highly trained.

Question: *Does cremation affect the astral corpse?*

Answer: Yes it does. When you depart from your astral body, for a short while you are still interested in your physical body. When it is cremated you feel more free to continue your journey. Remember, until your body is cremated or decomposed you stay in your etheric body.

Astral corpses (not astral entities) are always attracted to physical corpses, and they carry certain germs to the astral plane. Cremation stops such action.

Question: *How does a planet become sacred?*

Answer: When the Planetary Logos takes the Planetary Fifth Initiation, which means when Its humanity reaches to at least the Transfiguration, the planet becomes sacred.

Question: *Does Hierarchy decide our future?*

Answer: No. Hierarchy presents those steps to us which can lead us to planetary brotherhood, prosperity, health, and happiness. But if you do not want to survive, they can do nothing. If you ask for Their assistance with sincerity and follow Their wisdom and plan, They help you.

Question: *Does "OM" damage us?*

Answer: No and yes. When you are in irritation, hatred, jealousy, in the fever of greed, or revenge and try to sound an OM, the OM increases your vices and damages you. Remember that an OM brings energy into you, stimulates your whole nature, and cleanses you from decomposing atoms. But if you are in such states of agitation, this purification does not take place.

Do not sound the OM unless you have peace, harmony, love, and compassion within you.

In conclusion, try to live a life of dignity, nobility, and responsibility. Live closer to the subjective values and beautify your life with such values. Attacks often strengthen you. Do not be afraid, but also do not be wasteful. Do not invite attacks, but try to attract benevolent forces of the Universe by living a life that is in harmony with Nature.

20

Psychic Attacks

When we talk about psychic attacks it creates some problems with people, not unlike medical students who, when they study about diseases, go home and think they have all the symptoms about which they heard. Similarly, those who hear about psychic attacks imagine they are under various kinds of attacks. They think they are obsessed, possessed, or confronted with evil entities in all the negative events of their life.

The truth is that

- most of you are not advanced enough on the Path to be under the attack of dark forces

- most of you are protected because of your purity, beauty, dedication, and sacrificial life

- most of you are protected by your Solar Angel, Teacher, Master, Ashram, and by the Hierarchy, or by the benevolent forces of the Universe

- most of you are protected because of your loving heart

- most of you are protected because of the psychic energy you have or the psychic energy that your group has

- your prayers have built a strong shell around you; real, sincere, heartfelt prayers increase your psychic energy and attract invisible helpers around you

- meditation prepares your bodies in such a way that attacks cannot easily defeat you and often, when you get stronger, you defeat most of the attacks

- our good deeds in the past protect us; what we give, what we do to help people in dire conditions reaches us and helps us

One of the most powerful protectors is Christ Who, we are told, is a mighty warrior against dark forces, the center of which is in the Cosmic Astral Plane. He is continuously at war on behalf of humanity and, if we keep contact with Him, He will shield us by His mighty power.

The Great Invocation is a great mantram which protects you and others if repeated regularly with consecration and devotion. Of course, the sacred word OM and Om Mani Padme Hum have great power against attacks.[1]

All of these means have a great protective effect against dark forces.

---

1. For more information regarding mantrams, see *The Science of Meditation* and *The Psyche and Psychism*.

SUBCONSCIOUS ATTACKS

A very high percentage of attacks come from our subconscious mind. Most of the subconscious mind is full of our own fabrications.

Whenever we are in a posthypnotic state of mind, we collect lots of hypnotic suggestions and add to them with our own imagination and fabrications. All this goes into our subconscious mind.

There are a few emotional and mental elements that put you in hypnotic conditions. They are

- hatred

- anger

- fear

- jealousy

- greed

Whenever you are in these states everything around you — forms, sounds, words, colors, motions — turns into posthypnotic suggestions. You collect many posthypnotic suggestions from your radio, television, newspaper, friends, and enemies while you are under such emotional and mental elements.

In these states your subconscious prepares a videotape for you. All your environment, inner reactions, imagination, and fabrications are visually recorded on that videotape. For example, if you are in fear, the event causing fear in you is taped along with your imagination or fabrications. You may imagine that someone is going to kill you this way or that way, or that you are going to attack him to protect yourself somehow. You create a drama which later may seem like nonsense to you, but it is exactly recorded on your videotape. It is a reality within your subconscious mind.

On the tape you may say, "I hate him. I wish I could kill him with a rock. I know what may happen to me. Maybe his son will kill me . . . this way or that way . . . or they will put me in prison," and so on. The important thing is that all this has gone onto the tape as posthypnotic suggestions.

One day years later, you are sitting somewhere when your tape becomes restimulated and you suddenly feel like killing "that" person, this way or that way. You feel depressed as you imagine what will happen to you according to your tape. You do not know what to do to hold yourself together to avoid committing murder, and you call a friend and say, "I think I am possessed. I feel a deep urge to kill 'that' man. I know what will happen to me after that," and you tell the whole story. Your friend believes that you are obsessed. Once you believe that you are obsessed, you think there is no way out. Many crimes and murders are committed in this way.

Whenever you wish bad for others, it turns into a wish for yourself in the subconscious mind. The subconscious mind does not discriminate between you and others, but it forces the hypnotic suggestion to actualize itself every time it is restimulated. You become the target of your own arrows. In ten minutes of jealousy and hatred, you build a one hundred-foot long videotape recording in your subconscious mind.

Some of our sicknesses are built in the same manner. You identify with sick people and you imagine you are sick. You imagine the drama of being sick; then you play back the tape factually in your life and call it an attack.

In Asia it is forbidden to talk in front of children about the sicknesses of other people or to discuss surgical and hospital experiences. They think that a child may identify himself with what is told, record it as a posthypnotic suggestion in his subconscious mind, and years later fall sick because of the recording.

I remember a case in which a young girl of twenty-one years developed a serious skin disease in California. As the doctor was examining her at her home, a little neighbor girl was present with her parent. At night the girl told the parent that she felt she had the same disease. Of course the parent said, "Just close your eyes and sleep. Do not talk nonsense."

Twenty-five years passed and the girl, now a woman, developed the same disease. In conversation she said, "I do not know why I knew I had that disease in my blood since childhood."

The neighbor said, "It was an attack from Satan." It is true our subconscious mind works often as a Satan. But most of what we are is the playback of our subconscious recordings, which of course can be annihilated by advanced psychological means before they knock us down.

Whether you are in fear, hatred, anger, jealousy, or greed, you are seventy-five percent in a hypnotic condition. If you understand this, you will be very cautious not to ruin your future, recording for yourself future troubles. It is evident that Sages, knowing this, have advised us not to fall into such "sins."

Many people think that one can escape from these suggestions. They say, "Look how happy I am." It is true they are happy now, but the subconscious mind has its mysterious laws. A portion of it can sleep for a few incarnations and emerge suddenly when all was in perfect condition and load the person with additional taxation. This is why we see great misfortunes come suddenly to a person when he seems in perfect condition.

You see two happily married people, and suddenly they divorce without any apparent reason or with a reason that is not related directly to them. Many people consider this a psychic attack of the same sort, but it is not. It is an attack by their posthypnotic recordings and actions. All such playbacks can involve your three bodies simultaneously because they are built by the chemistry of your thoughts, emotions, and actions.

Subconscious elements act as some viruses do. They hide in many forms to avoid identification. We must remember that the suggestions that other people plant within us are not as dangerous as the suggestions that we plant within ourselves. If you were able to observe yourself during the occasion of anger, jealousy, and greed and see the recordings that are taped in the physical, emotional, and mental dimensions, you would be horrified. We think we are harmless human beings. You will not think so once you see your recordings!

It is very important to understand that the main target of all our subconscious suggestions is ourselves. Of course in various situations we harm others under restimulation, but in most cases we harm ourselves in various ways. The subconscious elements are clever enough to manifest in our life in such a way that they escape the detection of the conscious mind. In most cases the conscious mind or the conscious man does not see the causes and the process but sees the effects and wonders, "How can such things happen to me?"

The subconscious mind is composed of unrelated circuits or tapes, but the strange thing is that once they are stimulated they unite as one unbearable noise. It is possible that in different weeks or years you are stimulated in different circuits, but it does not make any difference. "Once you awaken a dog, all the dogs begin to bark" and the posthypnotic suggestions guide your life according to the thoughts and feelings that you have at that moment in your conscious mind.

Let us say that in your recordings you have your father, mother, sister, lawyer, neighbor, jewels, bank books, and house. If one of these inputs is restimulated, all are restimulated, and though the entire recording cannot play back simultaneously, it supports the portion that begins to manifest. All this can be learned only by observation. Just try to learn how to observe yourself and others, and you will learn a super wisdom. Observe what is happening, find the cause, the process, the result, and go deeper. This is a supreme game.

It is possible that you built a videotape of yourself when you were nine years old, and it so deeply impressed in your subconscious mind that, throughout your life, it forces you to act as a nine-year-old girl in various ways, even when you become sixty years of age. Your recording sticks in its track and plays back the same recording through various actual performances. No matter how much you want to grow, part of you acts like a nine-year-old girl.

Such tapes are restimulated when the person becomes physically sick, falls into desperate conditions, or is emotionally excited. For example, you are forty years old. You dress like a lady, but you go to a party and act like a teenager to the embarrassment of your friends. Sometimes such videotapes are released in the presence of those people who provide the right atmosphere and chemistry to playback your teenage videotape.

Observe yourself and you will see how true this is. Such tapes are often innocent, but they stop your growth and expansion. Even if you escape from their influence and grow, occasionally you still act as a child or as a teenager.

Some people are able to observe themselves although they cannot stop acting silly, but they see what they are doing. Often they blame dark forces who "at a certain moment of their life attacked them and made them act silly." Many psychologists or psychiatrists, seeing such phenomena, think that psychic attacks or attacks of dark forces do not exist until one day they experience such attacks themselves.

We cannot protect people who want to hurt themselves. Hurting oneself is usually based on one's own past heavy karma. If one thinks that he is not punished enough for the things that he uncovered, he tries to find ways to hurt himself. Many people even consciously hurt themselves and blame the dark forces. It is true that our minds can be controlled by outer agents, but before outer agents can conquer us we destroy our inner fortress and surrender to them.

Question: *Can you tell us how many ways our subconscious mind becomes activated?*

Answer: By a number of ways, but there are five major ways:

1. *There is stimulation through association*, which we spoke about.

2. *There is increasing pressure* within the subconscious mind. Sometimes the hypnotic events are so pressurized that they explode and lead man into insanity, into confession, into renunciation, and into certain unexpected behaviors.

3. *Karma*, when the time is ripe, works through the subconscious mind to bring man into balance and equilibrium or for him to meet and pay his debts.

4. *The Teaching increases the fire of the higher mind* to such a degree that it breaks the protective wall of the subconscious mind and releases the elements lying there for centuries. This is why you can see very weird behavior sometimes in a person who really engages himself in the Teaching. Sometimes he can control these currents of the subconscious mind, but sometimes he becomes their victim. He feels he is in the rapids and either must die or save himself. Some of these people disappear into forests, caves, or resign from their duties and responsibilities and become wanderers.

Some Teachers, if they see the danger, can help such people to pass over a dangerous bridge relatively safely. But if the person does not notice the coming changes, the current takes him away into the rapids. This is why we need a Teacher to protect us in the moments when the dam of the subconscious mind breaks down.

5. *We also have the influence of disciples and Initiates.* Apparently normal students of wisdom who come in direct contact with advanced disciples suddenly demonstrate very unusual behavior. The disciples, because of their psychic energy, indirectly restimulate all that is good and bad in people, leading them into a desperate condition.

One day a great Teacher visited our organization. The leader of the group asked a very curious question of him. He asked, "Are you turned off?" The Teacher whispered, "Yes, yes, yes." Then he was led to the class where he stood almost like a statue and gave a remarkable talk about how to build our future. Later when he departed, I went to my Teacher and asked the meaning of the short conversation he had with the visitor. My Teacher in surprise said to me, "You have dangerous ears. Sometimes you must not hear things that are whispered."

"What does that mean, 'Are you turned off?' " I asked. For six months or more he did not give me an answer, but one day when we were alone in the forest, blocking the flow of the stream he said, "This is what it means to cut off or turn off. The Teacher who came could hurt us drastically if he did not turn off the currents of his psychic energy. This is why they live in caves, jungles, or forests. He came here to talk but he was able to turn his energies off, as I am able to cut off the flow of this stream for a while." This created serious considerations in me, and I wanted to know more. . . .

These are the five major means which can restimulate our subconscious mind.[2]

Of course, this does not mean that we must escape the Teaching and escape from the Teachers, but we must take it easy and be cautious. If you are daring and courageous enough, you must not be afraid of the subconscious flood but face it, control it, and not lose your mind. The best way to get rid of the subconscious flood is to persist in the Teaching no matter what happens to you and around you. Remember you must take the Kingdom of God by violence. The spiritual life is a battle, and from the beginning you are going to prepare yourselves as warriors. Keeping your balance, equilibrium, purity, and sacrificial service and following the wisdom of your Guide, you soon will pass the dangerous period and help others to pass also when their time comes.

Observation is the art of detachment from all those unconscious things that are going on within your nature. For example, you must learn how to watch the videotape of your subconscious mind. Of course this is not easy, but gradually you begin to see that things are automatically going on within you without your conscious participation. Here you must stop and watch.

Your body, your emotions, your mind suddenly act "weird." Stop and watch how that is happening. Once you learn to separate your conscious mind and watch your mechanical action, you are a hundred years advanced, and you are on the path to becoming a superior man or woman.

Sometimes when I watch the activities of my subconscious mind or my past fabrications I am surprised at how clearly they are put together and how much effect they can have upon us if we do not observe them. Some

2. See *The Subconscious Mind and the Chalice.*

of my poems and articles were written after observing the activities of my subconscious mind.

The elements in your subconscious mind can act as real enemies to you if you let them control your life, but once you learn how to observe them, control them, and use them, they become the source of your inspiration and solemnity and lead you to the science of knowing your True Self.

There was a man who wrote a very precious book, which is considered a masterpiece today. If you read it carefully, you will see that he is using all his subconscious storage to teach people about the true life and sometimes even shedding light onto them from the treasury of his Chalice. All that we passed through, all that we did wrong or right, eventually can turn into diamonds of wisdom for us if we conquer it.

Question: *Can you tell us if desire builds up the elements of the subconscious mind?*

Answer: Of course it does. Actually all our suffering, pain, wars, and revolutions are based on desire. Desire is of two kinds:

1. *Desire for physical and emotional objects.* If you analyze this first desire, you will see that its root is fear — physical fear, emotional fear, and mental fear.

2. *Desire to liberate oneself from limitation and karma created by the desire of objects of these worlds.* If you analyze this second form of desire, you will see that its root is your spirit which is striving toward joy and freedom.

In relation to the first fear, you desire more and more money because you have the fear that all that you have will not give you security or you will not be magnetic, welcomed, or loved or you will not have enough education to provide your necessities. It is all fear.

Of course, your many desires are programmed by your posthypnotic suggestions. They hypnotize you to have, to have, to have or else calamity will come into your life.

One day a lady was buying clothes. She said to her girlfriend, "I want this, this, this, and that dress."

"Oh?" said her friend.

"Yes, or else he will not fall in love with me."

How can we overcome our lower desires? The answer is by working on our higher desires. The higher desires will eat our lower desires.

There is a wonderful method which you can use to protect yourself when you are attacked by the posthypnotic suggestions of your subconscious mind. I learned this from the experience of the temptations of Jesus in the wilderness. I thought that Satan tempting Him was the embodiment of all that was remaining in His subconscious mind, and that Satan was making one last attempt to destroy Jesus.[3]

The significant thing is that every time Satan tried to trap Him, He answered him by repeating some verses of the Teaching that He had learned in childhood. He did not analyze Satan's words because, first of all, the subconscious elements cannot fall under the power of analysis in general and, if they do, they gain strength and power because of your attention. Second, He answered him with words of wisdom which are the accumulated experience of ages.

All the epistles of the "Temptation" say it is a story of the subconscious mind and gives the method to deal with it. When temptations and attacks come to your life, answer them with the words of Christ, with the words of the Ageless Wisdom. I often answer my attacker with the words of the Great Sage or with the words of the

---

3. See Matt. 4:1-11

Psychic Attacks

Bhagavad Gita or even the *Koran*. One day I had an attack of unforgiveness. Then I recited a verse from the *Koran* which says, "God is all forgiving." The attack was gone immediately.

There are wonderful verses that you can learn from the *New Testament*, from Agni Yoga literature, from the *Bhagavad Gita*, from the *Upanishads*, or from any wisdom Teaching, which can save your life during attacks. Remember that the words of Great Ones have great power which can disperse any subconscious or outer attacks.

I believe that Jesus told about His experience in the wilderness, and they dramatized it by the story of Satan tempting Him. He brought out the principles through memorized words and rejected the attacks. The words of the Ageless Wisdom stand as principles and powers against any kind of attack if they are used with strong faith and obedience.

Try to collect from the Teaching those verses or words that

- ◆ remind you of fearlessness
- ◆ remind you of unity and love
- ◆ remind you of forgiveness
- ◆ remind you of service
- ◆ uplift you from depression
- ◆ urge you into cooperation
- ◆ make you inclusive, daring, and courageous and use these virtues on the right occasions

Such collected words will go to your superconscious mind and at the right time will resound and protect you.

One night we were traveling on the freeway at sixty-five to seventy miles per hour when suddenly we saw a car

339

500 feet in the distance put on its brakes and stop in the same lane. The car spun around twice on its wheels and stopped against the traffic. I jumped out of the car and said, "My Angel is my protection," and stood against the traffic, waving my hands to stop the oncoming traffic. Hundreds of cars stopped, some five to ten feet away from me. I had the courage to stop the traffic and save five people in the other car by reciting the words, "My Angel is my protection."

When the cars behind ours stopped, I gave a sign to the driver to turn back into traffic and enter the right lane. Then I jumped into our car, and we continued our journey. The people in the car with me were very grateful, but they said minutes after I jumped out they were expecting to see my body fly by on the freeway in pieces. Of course this was an extreme case, but my words of power helped me to be courageous.

One day a woman's son died. She was extremely grieved. I visited her and gave her the second chapter of the *Bhagavad Gita*. After reading it she took a deep breath, smiled, and said, "You saved my life. These words are so precious." That night she read the chapter more than five times. In the morning she was victorious, and she went for a short vacation with the book. She wrote me a letter filled with deep gratitude.

The Teaching can be used on every occasion, even if you are flooded with good fortune, position, and success. There are verses that can keep your vanity and ego down and lead you to sanity and simplicity.

Sometimes success is a greater defeat than the defeat itself.

Once I told a man to say, "Revenge is Mine, said God" a few times. Then one day he had an opportunity to kill a man who had stolen his money a few years ago. Immediately the words came to his mind, and he did not kill the man. Later he told me that the words saved him in the darkest hour of his life, and he was protected from being a murderer.

Question: *How do such sayings or mantrams help us?*

Answer: The secret is this: Whenever you are under post-hypnotic suggestions, you need someone to help you avoid harming yourself or others or avoid being trapped in various problems because your consciousness is asleep.

If there is no one around you who can do this for you, and if you are wise and quick enough, you say the mantram and warn yourself. For example, if you are trying to quit drinking and you see a bottle of alcohol before you, take the bottle and say, "Lord, lead me not into temptation" or another mantram that you know.

While we are under posthypnotic suggestions our conscious mind does not operate, and we need someone to guide us until we are out of it. Mantrams can help us if we do not have a wise friend close by. In repeating the mantram, you can make a contact with your Higher Self and put It into action to guide your conduct.

Observation can help us if we are conscious to a certain degree. If we are acting under the subconscious mind, observation is not possible. You have to have a friend or immediately repeat a mantram. It may be that you automatically repeat your mantram when you feel danger is approaching. That is good. The mantram is there to help at the last moment.

Observation is very useful, but we need immediate action to come out of a bad condition.

The subconscious mind does not work with logic. It has no space-time concept, and any man is every man. For it, there is no loss or gain but only mechanical discharges of subconscious elements.

It is dangerous to work on the subconscious mind. You pull out one thread and you say, "I found the cause of the disturbance," but later you realize that the one thread is tied to a thousand threads. When you pull them out, you see that you are in the hornets' nest.

Once the subconscious mind is agitated, the person goes crazy because he alternately tries to fulfill the contradictory demands of the suggestions. You see in his behavior a lack of continuity. You see in it constant change, lack of stability and direction. That is what the subconscious mind does.

In your videotape you have many other dangerous elements. For example, when you are angry with your husband you think, "I wish I would become sick so that he pays attention to me or nurses me" or "my sickness will become a punishment for him" or "I wish I would die so he would understand my value." Such thoughts are common, but we must remember that they go and sink into our subconscious mind as posthypnotic suggestions, and after a while we act stupidly and we condition our life in a way that we become sick or we die. Such suggestions control us to such a degree that we think that is exactly what we want, and we do not let them go. We do this either for self-punishment or for revenge.

There are other steps that we can take to avoid being the slaves of our subconscious mind. One of them is to see our negative attitudes and change them immediately. When, for example, I am ready to curse you, I make a strong effort to bless you. When I am ready to hit you, I hug you. When I am ready to call you on the telephone or write you using foul language, I use my telephone to make you happy or write a pleasant letter instead.

The next step is to work on your virtues and try not to allow your vices to take over. Reading religious books and books of the Ageless Wisdom gives you plenty of support to live a conscious life or at least a life that is controlled by high standards. It is also good to have friends that are sincere and loving and who dare to point out your weaknesses with loving understanding and without hurting your feelings. But the most practical method is to build your ideal image every day, making it better and better and trying to actualize it life after life.

One of the Wisdom Teachings of the Far East suggests that we try not to create enemies but to increase our friends. If we have good friends, we increase the possibility of our survival and success and, at the same time, help our friends to live a better life. Thus, the less enemies we have, the less chance we have for attacks. But people are careless, and even without intention they create enemies through their gossip, slander, bad behavior, exploitation, manipulation, and unrighteous and selfish attitudes. Remember that the more enemies you have or the more enemies you create, the more attacks will reach you through their evil thinking, negative emotions, and destructive actions.

My Father used to say it is better to lose money than to make an enemy. The dark thoughts of an enemy, like arrows, penetrate into our aura and create inflammation there, which in time become seeds of various ailments. That is why Christ advised us to come to an understanding with our enemies before sunset.

Of course, sometimes it is impossible not to create enemies because of your beauty, success, and achievement. But it is possible to minimize their numbers with your tactful relationships. If you created an enemy, do not agitate him, but let time pass for him to calm down.

Most of our depressions originate from the negative thoughts and hateful emotions of those people whom we hurt in various ways throughout our years or lives. It is better to be surrounded by good thoughts and joyful emotions because they bring you health and happiness. Why contaminate your days and years? Thoughts and emotions are living entities that may bring viruses from their sources and contaminate our life.

Our problems and difficulties must be used as devices to improve our life. Instead of thinking that the conflicting situations in our home, business, and environment are situations to be hated or fought against, we must intelligently use them to refine ourselves by bringing forth the divinity latent within us. We can use them to cultivate various virtues, though attacks are really aimed at us to weaken or destroy us.

This does not mean that we welcome negative people and conditions and slowly get involved in their treason, but our attitude will be an extreme alertness and a cultivation of those conditions and virtues which will allow us to disarm them and eventually challenge them to enter the path of transformation.

Some of our videotapes not only exercise pressure on us through posthypnotic suggestions but also provide vehicles for astral corpses, astral entities, or those entities that are earthbound. When our own thoughtforms serve as bodies for such forces we are in a very dangerous situation. We invite dangerous lower entities to obsess or possess us through the vehicles we build, through our thoughts and emotions, and through our imagination.

Sometimes our dead friends or parents come to our dreams and give various advice or warnings. This is another important point in which we must be watchful. Once a person is dead, he cannot come in contact with the physical world except if he is trapped in the etheric domain. The only way to communicate with the dead is to develop an ability to travel to Higher Worlds after building our Antahkarana. It is probable that the corpses of our friends and parents can be attracted to our subconscious thoughts and emotions. Once they are in the network of our subconscious elements, these elements reactivate the diskettes of the corpses and make them communicate with our etheric brain during sleep. We need not be deceived by such contacts but instead need to strive for new achievements in our spiritual nature.

It is also possible that dark forces or other entities use the corpses of those whom we know to come in contact with us. In such cases the entity can activate their diskettes and know all about their life and yours, thus giving the impression that your departed one has valuable advice and guidance for you. Such entities first approach you in very pleasant ways, stimulating your expectations and dreams, but once you are hooked to them, they begin either to play with you or to use you for their concealed goals.

You can highly please your departed ones and receive their blessings if you do philanthropic work in their name: publish books dedicated to them; give a yearly dinner to a poor one in their name; send poor children to college in their name; help the needy families in their name; help orphans and widows financially in their name. Such behavior is very common in the Far East. They even build schools and hospitals in the name of departed ones. This is how you express your deep love for them.[4]

In Armenia they built fountains in public places in the name of their departed ones, or they built shelters on the highways for the protection of travelers. They also built libraries in the name of their departed ones. Anything done with gratitude to the departed ones is never lost but brings in their blessings. Moslems build mosques such as the famous Taj Mahal and other sanctuaries. This builds a high-level consciousness between those living and those who are departed.

4. See *Other Worlds*.

One of the things that can be suggested here is *do not desire to contact the dead* because your desire causes a way for such entities to contact you. We attract the corpse through corresponding vices, and this is very common. If a corpse owner was a prostitute, murderer, alcoholic, liar, and so on, we attract them if we are involved with the same vices or, as religion puts it, with the same sins. That is why a vice is not only an internal enemy but also can be linked with an outer enemy.

Certain corpses want to feel tobacco, liquor, drugs, sex, blood, violence, and we attract them by falling into such vices or even by thinking about them. Our criminal thoughtforms bring the corpses of the ensouling entities close to us, eventually to obsess or possess us.

Corpses come to us because of chemical affinity. They approach our aura, and our aura provides the energy for them to play back their recordings. If you are in close contact with fortune tellers, past life readers, lower psychics, mediums, and ignorant channels, be extremely careful. It is better to depend on your logic, reasoning, intuition, or feeling than to depend on them. It is also wise to keep their belongings out of your house because such entities are hooked to their belongings, and they use such threads to come in contact with you.

Such an explanation is in no way intended to tell you to cultivate hatred or to look down on those people who are engaged in the unfortunate business of coming in contact with corpses. Actually, this information is a valuable service for them to warn them about the dangers in which they are involved. A group of aspirants and disciples create an electrical atmosphere which repels such entities. This is why groups are protective shields for those individuals who are susceptible to attacks.

Question: *Is the astral corpse an entity?*

Answer: Yes and no. The astral body is formed by astral elementals, living, tiny beings, but the human soul is not in it any longer. It may happen that an entity or a dark force can use it and make it act as an entity.

Question: *Is there light or are there pure entities that help us, inspire us, and lead us toward greatness?*

Answer: Of course there are. They are those whom we call, in general, angels. Angels to us are thoughtforms, aspirations, and the treasury of our Chalice which inspire us, protect us, and lead us. Some people continuously live in their presence and feed them with their lofty thoughts, emotions, and aspirations and build a close friendship with them.

Their presence and contact give us great joy and upliftment. They do not obsess or possess us. They encourage us to have our free will and live a noble life. But when we are under the control of astral entities, we feel weird; we feel like slaves.

When one is obsessed sometimes he notices that he is doing things independent of his volition. Such observations last a very short moment, but you see that some part of your nature is doing things in which you are not involved. You say things without willing to say such things. You feel the presence of a force using you without your permission.

A medical doctor came to me one day and said, "Would you look at me? I feel I am not myself. Some force is trying to push me out and enter into me." Everything possible was done for him to make the entity leave. After three months he was free. In those three months he stayed in my home and I closely studied him. He was observing his other self and reporting his feelings to me.

On such occasions, first, you feel that you are not yourself. Secondly, you see that you are doing things that you actually do not want to do. Thirdly, you rapidly change your moods; you become angry, happy, depressed; you fight; you love someone one minute and hate him the next. These are the symptoms that you can observe. Remember, observation and striving can clear away obstacles.

If you are lucky, you will have a Teacher, a friend, a guide who really loves you and will take care of you. You do not need to go through the experience of obsession and possession if you follow the path of Beauty, Goodness, Righteousness, Joy, Freedom, striving, and gratitude from the beginning.

Once we had a friend who was a medium. He suddenly shot himself. When I asked my Teacher about it he answered, "When an astral corpse attaches to someone, other astral corpses also form a chain with him and sap the energy of the medium to such a degree that the person wants to die, thinking that he can escape from them through death. Sometimes it happens that when the soul of the person leaves the body and entities obsess him, he is no longer present. The entities kill him in order to have an astral body to live in."

There are other phenomena which are related to thoughtforms. When you have a Teacher, you build a thoughtform of him which lives in space for many years. A dark force enters into it and appears in your dream or at the time of your prayers or meditation. You receive various messages, then slowly the good changes into mediocrity, then into evil. Most of the people who come in contact with "Masters" are coming in contact with the thoughtform of the Master, built with the mental substance of his disciples.

If true Masters want to communicate with you, first They make you ready during a few incarnations, then

They pass you through fiery tests, and then, in most cases, condense Their bodies and come in contact with you on the physical level. The contact of a Master puts you under higher responsibilities and labor. They do not come to flatter you or read your future but to challenge you to do something daring for the sake of humanity.

Remember that the Hierarchy is the greatest shield and source of life. Abide in the Hierarchy and live in the Light of the Hierarchy. Stand in the center of the five-pointed star and love all creation. Those are the steps that will protect you from attacks.

Question: *Would you tell us how the subconscious recordings take place?*

Answer: One of the ways they take place is when you fabricate while you are in a posthypnotic state of consciousness.

Let us dramatize: "Now it is dark and I am in fear and I see something moving in the dark. I imagine that the moving object is a man who possibly has a gun, and he is going to kill me. Maybe he has other men behind him. I do not want to surrender when he approaches, so I will try to put my dagger into his body. Maybe he will shoot me or maybe I will die in pain and suffering or maybe I will kill him."

Now this is a fabrication, a videotape that goes into my subconscious mind as a posthypnotic suggestion. Plus, there is the feeling of warm air on my face, the smell of trees outside, the color of the furniture and its form, the outside noise. All are on one tape. When this tape is re-stimulated and played back, I will have a very hard time resisting it because there is not a man out there. It is me. I was the theme. The subconscious mind cannot discriminate between you and your fabrications.

Now what happens is this. Any time the videotape is

restimulated, you feel afraid of yourself. Sometimes you feel you are a thief, and you are going to kill yourself or kill the thief. Such recordings are the origin of most nightmares.

Question: *Does the subconscious mind record only negative things or also the positive?*

Answer: The subconscious mind records positive things, too, if they are attached to the negative ones. For example, you are in a marriage ceremony and you feel as though you are in seventh heaven. Suddenly, a man with a gun kills your wife. After this experience, for years and lives you are afraid to marry because your joy was poisoned by a negative event. Every time people talk about marriage ceremonies you feel weird, even if you have forgotten the event.

We must add also that groups and nations are like human beings in that they also have their subconscious mind and conscious mind. For example, in a group, sixty people represent the subconscious mind, thirty people represent the conscious mind, and ten people represent the superconscious mind. The same thing can be said for a nation. The success of a nation and group depends on increasing the number of conscious and superconscious people.

Subconscious people are the sources of trouble. Most of the trouble in groups and between nations is the result of the clash between the subconscious and conscious minds. It is deplorable that people, organizations, and governments use fear techniques which make people unconscious and prone to posthypnotic suggestions to a certain degree. This is why we must be careful not to decrease the consciousness of people through thoughts, words, and actions that are related to fear, anger, hatred, jealousy, revenge, and greed. I call these the six vipers. Once you make people less conscious, they become more dangerous because they can be used by their subconscious mind and by entities who search for those who have no conscious control over their life.

In conclusion, attacks are intended, first, to violate your freedom; second, to misdirect your will; third, to obsess you; and fourth, to possess you.

21
Dark Poisons

Jealousy, hatred, and feelings of revenge are very dangerous poisons for the etheric centers, senses, and subtle planes. The poisons generated by these vipers penetrate into the protective shield of the aura and the etheric disks between the centers and eat them as termites eat the wood. Such poisons are detrimental to the etheric, astral, and mental centers. They destroy certain parts of the centers and senses.

Such a slow but progressive disturbance causes confusion and imbalance in the entire electrical system of the human psyche. It disturbs the chemical balance in the physical body. It disturbs the process of reception and the responses of the astral centers. It disturbs the process of reasoning and logic in the mental body.

The overall effects of such a poison are decaying health problems, negativity, irritability, insensitivity, crime, destructive activities, and insanity. Such a condition comes out slowly in one life, and the subject cannot notice it clearly, but people around him see it.

When such a condition of self-poisoning continues, it affects the course and conditions of future lives. Most of the sad conditions of babies are proof of it. Dark poisons lead people to alcoholism, to drugs, to license, and eventually condition the babies being born through them.

Those who are revengeful, full of hatred and jealousy, must be prevented from working in higher leadership positions because their decisions and judgments will be illogical, unreasonable, anti-survival, and destructive.

Jealousy, hatred, feelings of revenge, and the resultant gossip, slander, and treason make your higher centers and senses dull and insensitive. When you read higher literature, listen to inspiring and uplifting lectures or talks, or listen to advanced music, you flood these senses and centers and stimulate them to such a degree that they become illogical and disturbed. You become an automaton under their illogical and disturbed influence. Thus, the chemistry of the psyche is disturbed, and the centers and senses cannot do their predestined job. This leads the person to destruction.

Our nature operates in right chemistry. Wrong chemistry creates unending problems. Destruction is the way for Nature to save through the Law of Economy. Outdated forms must perish so as not to hinder the advancement of those forms which have enough potential to unfold and progress.

Often such a poison accumulates in the aura and is projected by an evil intention to certain victims. Sometimes the poison, verbalized by anger or hatred, goes into the mental body of the victim and acts as a posthypnotic suggestion, devastating the life of the victim. Such a link ties the aggressor and the victim with psychic ties and often, even when the aggressor dies, he continues to poison the victim. Also, this person, if loaded with the projections of many people, for a time destroys the protective net of the victim, leading him into continuous accidents and difficulties.

One can repel such poisonous currents with his psychic energy or with vigilance and prayers. Some leaders disappear in isolation in order to destroy such accumulations. Some remain at their duties and become a living sacrifice. However, they learn much and, in due time, they learn the art of fighting. Sometimes, Those Who are watching a leader do not help him to see if he is able to mobilize his own resources and destroy the attacks. Remember, in the future we are destined to be warriors against all destructive forces. As for people who do not have good words for us, we send love to them.

People try to find the reason for certain phenomena because they think that if the cause of any event is found, it will be possible to repeat that event or prevent it from reoccurring. For a long time people try to find out why and how people became traitors or why they enjoy slandering people. The reason is very simple. Those who have a tendency or urge to gossip about people, slander them, or turn into traitors are those people who

- are full of criminal records

- have a damaged brain because of accidents or alcoholic parents

- have several health problems, inherited or developed

- have unhappy family relationships

- used drugs, heavy tranquilizers, or other medication

- are attacked by their parents and by their close friends

- have a sick ego, heavy vanity, or an inferiority complex

It will be a great release for such people to understand that their problem exists within themselves. Once they see that this is the cause, then they can go to certain professional people to seek healing.

One must not be angry upon seeing these attacks but feel sorry for them because, though they slander and use malice and treason, they eventually create heavy health problems for themselves.

One can see clearly how unhappy such people are. They are unhappy with their parents, unhappy with their friends, teachers, with their husbands or wives, with their children and associates. And because they are unhappy, they want others to be unhappy. The happiness of others aggravates them more than anything else, so they use their poisonous weapons to hurt others.

But Nature works in different ways. Slanderers, traitors, and people of malice first of all disturb their own chemical balance. They put within their nature the seeds of certain malignant diseases and prepare an unhealthy and miserable life for others. It is true that they can damage the reputation of people, but their own damage is greater in comparison to the damage they do to others.

Sometimes they even lose their souls and become prey for possession. They not only hurt themselves but also their souls. This is why when you see such people, pray for them and feel sorry for them. They are paying the karma of their dark deeds, negative emotions, and dark thoughts. We grow by the attacks of such people. And we welcome them when they come to their senses.

PART 3

LIBERATION

22
Victory Over Darkness

People want security and safety. We see this every-where. People want to be secure and safe in all aspects of their lives, but they do not want to bother fighting against darkness. The reality is, if one does not fight against dark-ness, he eventually defeats his own security and safety. This is a very fundamental principle. If we do not fight against darkness, we will not have security or safety. Actually, our safety is rooted in our fight against darkness.

When we use the word "fight," we do not mean to use guns and atomic weapons to destroy each other. The fight begins within oneself. The fight is to increase our light, beauty, goodness, intelligence, and consciousness. When one fights for higher standards and principles, he increas-es his beauty, consciousness, intelligence, and wisdom. Everything within us that stands against Beauty, Goodness, Righteousness, Joy, and Freedom is an element which must eventually be destroyed. The fight must first be within oneself.

One must learn how to fight intelligently. Sometimes we do not observe and perceive how intelligent the lower self is. Our body, emotions, and mind find various methods to escape or attack. The first battle one must learn is within himself. Only those who have fought the inner battle can be fighters in greater fields. It is said that until one conquers himself within himself, he cannot be a "warrior."

People often start fighting in outer fields, attacking external matters, before they have learned the technique of fighting within themselves. As long as the lower self is not defeated, one cannot be a fighter because in the field of battle the first one to knock you down will be your lower self. You cannot enter the battlefield with an enemy inside yourself and expect to win.

Our security and safety depend on how much we can conquer ourselves, how observant and awake we are to the enemies that exist within. Some people, even some psychotherapists, flatter others by saying that they are all beauty, inside and out. But actually, there is beauty and ugliness within us. We are a mixture of darkness and light. Eventually we will conquer the darkness within ourself by our own efforts. If the darkness within a person is conquered, he is ready to be a warrior. At that point in time he knows how to fight; he is an integrated, wholesome person who starts fighting the good battle in his community, nation, and in the world.

The tragedy is that people are fighting in international fields before they first conquer themselves. For example, a man of vanity, pride, superstition, and prejudice is put into a great and powerful position in which he uses powerful ammunition. But he is also fighting so that his lower self wins. We must ask ourselves if the battle is being carried on to make our light side win or our dark side win. If the dark side is not conquered, why fight?

In ancient temples people passed through very heavy disciplines before they were given any science, geometry, algebra, chemistry, or physics to learn. Why was this? Unless one's animal side is conquered and harmonized with his Divine side, he will always satisfy the animal side by using all his knowledge and power during the battle.

Who are the real fighters? Fighters are those who have won the battle within themselves. If a group has won this battle within itself, it can be a warrior in a nation. A nation that has conquered the enemies within itself can be a warrior within the international field. Any family, group, church, or nation that is dark and light mixed together is nothing else but a ruinous, disintegrated organism. This is why one must learn about the battle of life.

The Great Sage often refers to His "warriors." Once when I was speaking about warriors certain people thought that I was recommending revolution. After the lecture one of them approached me and I said, "You haven't won the battle within yourself." "Why?" he asked. "You smell so bad with cigarettes." "Oh, that's what you mean," he said. "That is easy." But I said to him, "If you win that battle, later we can discuss how to win battles in other fields."

Signs of a Warrior

1. *The first quality of a warrior is to be victorious in the field of his own battle.* Sometimes I counsel with people who do not want to see the enemy within themselves. They want to cover it up and close the doors so that the counselor does not see any darkness in them. How can the counselor help them under these circumstances? He is going to increase their light to such a degree that they can see the darkness still hiding in their hearts.

Our first defense mechanism is to abandon the field of battle within ourselves and stick with our rationalizations and showing off, trying to demonstrate that we are really conquerors. This is the first way to defeat ourselves.

2. *The second quality of those who are going to be fighters is knowing how to think.* As we progress in this civilization, we will see that the battle is not really on the physical plane but on the emotional plane. Eventually the battle will move to the mental plane, then to the higher mental plane.

You must have weapons to fight. One of these weapons is clear, pure thinking. If a general is going to win a battle, he must know clearly what the situation is on the battlefield. For example, he must know from where the aircraft are coming. He must have clear thinking and know the conditions of his own situation as well as that of the enemy. The first battle is within yourself.

Sit and observe how many enemies you have within your own consciousness and subconsciousness, within your habits and automatic reactions and responses. How many enemies do you have? You will find the number hard to believe. You think that people respect and adore you because, like an ostrich, you put your head in the sand while your ugliness is exposed for everyone to see. You are going to think clearly and ask, "What am I? What am I doing? What things exist within me against which I am going to fight?"

3. *The third quality of a warrior is wisdom.* Without wisdom, you cannot be a good fighter. Wisdom is the collection of all your experiences, plus intuition, intellect, and great love. With wisdom a situation is not confronted like a cliché, but in subtle ways of thinking and adapting yourself and seeing conditions as they exist.

Once, in the Royal Air Force, we were watching the enemy approach. The captain said to the general, "Let's wipe them out!" The general smacked the captain in the mouth and told him to shut up. The captain said, "But they are in our hands!" The general called for the guards and had the captain put in prison. If we had followed the captain's suggestions, we would have been in grave danger of annihilation. The general was seeing and thinking clearly. He was very wise.

Start developing these weapons and ammunition. To be integrated within yourself is more powerful than an atomic bomb. To know how to think is the greatest weapon within you. To have wisdom means to have an abundance of every type of fighting method.

4. *The fourth quality of a warrior is daring.* A warrior must be daring. If you cannot dare, or if you don't have courage to face yourself to see exactly what you are and where you are failing, there is no hope for you; you cannot fight. Daring means that you are ready to perform an unselfish act. As long as you are stuck to your skin, you cannot be a daring person. People sometimes think that daring is equated with foolishness. It is not to this sort of daring that we refer.

5. *The fifth quality of a warrior is insight and foresight.* You must develop insight which means that you can see clearly the situation within yourself, your family, your church, and your nation. Foresight is the future. For example, you ask, "How will this condition manifest in the future of humanity?"

6. *The sixth quality of a warrior is control.* This refers to control of your thoughts, emotions, and actions. In giving some instructions to his students a great Teacher said, "I do not want this information to enter your lower mind because 'blackbirds' will pick at and steal it, and then organize actions against you." This seems impossible. For example, I have just given you a very important secret. It is now in your mind. How are you going to protect that secret and prevent dark forces and entities from stealing it from your mind and organizing counteractions against you? This is all in the science of controlling your physical actions, your emotional actions, and your mental actions. This is one of the greatest secrets of winning the battle. For example, you have something in your mind and no one knows about it, not even your enemies. But, if your enemy is intuitive and telepathically sensitive, he can take it from you in one second.

FORMS OF DARKNESS

Darkness is the absence of light. We must know what is darkness and what is light. Inertia, apathy, laziness, and depression are darkness. Intelligently, daringly, with wisdom and thinking, in slow motion and diplomatically, use whatever you can to fight against this darkness. Once you see that these weeds exist within you and you do not take them out, they will increase a million times. The same principle exists in your group, in your nation, and in humanity. Inertia, apathy, laziness, and depression are signs of an insensitive nature. It is a sign that the person does not know what is going on around him.

Darkness is matter. For example, you cannot see outside light without windows in buildings. The matter within you is attachment to material values. Worship of matter, the "golden calf," is darkness within you. Worship of all material values is darkness. You can use them but not worship them by not letting them control and use you.

Absence of communication is darkness. For example, when people come for counseling I often advise them to communicate with each other, talk with each other. When we open our hearts and communicate, there is light. But if we close ourselves to another person, there is no communication and darkness settles between us. We prevented China from entering the United Nations for many years before giving permission for their entry. We have called nations "evil empires," yet we are now communicating with them. Communication is light, and light gives life and survival.

If God is in everything and in everyone, why do we not communicate with Him in everyone? What kind of philosophy is it that forbids us from attempting to communicate with the God in everyone?

A man married a girl whose sister was married to a black man. One of the man's friends wrote to some people in South Africa who knew the man and gave them this information. As a result, the man began receiving angry letters from people in South Africa simply because he was married to a girl whose sister was married to a black man. There is such a great tragedy in this. We must try to communicate with the God in everyone. In communication everyone knows where they stand. Only in communication can you come closer to eliminating those things which separate you from others.

Absence of consciousness is darkness. Anything that dims or depletes your consciousness is darkness. For example, hallucinogenic drugs and hypnotism darken your consciousness. Whatever dims your consciousness is darkness because the light is going out in you. You must keep that light bright and shining.

Spiritual sleep is darkness. Spiritually, you must be awake. Christ said, "Pray and be watchful." Prayer is to penetrate and contact the Almighty Mind and then be watchful. If you sleep spiritually, you are entering into darkness. You do not know where you are going and from where you are coming.

Lack of sensitivity is darkness. We lose our sensitivity through egotism and self-worship. Eventually, we think that no one else exists but us. Insensitive people are totally self-centered. If you say to them, "Why are you doing this? It is hurting someone," they will say, "I don't care. I am thinking about myself." Such people are insensitive because they are too self-focused. Sensitivity means to radiate your rays. Each ray brings certain impressions to you. But if you are insensitive, you are like a tortoise covered with a big shell.

Separatism is darkness. When I was nine years old I read one of the Teachings of the Great Teacher. It said, "If you think that you are holier than a dog, you are worse than a dog." I ran to my Mother and Father and asked what it meant. From that moment on I said to myself, "It is not my business to judge people." Judgment must vanish. People are what they are. Just mind your own battle, and when your battle is won you can create battles in others so that they can fight their own battles within themselves.

One of the techniques of battling is this: You don't fight for others. You don't make others fight with others. You make a person fight with himself. You make a group fight with itself. If you are planning fights for them before they have become the conqueror of themselves, they will mess everything. The science of fighting is very subtle.

Exploitation is a very subtle form of darkness. You use your love, your wisdom, your money, and your gratitude just to exploit people. You say for example, "How beautiful you are. I am so grateful," because you are thinking of asking that person for three thousand dollars. The history of humanity is not progressing the way it should because we have millions and millions of people exploiting each other in all ways. If we start revealing how people are exploiting each other it will create an explosion.

Try not to exploit others with your gestures, your maneuvers, and other subtle ways and means. Exploitation increases your darkness and the darkness of others.

A person who has been exploited will attack you with the weapons of darkness because he has become dark.

It is said that it is better to have an intelligent enemy than a stupid friend. A stupid friend is worse than having no friend. But if you have an enemy who is intelligent and thinks clearly, it is possible to eventually make him a friend. We see this in history. Intelligent nations will find each other, even if they are enemies. Intelligence works for survival. Intelligence does not work for destruction.

Manipulation is another dark technique similar to exploitation.

Absence of the sense of responsibility is a great darkness that you are going to fight within yourself. Do you have a sense of responsibility? Let's say that you have become a member of a group. Are you fulfilling your responsibilities in that group? If you don't have this sense of responsibility, you are living in darkness. Let's say that you started to see a great value, a great source of wisdom in someone. Are you respecting and developing gratitude toward him, her, or the group? If not, you do not have a sense of responsibility. You are undermining yourself. A sense of responsibility is the ability to see the needs and requirements of others and of situations and to try to meet those needs in a spirit of nobility and beauty.

Hatred is a great darkness. Whenever there is hatred in a home, a group, a church, and in humanity, we are in darkness. In darkness we do things without knowing what is going to happen. In darkness we throw a stone. That stone destroys the most valuable thing in our home. But if we are in light, we know where to throw the stone and whether or not to throw the stone.

Malice is dense darkness without the stars. *Slander is like a mire.* When you see that hatred, malice, slander, separatism, exploitation, and manipulation are slowly sprouting within you, immediately cut them if you want to be safe and create safety. Also awaken others to see these things and take action against them. This is where your safety is.

I remember an incident with a family living near us in California. I noticed that one of the boys was smoking. I went to the father and said, "Something sneaky is going on. Your boy came to my son and they entered our garage. When I went into the garage I smelled something unusual." At the time I did not know what marijuana was. He said, "It is just some kind of grass that they are puffing on. It is harmless." I said, "Okay." Six years later all five children in that family were heroin addicts. I said to the father, "Now do you see what happened? Because you didn't stop the first sign of darkness you must now confront a dragon."

Some people say, "A little hatred, a little malice, a little gossip, a little treason will not matter. These things are human, natural." Well, some kinds of poison found in Nature are also natural, but you do not swallow them.

Ignorance is real darkness. For example, two brothers are raised in the same home, but one of them becomes a great scientist and physicist, while the other becomes a bum. This is the difference between ignorance and light. Every one of us must increase his knowledge and use it in the right way. I admire some people who, in their middle and later years, go to universities. I know a man who is now seventy-six and his wife is seventy. They recently became chiropractors. It was a joy to know this. They are increasing their knowledge and expanding themselves. Do not stay where you are because wherever you stop is darkness for you.

Sometimes we think we know everything after reading only a few pages or listening to part of a lecture. In this condition we are in darkness because we are in apathy, depression, laziness, and inertia.

Ugliness is a great darkness. Think and discover if

you are ugly. Are you seeing ugly things? Ugliness must not have any way to survive.

Totalitarianism is also darkness.

What does darkness do?
- Darkness separates people from each other.
- Darkness destroys culture.
- Darkness confuses the mind.
- Darkness creates inertia in the soul of a person.
- Darkness brings pain and suffering to humanity.

What does light do?
- Light unites people and creates integration and synthesis.
- Light causes creativity on all levels.
- Light clarifies and brings certainty.
- Light brings in enthusiasm — the fire of striving.
- Light brings in happiness, joy, and bliss.

Question: *Can you comment on the relationship between love and wisdom?*

Answer: Sometimes love is emotional, and there is no analytical reason and logic in it. Wisdom is love plus analytical reason and logic. For example, you are a celibate and you fall in love with a married woman. Love at a certain level says, "Grab her and marry her," but reason and logic says, "She is married. She has children and her husband is beautiful." This is wisdom, but we do not become wise in one day. We must go through many failures, experiences, and defeats so that eventually we come to our senses and understand our lives and environment. When we say that you are going to be fighters, this does not mean to take a bottle and hit someone's head and say, "This is what it means to be a warrior."

Question: *Can you clarify what you meant about the captain's suggestion to the general that they attack the enemy immediately?*

Answer: The captain was judging that situation at that moment from a very short-sighted and limited viewpoint, but the general was seeing the consequences and the issues behind the situation. He was saying that if he attacked, it would let the enemy know his location.

Do not jump to a conclusion or an action until you measure and see all sides of the situation. Then you are slow but sure of your actions and their results.

Question: *Do you think that all darkness is coming from our ego and illusory levels?*

Answer: It doesn't matter from where it is coming. It is there. First you confront it. When you annihilate darkness, who cares from where it came? The source and roots of darkness can be five hundred lives ago. Sometimes the roots of darkness are in your subconscious, in your mother's genes, in your past lives, or in your ancestors. How are you going to find them? Psychology and psychiatry try to find these things, but for me it is not necessary. The important thing is to clean the darkness from our nature.

Of course knowing the roots of darkness helps, but you will need three hundred lives to find them. Let's say that you have a tendency to lie. Lying is darkness, a form of manipulation. First you start lying to yourself. I have noticed this in myself. Before I lie to someone else, I first lie to myself. If I am unable to lie to myself, I am unable to lie to others.

First, the enemy within must be defeated. This is a very great science that is related to politics and to all other fields of human endeavor. In the future, all politicians will be wise leaders. Plato said that the future rulers of the world would be philosophers — lovers of truth and wisdom. Wisdom cannot be accumulated if you don't have the experience within you of how to fight.

A Teacher once told me, "You are going to walk for six months from this wall to that wall." For the first two or three days I was really cursing everything as I walked, mumbling, "What kind of discipline is this?" Then I saw the whole science and psychology behind it. Three years later he told me to sit on a street and watch people walk. After a while I could see why people were walking in certain ways because earlier I had watched myself walking. When I am nervous, afraid, or happy, my walk reflects these conditions. When people passed by me, I knew the psychology behind their walks.

First, learn in the book of your own self. When you learn to read the book of your own self, you can read the "books" of others.

Question: *Is service done during or after the battle?*

Answer: Service is done at all times — before, after, during and in the future. Service is annihilation of darkness. Before fighting you think, plan, reason, and feel. This is service. In thinking, in talking, in feeling, and in acting, you clean darkness on various levels. Service is radiation of your Light. The more you radiate your Light, your Divinity, the more you enter into Light. This is why we need to battle.

A friend and I went to a large store. He saw some very beautiful watches. I was occupied with buying something, but I noticed that he was taking a watch and starting to put it in his pocket, then he put it back on the counter. Finally, he put the watch in his pocket. If you play his actions in slow motion, you will see his physical, emotional, and mental actions and reactions and what is happening in the psyche of that person as he tries to steal that watch. If he observes these actions and reactions and conquers them, then he is finding himself. We can say that losing yourself is falling into darkness, while finding yourself is finding the Light.

Question: *Can you say what the source of the Light is?*

Answer: The source of Light is you. Every person is Light wrapped with many, many blankets of physical, etheric, emotional, and mental trash to such a degree that the light is dimmed. As you conquer the pressures and inclinations of your vehicles and stand as the Self, you are Light. Light is "seeingness," "knowingness," "touchingness," "smellingness," and so on. Love is light. For example, Saint John said, "There is no darkness in true love." Every time we act against love, we fall into darkness.

Question: *Would you speak more about overcoming inertia and depression?*

Answer: Inertia and depression are conquered by striving toward light because light is action, radioactivity, and movement. Darkness is static. The more you strive toward light, the more energetic and dynamic you become. I believe in prevention.

There were two sisters with a difficult home life who wanted to learn meditation. I said, "If you learn to meditate and try to study the Teaching, you will prevent any kind of depression, inertia, and apathy in yourselves in the future. You will become *sattvic* — radioactive." The younger sister laughed, but five years later was in a hospital because of depression, having fallen under the influence of her home life. The other sister, who did meditation, stood like a beacon.

Prepare yourself now so that you do not fall into these dark conditions. People start taking vitamins, exercising, and eating well when they become ill. Before you fall ill, start preventing that illness. When people say, "Oh, when I go to the hospital I will take care of myself." At that point it is too late. Take preventative measures and avoid going to the hospital.

Start now to follow the path of striving. Striving means to take those actions which improve yourself. This means not only listening to lectures and reading but actually doing things.

Question: *So many people talk about the benefits of listening to subliminal tapes. What can I tell them about this?*

Answer: Subliminal messages are a form of hypnotism. You are going to fight against your own darkness without inhibition and without exercising pressure upon it. If you are lying and I slap your face and say, "Do not lie," you may never tell a lie around me again, but my action will not have cleaned out the roots of lying from you. Because I inhibit you by cutting the leaves and stems of your lying without removing the roots, lying will grow and become a cancer in you. Subliminal messages create psychic cancers. Suppression is not evolution.

We are talking about releasing people from their darkness. Everything that is suppressed in your nature will gain ten times more power by hiding itself in various molecules and manifesting as different diseases and complications, the way that AIDS expresses itself as insanity or blindness. The illness is no longer just AIDS; it has put on other masks and started to work in different ways. We must expose the darkness. Subliminal messages are one of the greatest evils that humanity confronts at present.

The ladder of light is built with the steps of

- joy
- enthusiasm
- striving
- sincerity
- aspiration
- worship
- dedication
- devotion
- solemnity

23 Protection

We can protect ourselves from the dark forces through

- purity
- increasing our psychic energy
- learning the ways of the dark forces
- blessing others
- prayer and high-level reading
- fasting
- hiking
- retreat
- heavy labor
- listening to special music
- eating proper food

- periodic abstinence from sex

- keeping silence periodically, for three days or more

- intensifying our observation

- forming triangles

- organizing goodwill activities

- working harmoniously with a group

- meditation

Purity. Purity repels dark forces. They can come closer to us because of physical impurity, emotional negativity, and mental pollution. Right and clear thinking, loving emotions, and physical purity protect us from their attacks. Nasty or ugly words, lies, malice, and slander create invitations to the dark forces. Those who are loaded with karma are like magnets for the dark forces.

Increasing our psychic energy. How can we increase our psychic energy? The simplest way is through love, striving, and sacrificial living. Psychic energy also increases by living under the light of the Transpersonal Self and directing all our activities by the light of goodwill.[1]

Learning the ways of the dark forces. This has been discussed in previous chapters.

Blessing others. Blessing is an act of sending psychic energy to one who is afflicted by obsession or possession, or to one who is under attack. Psychic energy casts the intruder away. When one is under attack, he can also pray for the blessings of the Great Lord.

Blessing is a fiery energy by which everything in the home and office must be charged to prevent the approach of the dark forces. You must bless your clothing, your

---

1. For more information regarding psychic energy, see Ch. 25 in *The Psyche and Psychism* and *A Commentary on Psychic Energy.*

dishes, your appliances and equipment — everything that you use. You must also bless your home.[2]

Prayer and high-level reading. If you are under attack you must pray. The Great Invocation and the Lord's Prayer can be used. You must pray for those who are under attack, asking the Lord to send His protection. Reading highly charged inspirational books or prayer books helps immensely.

You can also read for those who are under attack. In Asia, holy ones read from spiritual books, such as the *New Testament*, the *Koran*, the *Bhagavad Gita*, the *Upanishads*, and so on, over the heads of those who are under attack.

Fasting. Fasting is a great means to avoid the attacks of the dark forces. Fasting periodically is very helpful. Real fasting is the act of closing your mouth and not accepting any kind of food or liquid, including water. Of course you must plan your fast carefully and carry it out only with the advice of a specialist.

Hiking. Taking hikes in forests, on riverbanks, at the seashore, in the mountains and deserts is very beneficial. You can do this for hours or for days. It rejuvenates your psychic system and repels psychic attacks.

Prana, negative ions, pure air, and deep breathing work miracles for your nervous system. You can also drink valerian tea or drink a few drops of wormwood oil in a glass of water, if your doctor permits it.

Retreat. Occasional retreat is very important. It integrates you and isolates you from people and objects which are conducive to attacks. It also strengthens your entire system and refocuses you upon spiritual values.

Heavy labor. Hard physical labor is one of the best means to repel dark attacks. The moment you feel that you

2. See Ch. 19, "Blessing All Humanity," in *The Science of Meditation.*

are losing control of yourself, engage in heavy labor such as gardening, digging, cleaning, working on the car, painting the house, carpentry, and so on. Dark forces hate labor.

There is a story about a girl whom a devil tried to possess, but whatever he did it was impossible for him to possess her. He finally went to his boss and said, "Why can't I possess her?" Satan answered, "Because she is always occupied and clean."

Listening to special music. The right music is very helpful, especially Gregorian chants, Eastern Orthodox church music, and the music of Sufi masters and certain esoteric Teachers. Dark forces hate harmony and rhythm.

Eating proper food. Eating right is one of the best methods of repelling evil forces. Meat, bloody dishes, oil, sugar, and salt attract the dark forces. You must also move your bowels and urinate frequently. Any impurity in the body attracts them.

Periodic abstinence from sex. Abstaining from sex increases the energy in your aura and nervous system and keeps you away from certain pollution. When sexual energy is sublimated, it helps your pineal gland to contact higher spheres of energy.

Occasional silence. Occasional silence is imperative. It cleanses your aura, seals the cracks in your etheric body, and prevents dark forces from contacting you.

Intensifying your observation. The intensification of your observation helps you see those signs which make you aware of the activities of the dark forces in your environment. One must be alert in order to observe the first signs and take precautions as soon as possible.

Forming triangles. The formation of triangles is a great protection. The Great Invocation builds a shield around you which prevents dark forces from penetrating your environment.[3]

Organizing goodwill activities. Goodwill activities allow benevolent forces to be around you. Also, such a labor releases many high-level energies from your Core. An individual who is highly charged with the energies of goodwill repels agents of darkness.

You can organize various goodwill activities such as supporting the poor, the hungry, orphaned or homeless children, the sick, and the aged to try to meet their needs as much as possible.

Working harmoniously with a group. Group work is very important. The strongest tower is a group dedicated to higher ideals. When such a group is harmonious, it creates a field of electromagnetic energy which repels dark attacks.

Meditation. Meditation is a technique to draw energy from the Higher Worlds. Light, Love, and Will energy come to those who meditate on a regular basis. Meditation increases the protection of your Solar Angel. Meditation increases your radiation to such a degree that the dark ones are afraid to approach you.

These methods of protection are some of the ways you can protect yourself from the dark forces. Your Master or Christ can also protect you.

There are seven diamonds from which the dark forces flee:

1. *The first diamond is beauty.* Dark forces hate beauty in any form. If they "love" beauty it is only because they want to use beauty as bait to fish for people, to catch them, and to use them for their own purposes.

Beauty shatters the constitution of the dark forces, so be beautiful. Think beautifully, speak beautifully, live beautifully, and they will never be able to hurt you.

---

3. See *Triangles of Fire.*

2. *Goodness is the second diamond.* Fill your mind, your emotions, and your words with the spirit of goodness, and dark forces will not be able to approach you.

3. *Righteousness is the third diamond.* Be righteous in your thoughts, words, and actions. The dark forces will never come close to you. If you play at being righteous without being righteous, they will get you.

4. *The fourth diamond is joy.* Joy is psychic energy, and psychic energy burns evil. Increase your inner joy. Be joyful. Spread joy everywhere. Do not let petty things in your life obscure your joy. Joy is a line of direct contact with your Divine Core, so always strive to be joyful.

5. *The fifth diamond is freedom.* Dark forces are afraid of a person who is free from his urges and drives, his glamors and illusions, his vanity and ego. It is impossible for them to reach a person who is a free soul.

6. *Light is the sixth diamond.* Light destroys darkness; it kills the dark forces. Try to stand in light. Strive toward enlightenment. Do not let any dark corner exist within you. Live and move in light, and let your light shine.

7. *The seventh diamond is contact with Christ.* Christ is the Commander of the Celestial Armies. If you stand with Him, if you contact Him daily through your meditation and prayers, the dark forces will not dare approach you. That is because those who stand with Christ have a secret sign on their souls which frightens the dark forces. But if you play games in the name of Christ, you will soon fall into the traps of the evil ones.

These are seven diamonds which you must carry on your chest as your shield against the enemy.

24 Liberation

The enlightenment and progress of a human being is achieved only when he is liberated from obsession and possession. When you think, act, and speak as a liberated soul but all that you do is mechanical and artificial, your spirituality has no real value — because you are not the doer.

The difference between liberation and freedom is great. In freedom you free yourself from your own

- inertia
- glamors
- illusions
- vanity
- ego

In liberation you liberate yourself from obsession and possession, from serving those who are obsessed or possessed, and you make efforts to liberate those who blindly serve obsessors and possessors.

These are the tasks of every disciple in the world. Liberation cannot be achieved until all people can free themselves from the fivefold chain of inertia, glamor, illusion, vanity, and ego. These are all rooted in the subconscious mind. This fivefold chain is called Satan's ladder. If this ladder is not constructed, Satan cannot climb into your building. As long as one does not fight for freedom and liberation, his essence cannot grow. He can, however, do mechanical things like influence people, have things, and give things while his essence remains the same. All his relationships promote slavery and encourage him to exercise control over other people.

There are seven immediate obsessions which must be avoided

- alcoholism
- drugs
- extreme, abnormal, and immoral sex
- gluttony
- greed
- possessiveness
- violence

A free and liberated person creates those conditions in which other people find opportunities to free themselves. *The greatest freedom is freedom from obsession and possession.* Actually, in these two factors all forms of slavery are condensed.

Obedience to entities which are inferior to our development makes us work against our own best logic and reasoning. Not only entities may obsess or possess us but also our virtues may obsess and possess us. We can even be the slaves of our virtues if

- we do not actualize them
- they become a limitation for us
- we use them for our self-interest
- we use them to enslave or influence others
- we do not manifest them on higher planes or in all of our relationships

For example, solemnity is a virtue. We appear solemn during certain occasions but then live a very unsolemn life in our homes, in our imagination, in our thoughts, or in private relationships. A virtue must express itself on all planes and in all relationships so as not to be a hindrance in our psyche.

We can also be obsessed by the quantity of objects, as if quantity is the most important factor to determine success. In this way we lose the opportunity to see those few items that can change the condition or direction of life.

We can be obsessed by the image of position, as if a certain position denoted freedom or progress. Certain positions kill our soul and bankrupt our spiritual treasury.

We can be obsessed by jealousy. Through jealousy we make the image of the person toward whom our jealousy is directed live or dwell within us and control our life. Even after the person dies, we draw his elementals into our aura through that image and make it obsess us. It also happens that if we die before the other person dies, we may try to possess him because of our hatred and jealousy.

Chanting without conscious participation may create obsession and possession in the following ways:

- It puts into action your physical, emotional, and mental mechanisms, making them act mechanically.

- If you are invoking an entity, that entity may eventually find you through your voice and emotions and possess you.

- If your chanting is related to your individual interests, the image of those interests obsess you and make you refuse to consider the interests of others.

- If you are not conscious and concentrated during chanting, your other thoughts, thoughtforms, and dreams absorb the energy created during chanting and eventually obsess you.

While you are chanting, if your thoughts are related to sex, hatred, fear, jealousy or revenge, they receive energy from your chanting and become firmly rooted in your aura. This is why chanting can only be done when your mind is focused and when you are conscious about what you are chanting.

Freedom is the absence of interfering influences which try to control your will and use you against your own interest and future well-being. Chanting eventually turns into a crutch on which you lean, instead of developing your beingness and potentials.

Obsessing and possessing forces and entities cannot penetrate an aura which is harmonious. Harmony in an aura is a great protection and power against obsession and possession. Whenever harmony is disturbed, an opportunity is given to obsessing forces and possessing entities.

Obsession and possession occur when, through internal conflict, a person weakens himself. Disturbances in our aura occur when a conflict begins between our thoughts and our actions or speech. If the thought is fabricated, reversed, or disturbed through our verbal expression or action, then conflict comes into being between the mental and etheric matters. Such a conflict creates weakness in our energy system which, if repeated, frequently causes greater damage to the etheric and mental centers. This is why Christ said that when we say yes, we should mean yes, and when we say no, we should mean no. In other words, no conflict must exist in our being.

Conflict also comes into being when one acts against accepted facts. If a person knows that what he is doing is wrong, he creates conflict within his aura. There are other factors which create conflict, such as saying one thing and doing something else, talking about high morality to others and then living an immoral life, or personally and deliberately leading people in the wrong direction. Conflict also occurs if we stand as a false witness or tell lies.

The progress of a human being toward his destination can only be achieved through discipline and self-control. Self-control can be defined as control over the mechanisms which the Self created to use in order to manifest the deeper creative powers latent within Itself. But, during the construction of the bodies, the Self temporarily forgets Its purpose and becomes controlled by the bodies and their tendencies, by the substances of the bodies, and by those who are active in the substances out of which the bodies are built.

There are three kinds of people:

1. *Those who are controlled* by their physical body, emotional body, or mental body.

2. *Those who fight against controlling forces*, such as between an entity and the substance of the body, emotions, and mind, or between those negative forces which try to use these substances to capture a person and use him as an agent for their plan. Because of their human birth, they can still be an efficient tool in the hands of the dark ones.

3. *Those who are in control*, although the one who must be in control is the Self. The body must be subjected to the will of the Self. The emotions and mind must also be subjected to the will of the Self.

In the past, either the body, emotions, and mind controlled the Self or the will and desire of those entities who inhabited the etheric, astral, and mental realms of the person controlled him.

Approximately sixty percent of humanity are controlled. Thirty percent are fighting against being controlled. Ten percent are on the verge of achieving control or are already in control.

One day Satan and a man became friends. They worked all day to cultivate a field, and at dusk they were ready to make the five mile walk home. Satan said to the man, "I see that you are tired. You can sit on my back and sing a song, and as you sing I will carry you home. But when your song is over you must climb down, and I will jump on your back and sing my song. Then when I am through, you will take your turn, and so on." The man agreed, jumped on Satan's back and began to sing. But after half a mile his song was over, and so he had to let Satan ride. Satan jumped on his back and began to sing. The man walked one mile, two miles, three miles, and Satan was still singing. "I am tired," said the man. "Please finish your song." "What are you talking about?" Satan asked. "We have an agreement. I will not climb down until my song is finished. You have no right to interrupt me." The man carried him for another mile and then fell to his death.

This is the story of materialism. The materialists have a song that will never finish until its carrier is killed. The problem is how to control the earthbound intellect. Materialistic science is like the bottle of Solomon which when opened released a giant so large that no one could force it back into the bottle.

Satan is a symbol of anything that has control over you. Freedom from this control can be achieved only by knowing the factors which are trying to control you through obsession or possession. The ultimate goal of the human being is liberation and freedom. Only through striving toward liberation and freedom can one release the divine potential within himself and walk toward his glorious future.

25 Combating Evil Forces

The first method to combat evil forces is regular meditation. They say that the bear has one song which it always sings. I sing one song — meditation, meditation, meditation. Meditation is a science to increase Light within you. Meditation makes you feel principles. Meditation makes you obey Higher Guidance. Meditation makes you sensitive toward Beauty, Goodness, Righteousness, Joy, and Freedom. Meditation makes your aura so sensitive that you build a warning system against dark forces. This system acts as an alarm, and you can immediately feel dark forces approaching you. Many people do not have this mechanism. Once you have it however, certain people can enter your home, shake your hand, and bring you a gift, but something they do makes you realize that they are dark. Lawyers and judges, in particular, have developed this mechanism to a certain degree, and after years of experience many of them can tell immediately if a person is guilty or innocent, no matter what proof exists to the contrary.

Through meditation you build an alarm system and perceive dangers. You feel the motives behind the actions of others. If this mechanism is built-in, you are safe. Sometimes however, by associative thinking, you judge wrongly. For example, let us say that in the past you saw a criminal whose nose was crooked. Because of that experience you tend to judge everyone with a crooked nose as a criminal, which is not right. It must be real proof that you are developing an alarm system.

In some esoteric schools, teachers require their students to sit on street corners and observe how people walk. For the first two months I did this, I disliked it. Then it became interesting. People are so strange when they walk. Not as many people walk in America, but in the area where I lived everybody walked an average of two or three miles a day. It was interesting to observe how people walked, especially if you watched one person for three or four consecutive weeks. You could detect changes in his walking. One day he was mad; the next day he was excited. Sometimes he was depressed or hopeful. What caused these changes in his walking habits? I started developing some kind of sense to observe and measure people — not criticize them, just measure them.

By watching your friends and other people, you can do the same thing. Ask them why they are moving in a certain manner. Search for the cause of facial expressions and their style of walking. When you find the cause, you become a reader of the hearts of men. It is said of Christ that He knows the hearts of people immediately. When He looks at a person He knows what is going on in that person's heart. The heart is the central station of all the activities of a person.

The second method to combat evil forces is exorcism. To do this, you can read certain verses of the *Bhagavad Gita*, the *New Testament*, or other great prayers. The Great Invocation is very powerful, as is the Lord's Prayer. Some Catholic churches have very wonderful and powerful prayers. Strong prayers can also be found in the *Vedas*. There are some masterpiece prayers in *The Spirit of Christ*, a book written by Andrew Murphy.

You can stand in the middle of the room and say the prayer, "Love to All Beings," while visualizing that you are like a prism and that Divine Light is coming to you and spreading everywhere. This prayer should be repeated every day for three or four days, using three or seven lighted candles, eucalyptus oil, peppermint oil, and incense. Frankincense is good, but the most powerful incense is sandalwood. Burning sandalwood powder on charcoal makes a very strong and effective scent.

Another method of protection, which is extremely powerful against dark forces, is dried cow dung. Cow dung consists mostly of very concentrated herbs which, having passed through the four stomachs of the cow, absorb a substance that creates a very beautiful scent when it is burned. This substance is harmful to astral forces. I have tested it on many occasions, and it is a masterpiece. It is best to collect the dung of cows which graze in the high mountains. After collecting the dung, dry it, then burn a small piece of it. The fumes smell very, very good. The following advice is written in the Vedas: "Putting a little rice and ghee upon it, you must burn cow dung at sunset and sunrise." This is known as an Agni Havan ceremony.[1] Do not think of cow dung as a waste product because it has a different chemistry.

Have you ever noticed a foul odor in your house for no apparent reason? Dark forces can dump astral corpses in your home. As these corpses degenerate, they become like fleas. The herb that effectively fights these "fleas" is

---

1. This means to purify by fire.

bay leaves. Bay leaves are also a great insecticide. Just rub the leaves and let the scent fill the infested areas.

Blessing is another form of protection. You must bless everything you use. As mentioned previously, there is a prayer for blessing money and also one for blessing water. Do not drink water before blessing it either mentally or physically. You can physically bless the water by uniting your thumb and ring finger of the right hand, making the sign of the cross over the water and saying, "In the name of Power, Love, and Light, and in the name of the Church, let this object be blessed."

Question: *Why do you bless water?*

Answer: It is important to bless water because the cup in which it is contained may have been used by a person whose emanations are still there. The emanations of a person remain for at least two months, no matter how much you wash it. The emanations of dogs remain on the objects they use for three years. Jewelry carries emotional emanations. Be careful in using the jewelry of people you do not know. Blessing helps, but sometimes you cannot clean away all the emanations. You can pray, using these words, "In the name of the Almighty Power, I command the dark forces to disappear from this object, from this place," and so on. There are also some very powerful prayers in the *Koran*.

Fasting protects you. If you are under any attack from hatred, malice, jealousy, treason, disunity, anger, and so on, go on a fast immediately and drink only water. Dark forces do not like fasting. They like the byproducts and decay of digesting food in your stomach. They live with decay. When your mouth smells badly, they love it. You must also clean your stomach for two or three days by fasting on yogurt. Eat lots of yogurt, day and night, so that you clean your whole body. Sometimes garlic is good to use along with yogurt to clean away the smell.

Question: *Is buttermilk equally good?*

Answer: Yes. It cleans odors from the body.

These emanations are very bad. Frequent bathing and a change of clothes during the period of attack is essential. Maintain physical cleanliness. During their menstrual periods, women must keep themselves extremely clean.

Hiking and mountain climbing are very good. Dark forces hate climbing and hiking. That is why Socrates, Plato, Pythagoras, and Jesus, for example, gave Their highest Teaching while walking and climbing in the mountains. Their students and disciples would hike with them. While great Teachers talked, Their disciples listened. In this way, the words of the Teacher sank directly into their higher consciousness.

If you are under attack, living in nature for a while is beneficial. Say, for example, that you are under attack and fighting with your husband or wife. Take a vacation for three or four days. Go to the mountains or to the seashore for a rest, and then come back. You will see a great improvement in your relationship.

You must also listen to higher music. Some classical music is also good. Harp, piano, and flute music are good. It is your choice. Sounds produced in music such as rock and disco are very disastrous. Actually, such music encourages evil forces.

Consuming food that is not contaminated with poisons or chemicals is very important because poison and contamination are agents of the dark ones.

Periodic abstinence from sex is a good protection. This deters dark forces from locating themselves in your sacral center. If your sacral center is under your control, they will stay away. But, if sexual abstinence is overdone, the dark forces can take control of your heart. Then they petrify your heart against your husband or wife. Be very careful with your sexual energy.

Silence, instead of arguing or reacting to the comments of others, is very good. For example, if people are gossiping and speaking about ugly things, do not respond to them. Instead, maintain a sweet, blessing silence. In this way you will not invite dark forces, which always wait for a reaction from you. When you react, they are drawn to you.

Observation is another effective method to combat the evil ones. Observation clears up a lot of things. Ask yourself, "Why am I doing this? Why do I talk this way? Why am I sitting next to this person?" Observe very clearly. If you do not like what it is you are doing, do not do it anymore. Follow your heart.

Triangular sounding of the Great Invocation is a very important method to combat the dark forces. Find two other people besides yourself with whom to say the Great Invocation, the Lord's Prayer, or any prayer. This is a very effective way to connect three strong people so that they are protected by their auras.

Goodwill is also very important. When you feel that you are coming under a dark influence, start helping people. Give them money, work for them, donate your time, and so on. For example, help the poor and the needy. By doing so, the dark forces will leave you because they hate goodness. Doing good deeds pushes them away.

Heavy labor is another activity that dark forces hate. In Asian monasteries, if the Teachers see any student gossiping or being hateful, revengeful, and so on, they subject him to eight hours of heavy labor, such as digging, planting, cutting, carrying. One month later the ones who worked became so beautiful. Evil ones hate physical labor. The Great Sage says, "Labor is the rejection of evil."

Group work combats the dark forces. Learn cooperation; do something with other people cooperatively. The first field of cooperation is learned in the field of the family.

Dark forces and enemies can only be censored by you. The first sign is your feelings. The second sign is that your conscience is bothering you. The third sign is that you see signals, such as geometrical figures in various colors. These sparkling, yet ominous figures can suddenly appear before your eyes when you look toward a dark person. The sizes and shapes of these figures are very important to note. If they are round, they are immediate. If they are square, they will take more time. If they are a square with a dot in the center and two pincer-like horns coming from the top two corners, they are in the future. So you are going to discover these signs.

26 Failure of Dark Forces

Just as the Forces of Light have their limitation, so do the forces of darkness. For example, the Forces of Light work with freedom. They try to illuminate humanity to stand for its happiness, success, prosperity, enlightenment, and to proceed on the path of perfection, but they do not force their will on humanity. Humanity is free to respond to the direction of the Forces of Light or not. Until humanity begins to respond to the Forces of Light, humanity passes through extreme pain and suffering introduced by the forces of darkness.

On the other hand, the forces of darkness obsess and possess people and force their will on them and lead humanity into separation, materialism, totalitarianism, pain, and suffering. But through all their techniques they see a great danger. They see that the more they exercise their techniques, the more humanity awakens, and the more humanity awakens, the more they see the futility of serving the dark forces and of obeying their techniques or discipline.

The Hierarchy of Light works slowly and awakens the sleeping Divinity in man. Because of this awakening, the efforts of dark forces are condemned to eventual failure.

Of course, many generations come and go — and dark forces feel secure in their success. But those generations that obeyed them and worked under their command are the first army which will eventually fight against their own dark lords and accept the Lords of Light and Their Plan for humanity.

The enemies of light, freedom, joy, and love are not only found in totalitarian, materialistic, separative, greedy, criminal circles. They also have their agents in religions and institutions everywhere, who are supposedly dedicated to the welfare of humanity. They are found in the fields of politics, education, communication, arts, science, religion, and finance. There are those people who, after serving these lords of darkness, hatred, revenge, and matter, will stand against these lords in a mighty army and destroy the strongholds of darkness.

The Teaching says that the Forces of Light are under the command of Christ. He works slowly but surely. Ages are days for him. In His mighty patience, He gathers His army and waits for the signal to destroy the enemies of Light.

The more humanity suffers, the more humanity develops the wisdom of how to destroy the source of suffering. This means that the failure of dark forces is guaranteed. They destroy themselves by their own hands. This is what happened in Germany, in the Soviet Union, and in ancient Rome. The mighty emperors were destroyed by the servants of darkness who awakened to the issue and rebelled against their lords.

The Light in the human being is invincible.

The following stories will illustrate:

There was a ruler in our city who used to make his men collect the best Armenian girls and bring them to the ruler for his enjoyment. After his satisfaction he gave them to his soldiers. The soldiers, following the example of their ruler, enjoyed the girls and then killed them. The Armenians did not know how to protect themselves from such an evil. They did not have guns, freedom to talk, freedom to sue such beasts. They knew only how to suffer. The slightest sign of dissatisfaction and anger resulted in hundreds of dead young Armenian men in the city.

One day, in a secret meeting, the Armenians decided to walk to the ruler's fortress and do whatever they could do, knowing that they would not return home. In this desperate situation an old man stood up in the meeting and said, "The evil is fighting in the ruler to destroy its own agent. You do not need to commit suicide."

We heard that after his sexual pleasures and drinking one day, the ruler was going from his bedroom to the bathroom with a gasoline lamp in his hand. He fell down behind his house and, with a big explosion, the house was annihilated to dust along with all his faithful guards and their ammunition. Only the mother of the ruler was alive. She told the authorities all that happened that night. In her desperation to help the ruler, her gown caught fire and she ran to the outside pool and saved her life.

When asked about her son, the ruler, she said, "He was from the beginning self-destructive. I could not help him." Later we heard that in intense pain and suffering she passed away with cancer.

There was a man in an Armenian village who was called "the dark face" by Armenians. He was a dictator and an evil man. Armenians estimated that he had killed approximately twenty-five hundred Armenian boys, causing intense suffering and pain to the families of the victims. This man, not satisfied with his crimes, made a will. In his will he wrote that after he died his corpse must be carried to the Armenian city and hung from a tree. A few years later he died, and his family hung him from a tree in the Armenian city. Five hours later the Turkish crowd attacked all Armenian shops and houses and leveled them to the ground. In his will the authorities found the following lines, "I will be more destructive after I die."

After discussing the destruction of the Armenian families and realizing the evil existing in such a man, his followers attacked the man's family members and burned twenty-seven people with all their belongings.

Evil is its own enemy. Those who bring harm to society, or prevent its progress and well-being, sooner or later pay a heavy price.

27 The Legend of Good & Evil

Some people believe that there is no evil and there is no good. Some people believe that there are both evil and good, a Satan and a God. They are both right if you accept them as the products of their level of beingness. There is also the other concept that there is only God and nothing else. Many people are perplexed and confused, wanting to know whether the evil is emanated or born of God, or if God is both good and evil.

The archaic teaching thinks that God is good and all that exists is good. Then from where does evil or the concept of Satan come?

We are told that there was only the Space and in the Space one fragment was condensed and the Spirit came into being. This Spirit traveled by forty-nine steps toward materialization, and eventually the seven major planes and forty-nine subplanes of existence came into being.

In every subplane or plane innumerable Sparks of Space were scattered. These Sparks were endowed with the seeds of Will, Love, and Light. Their purpose was to unfold the three potentials of each Spark and make each of them conscious of their *Will power*, *Love power*, and *Light power* so that, as these Sparks came back to Space, Space would use them as architects for Its Cosmic Purpose. So in the history of creation, when the Spirit reached materialization and the forty-nine levels of condensation were reached, a Cosmic shock was given as a signal for evolution.

Thus we had *involution*, which was the process of the objectification or materialization of the Spirit, and *evolution*, which was the unfolding process of Will, Love, and Light of each Spark and its journey back to the Source.

Each atom forming any plane is dual. There is the material side and there is the space side. The space side of the atom in any plane is in the process of developing "spacehood" consciousness, unfolding Will, Love, and Light. Then after the shock, or call of Space, the race started among all atoms.

If the Cosmic history is read by the Intuition, we will see that these Pilgrims, "unfolding units of space," were traveling in various forms. They were

- rotating around their axis
- revolving around a more advanced axis
- steadily forging ahead toward the Absolute
- losing their path and repeating in the labyrinth of the planes
- falling back to their former level of expression
- standing on the path of evolution of other Sparks
- trying to awake others to the fact of the evolutionary path

Those who advanced through the physical, emotional, and mental planes and did not want to go forward toward greater freedom, decided to stay in these planes and prevent those who were intended and ready to pass beyond them. Such preventers became identified with matter and with possessions. They did everything possible not to lose their possessions.

When they died and came back to the physical plane, due to karmic law, they developed every kind of art to live on the physical plane, to possess all that they could, and to be merciless to those who did not believe in their philosophy of life. Every time they reincarnated, they identified more and more with matter and material values.

Those who advanced onto the astral plane developed the pleasure seeking tendency and used all possessions to make their body and emotions enjoy pleasures of identification. Such Sparks, living in the world of possessions and pleasures, wanted to perpetuate their condition through all those ways and means by which they could increase their possessions and pleasures.

Some of them penetrated into the mental plane to discover all those ways and means by which they could manipulate others to increase their wealth, to make other pilgrims join them, and to prevent those who were determined enough to go ahead toward the Source.

An understanding was established between the possessors of matter and the pleasure seeking ones, guided by those who research ways in which material life pleases man and which man perpetuates. These mental plane Sparks, and astral and physical Sparks gradually formed a camp which opposed the ones who were determined to go ahead.

It is at this level that the clash started, and the "dark-faced ones," whose light of perpetual striving was obscured, determined to oppose any progress made by the progressing Pilgrims. Gradually, some part of this group concentrated itself on the mental, astral, and physical planes, communicating with each other through their motives, intentions, and plans.

The mental ones were guiding the astral ones. The astral ones were guiding the physical ones, and thus a hindrance was created on the path of evolution which was called the "Black Lodge."

Because the dark lodge is organized to a very advanced degree, they are able to create a life in the seven fields of human endeavor in which they control any resistance against their own will with a high degree of success. They developed a very high intelligence by which they employ even progressive Sparks to serve their intentions. Some of their plans are

- to pollute the planet

- to spread hatred, materialism, and totalitarianism

- to draw people into pleasures of the body and the emotions

- to create separatism

These are the four foundations upon which they raise their buildings or engage in their activities of all kinds.

People think that certain nations serve evil or are evil. The truth is the dark forces are in every nation, in every religion, even in every profession. The world is mixed up with dark and light Sparks, and the conflict of these forces is what we call world history.

Question: *Were the planets and solar systems in existence when this process started?*

Answer: That is a very profound question. Many pseudo-occultists tell us that "God created the planets, the suns, and so on and created man to enjoy them." This is not what the Ageless Wisdom teaches. The fact is that initially, when Space came to materialization like a Cosmic sphere through forty-nine levels of frequencies or planes, there were no suns, no systems, nothing but the matter of forty-nine levels. It is the advancing spirits that eventually built planets, suns, systems, galaxies.

That is why each planet has its Soul. Each Sun has its Soul. As the Spark advanced it built its bodies gradually on many planes as habitats for those Pilgrims who were advancing on the Path. After They built planets and systems with cooperation, we had solar systems. The Sun in these systems was the One who advanced a billion years ahead of those Sparks who were still in lower levels. A sun is the body of a Spark, who became especially radioactive due to its unfoldment on the infinite Path. Thus, an anthropomorphic god did not create the earth and heavens, but the real God in living Sparks created all that is on the path of Their journey to the Source.

Our Planetary Soul, or Logos, is One Who went billions of years ahead of our evolution and then provided His body so that we may live in it and proceed on the way of our evolution. This is a very unpopular concept, but in coming ages the best thinkers of humanity will discuss and write about it.

The Spirit that is the great Soul of a galaxy is within your essence. Advancing Souls are occupied in becoming planets, suns, and even in creating galaxies.

The destruction of those bodies are signals which demonstrate that the Soul of a certain body needs a new experience or that He graduated from His experience. Thus, we will steadily and continuously destroy and construct in Cosmic Space.

Question: *What will happen to the evolving Sparks when the Soul of a planet or solar system or galaxy leaves its body?*

Answer: All evolving lives will temporarily move to other planets in corresponding levels until the same Spirit, or Soul, creates a more adequate form to call his children back to school.

Question: *Can you tell us how planetary evil came into being?*

Answer: Our Planetary Logos evolves by creating a major scheme, which is formed by seven chains or forty-nine planets. Our scheme is spread through the physical plane to the Atmic Plane. This means that our Planetary Logos used atmic, intuitional, mental, astral, and etheric physical substance in order to build our planet, borrowing these substances from space.

Our chain is the fourth chain in the middle of seven chains. The first, second, and third chains were annihilated and the fourth chain was built. Our earth is the fourth globe of the seven globes of the fourth chain, and it is located on the physical plane.

When the Planetary Logos was building these seven globes to provide for the Spark a school of progressive unfoldment, He had many advanced Helpers Who helped Him educate the "students" of the first, second, third, and fourth globes in how to descend to the lowest frequency of matter and how to transcend the lowest point and ascend to higher planes within globes. Thus, the fourth globe contained the crucial point.

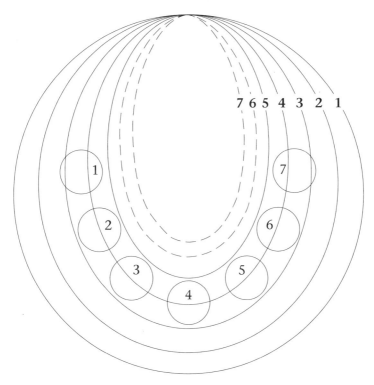

7 6 5 4 3 2 1

Diagram 2. The Seven Globes and the Seven Rounds of the Earth Chain

Descending from the number one globe to the fourth one was the involution of Sparks. Evolution is to climb from the fourth to the seventh globe. When humanity reached the middle of the fourth globe, many advanced Helpers refused to pass beyond the middle line and stopped on the path of evolution on this planet. The opposition started between advancing souls and the ones who, under the leadership of these nonprogressive units, decided to remain in the involutionary zone. On the three preceding globes they formed an organization to oppose the progress of advancing forces.[1]

---

1. See *Cosmos in Man*. pp. 29-31.

It is these powerful ones that organized all forms of dark and criminal activities in all fields of human endeavor in this world. Their prime purpose is to prevent the spiritual evolution of humanity, to keep humanity in slavery, separation, conflict, pain, and suffering.

It is said that great Helpers from other planets came and formed Ashrams to help advancing souls go ahead. Millions of Solar Angels came and dwelt in those advancing souls. Solar Angels were human beings who, in past cycles, redeemed themselves from the involutionary arc and then came to humanity to help it progress toward evolution.

Question: *What is the condition within the human being?*

Answer: These forces are active in human beings through their physical, emotional, and lower mental bodies. Until we surpass them and focus our consciousness in the higher mental and Intuitional Planes, it is possible that we serve them in many ways, except if we have the shield of our Master around us.

They use our vices, glamors, illusions, and negative emotions and gradually obsess and possess us and make us their servants. This is why Christ said, "Be watchful." This is powerful advice if one does not want to lose his path and eventually his Soul.

Question: *Is the existence of evil perpetual?*

Answer: For many cycles and in many planes the existence of evil will continue for a long time, until humanity progresses enough to make it impossible for evil to operate on the physical, astral, and mental planes, and until humanity makes it possible for planetary evil to see its failure and cooperate with the Divine Purpose.

Question: *Some place I read that if a human being lives an evil life, it may be that he will enter into the path of* *annihilation and lose his soul and become part of chaos. How is it that these planetary evil entities are still here after so many millions of years and are not annihilated?*

Answer: They will be annihilated or transformed at the seventh globe according to their attitude.

A part of Shamballa and Hierarchy have various activities to redeem them. Do not forget that they were coworkers of the Planetary Logos and through their service have a great amount of good karma. But destruction of evil human beings, who have no accumulated good karma, comes the moment that the light within them is completely extinguished.

Question: *Are they totally annihilated?*

Answer: Their identity turns into substance, and their bodies become part of the chaos. Nothing in existence ceases to be, but the formation of the diamond of the individuality melts away into the ocean of matter. For example, you have a clay pot. In relation to the clay, the clay pot is an individuality. It has the "I," but when the clay pot is melted into clay, the individuality is lost and the result of millions of years of labor is lost, but the clay is still there in order to serve in building another individuality starting from the beginning.

Question: *You say that advancing spirits eventually built habitats. Did those advancing spirits not have planets or globes to live upon?*

Answer: No, they are in our ocean of matter which we call a plane and are in a special low frequency of matter. It is after having control over the laws of matter and over matter itself that they build globes as the habitat for developing unfolding souls. Gradually, all these globes and systems come into being. We are talking about billions and trillions of light years. We know it to be so because the same process is going on now — new planets and new galaxies are in the process of formation.

There are globes which are formed on etheric planes. They are slowly becoming condensed and very soon they will be visible. Thus, all existence is in the process of construction and destruction, but the Sparks are on the path of evolution through all that is going on in the Universe.

Truly all the stars and celestial forms are the bodies of advancing great Souls on Their path toward the Source. In all of Them, Space is fulfilling Its Purpose.

Question: *In esoteric literature we are told that the Souls of the stars or even galaxies are called imperfect gods. Do you think that this is true?*

Answer: Absolutely, because these gods are the unfolding human souls progressing on the path of evolution for so many billions and billions of years. But because they are still on the path of evolution as pilgrims, they are imperfect. They are huge oak trees in comparison to men, who are acorns. This is why there is a secret tie between these gods and man.

Question: *What is the difference between being one with the All Self and being annihilated?*

Answer: In the All Self you have your individuality, though in perfect harmony with the Whole as a note in a Great Symphony. You reach the All Self as a conscious unit. In annihilation you lose all your accumulated experiences and the level of your consciousness. For those who do not have consciousness it is as if they do not exist.

Question: *What are the greatest sins?*

Answer: All acts, emotions, words, and thoughts against the Law of Unity, Love, and Light are the foundation of separatism and are the greatest sins.

Question: *What are the most important steps to develop for our spiritual evolution?*

Answer: ◆ building the Antahkarana[2]

 ◆ inclusiveness

 ◆ gratitude

 ◆ compassion

 ◆ purity of life

 ◆ righteousness

 ◆ service

These and all other virtues help to build our Soul and help us enter into the path of conscious immortality.

Question: A last question — how can we protect ourselves from dark forces?

Answer: We can protect ourselves by living in the closeness of the Hierarchy.

---

2. The Antahkarana is the connecting psychic link between the higher mind and the lower mind and between the higher mental and the intuitional bodies.

When all the cosmic forces are strained,
there can be no retreat without destruction.
When the Forces of Light are grouped around the
Light and the black ones around darkness,
there is no retreat.
Therefore, if the workers wish to conquer, they must
gather as a mighty force around the focus.
Yes, yes, yes!
If an ordinary physical form is kept together merely
by the cohesion of its particles, how much more
powerful is the force emanating from the Hierarch!
Hence, those who wish to conquer must adhere
closely to the protecting Shield, to Hierarchy —
only thus can one conquer.
Only thus, during this threatening time of reorgani-
zation, can one live through the manifestation of
turmoil. Thus, let us remember!

— *Hierarchy*, para. 111.

Index

A

Abortion 74, 97-98
  consequences of 97
Abstinence, sexual
  as protection 393
Adolescence 81
Adversary
  how to deal with 89-90
Agent of dark forces 88
Alcohol 81, 106, 108
  damage to solar plexus 107
Alcoholics 107
Alcoholism 81
All Self
  vs. annihilation 410
Ambition
  def. 302
Angels 347
  Mongolian tradition of 158
Annihilation
  of human being 408
  vs. All Self 410
Apes
  origin of 161
Arjuna
  and battle 156
Art
  target of dark forces 151
Astral corpse
  ridding of 391
Astral corpses 346-347
Astral entities
  and subconscious mind 344

Astral entities
  def. 324
Astral plane
  as clinics 48
Atlantis
  and evil 230
Attack
  vs. karmic debt 26
Attacks
  and karma 25
  and subconscious mind 329
  def. 199
  inner and outer,
    source of 315
  kinds of 25
  methods of 196-199
  outer 317-319, 321
  protection against 26
  psychic 327
  subconscious vs. evil 329
Aura
  and dark forces 47
  and slander 291
  of objects 67
  of victim,
    and poisoning 354

B

Baptism
  def. 163
Battle
  inner 155-157, 359-360
  stages of 274
Beauty 52, 218
  as protection 379
Bhagavad Gita 156

413

E

BIBLIOGRAPHIC REFERENCES

Agni Yoga Society. New York: Agni Yoga Society.
 Brotherhood, 1982.
 Hierarchy, 1977.

Bailey, Alice A. New York: Lucis Publishing Co.
 Esoteric Astrology, 1982.
 Esoteric Psychology, Vol. II, 1988.
 A Treatise on Cosmic Fire, 1989.

Lamsa, George M., trans. Nashville, TN: Holman Bible Publishers.
 New Testament, 1968.

Saraydarian, Torkom. Sedona, AZ: Aquarian Educational Group.
 Bhagavad Gita, 1974.
 Challenge for Discipleship, 1994.
 Cosmos in Man, 1983.
 The Psyche and Psychism, 2 vols., 1981.
 The Science of Becoming Oneself, 1996.
 The Science of Meditation, 1981.
 Spring of Prosperity, 1995.
 Triangles of Fire, 1977.

Saraydarian, Torkom. Cave Creek, AZ: T.S.G. Publishing Foundation, Inc.
 The Mystery of Self-Image, 1993.
 The Subconscious Mind and the Chalice, 1993.
 Other Worlds, 1990.

OTHER BOOKS BY TORKOM SARAYDARIAN

The Ageless Wisdom
The Bhagavad Gita
Breakthrough to Higher Psychism
Buddha Sutra:A Dialogue with the Glorious One
Challenge For Discipleship
Christ, The Avatar of Sacrificial Love
A Commentary on Psychic Energy
Cosmic Shocks
Cosmos in Man
The Creative Fire
Dialogue with Christ
Dynamics of Success
Earthquakes & Disasters:What the Ageless Wisdom Tells Us
Flame of Beauty, Culture, Love, Joy
The Flame of the Heart
From My Heart (poetry, Vol. I)
Hiawatha and the Great Peace
The Hidden Glory of the Inner Man
I Was
Irritation:The Destructive Fire
Joy and Healing
Leadership Vols. I - IV
Legend of Shamballa
The Mysteries of Willpower
New Dimensions in Healing
Olympus World Report. . . The Year 3000
One Hundred Names of God
Other Worlds
The Psyche and Psychism
The Psychology of Cooperation and Group Consciousness
The Purpose of Life
The Science of Becoming Oneself
The Science of Meditation
The Sense of Responsibility in Society
Sex, Family, and the Woman in Society
The Solar Angel
Spiritual Regeneration
Spring of Prosperity
The Subconscious Mind and the Chalice
Symphony of the Zodiac
Talks on Agni

Thought and the Glory of Thinking
Triangles of Fire
Unusual Court
Woman, Torch of the Future
The Year 2000 & After

BOOKLETS

The Art of Visualization
The Chalice in Agni Yoga Literature
Cornerstones of Health
A Daily Discipline of Worship
Daily Spiritual Striving
Discipleship in Action
Duties of Grandparents
Earrings for Business People
Fiery Carriage and Drugs
Five Great Mantrams of the New Age
How to Find Your Level of Meditation
Mental Exercises
Nachiketas
New Beginnings
Practical Spirituality
The Psychology of Cooperation
Questioning Traveler and Karma
Saint Sergius
Synthesis

LECTURE TAPES AND VIDEOS

The author has lectured extensively over the years on a wide variety of topics. Call or write the publisher for a detailed listing of available tapes and videos.

ORDER FORM

☐ **Please send the following books:**
I understand that I may return any book(s) for a full refund.
We guarantee your satisfaction.

QTY	TITLE

☐ **Please send me a FREE list of lecture topics available on tape and video.**

Name: _____

Address: _____

City: _____ **State:** _____ **Zip:** _____

Telephone: __(__)_____

Sales tax: Please add 8.5% tax for books shipped to Arizona addresses.
Shipping: $4.00 plus $1 for each additional book.
Payment: ☐ **Check** ☐ **Credit Card:**
_____Visa _____MasterCard

Card number: _____

Name on card: _____ exp. date: _____

✳ **Fax orders: (520) 282-0054**

✆ **Phone orders: 1-888-282-7400** *We accept VISA and MasterCard.*

✲ **On-line orders: nvp@sedona.net**

✉ **Postal orders: New Vision Publishing**
252 Roadrunner Drive, Suite 5 • Sedona, AZ 86336 USA
Tel: (520) 282-7400

Call Toll-Free and Order Now: 1-800-282-7400